**States and Schools**

# States and Schools

**The Political Economy of
Public School Finance**

**W. Norton Grubb**
University of California at Berkeley

**Stephan Michelson**
Harvard University

**Lexington Books**
D.C. Heath and Company
Lexington, Massachusetts
Toronto          London

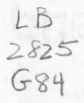
**Library of Congress Cataloging in Publication Data**

Grubb, W.        Norton.
    States and schools; the political economy of public school finance.

    Includes bibliographical references.
    1. Education—United States—Finance. 2. Public schools—United
States—Business management. 3. Education—Economic aspects—United
States. I. Michelson, Stephan, 1938—        joint author. II. Title.
LB2825.G84                    379'.1'0973                    74-10154
ISBN 0-669-93385-6

Published simultaneously in Canada.

Printed in the United States of America.

International Standard Book Number: 0-669-93385-6

Library of Congress Catalog Card Number: 74-10154

# Table of Contents

List of Figures                                                                ix

List of Tables                                                                 xi

Preface                                                                        xiii

**Part I**
**The Existence and Origins of School Finance Inequality**                     1

**Chapter I    Equality and School Finance**                                   3

   The Importance of School Revenues                             5
   Concepts of Equality                                          6
   The Relationship between Inputs and Outcomes                   7
   Arguing for Equality                                          8
   Levels of Resource Inequalities                               9
   Succeeding Chapters                                           9

**Chapter 2    School Financing Patterns and the Functions of**
**                    Schooling:  An Historical Analysis**                     17

   The Purposes of Education                                     18
   Education in the Colonial Era                                  19
   The Early Reform Era                                          20
   The Progressive Era                                           21
   The Structure of Public Education and the Development of
     School Finance                                     22
   State and Local Finance in the Twentieth Century              27
   Aid Versus Control                                            30
   Conclusions                                                   32

**Part II**
**Existing Distributions and Mechanisms of Redistribution**                    39

**Chapter 3    Distribution and Redistribution—A Primer**                      41

   Concepts of Distribution and Redistribution                   41
   Conclusions                                                   49

**Chapter 4 The Extent and Source of Revenue Inequalities** 53

Interstate Inequalities 53
Intrastate Inequalities 55
The Equalizing Power of State and Federal Aid 59
The Equalizing Power of State and Federal Aid—A Statistical Test 60
Intradistrict Inequalities 61
Conclusions 67

**Chapter 5 The Structure of State Aid: Mechanisms of Redistribution** 71

Basic State Aid Formulas 71
Formula Variations 75
State Aid in Practice 78
State Taxes and the Distribution of State Tax Burdens 80
A Theory of Distribution Restated 82

**Part III**
**Estimates of School District Behavior** 89

**Chapter 6 Elements of a Model of Public School Finance** 91

Variables 91
Functional Forms of the Estimating Equations 98
Sample Characteristics 105
Summary 107

**Chapter 7 Estimates of School District Behavior** 115

Variables 115
Equations for Local Revenue 122
Equations for Other Variables 128
The System of Simultaneous Equations 133

**Appendix 7A Estimation Procedures** 137

**Appendix 7B The Price Effects of District Power Equalizing** 141

**Appendix 7C Means and Standard Deviations of Variables** 153

**Chapter 8 School Revenue Distributions Under Alternative
State Aid Formulas** 157

The Limits of Simulation                                      157
Evaluative Statistics                                         158
Simulations:  Flat Grants and District Power Equalizing       159
Combining District Power Equalizing and Nonmatching Aid       167
Judging the Outcomes                                          171
Conclusion                                                    173

Appendix 8A   Simulations with Several Endogenous Variables    177

Chapter 9   The Implications for State Aid Programs            189

State Aid and District Behavior                               189
Modifying District Power Equalizing                          192
Distributing School Funds                                    193
The Prospects for School Finance Reform                      197

Cases Cited                                                  201

Bibliography                                                 203

Index                                                        219

About the Authors                                            223

# List of Figures

3-1    Distribution of Expenditures per Pupil Using District Averages,
       Massachusetts, 1968-69                                          43
5-1    Ratio of State to Local Tax Burdens by Household Income          81
6-1    District Budget Lines Showing Different Matching Rates           93
6-2    District Budget Selection: Tangency Solution                    94
7-1    Endogenous Variables: Hypothesized Interrelationships          120
7-2    Endogenous Variables: Empirical Interrelationships             134

# List of Tables

2-1    Percentage of Public School Revenue Derived from Federal and
       State Sources, 1890-1930                                              26
2-2    Local, State, and Federal Revenue as Percentages of Total
       Revenue                                                              27
3-1    Distribution of Expenditures per Pupil Using District Averages,
       351 Districts, Massachusetts, 1968-69                                42
3-2    Hypothetical School Finance Data                                     45
4-1    Percentage Distribution of Funds for Public Elementary and
       Secondary Education, 1971-72                                         54
4-2    Gini Coefficients Reflecting Interstate Inequalities                 55
4-3    Gini Coefficients Measuring Intrastate Inequalities                  56
4-4    Gini Coefficients for Hypothetical Distributions of State and
       Federal Aid, for Selected States                                    60
4-5    Regression Results Explaining Intrastate Inequality in Expendi-
       tures per Pupil, Forty-Nine States, 1959-60                         62
5-1    Sources of Revenue and Forms of State Aid, 1971-72                   73
7-1    Variables Used in Model Estimation, Massachusetts Sample           117
7-2    Correlations between 1960 and 1970 Values of Socioeconomic
       Variables                                                          121
7-3    Equations for Local Revenue, 159 Massachusetts Districts,
       1968-69                                                            123
7-4    Parameters Describing the Substitution of State for Local
       Funds                                                              125
7-5    Equations for Other Endogenous Variables, 159 Massachusetts
       Districts, 1968-69                                                 129
7-6    Effects on Property Value of School Revenues and Nonschool
       Revenues                                                           130
7B-1   Equations for Local Revenue, 159 Massachusetts Districts,
       1968-69                                                            144
8-1    Simulations of the Current Formula                                  161
8-2    Simulations of Flat Grants                                          162
8-3    Simulations of District Power Equalizing                            165
8-4    Modifications to District Power Equalizing                          166
8-5    District Power Equalizing with Minimum Tax Rates                    169
8-6    Different Formulas with Equal State Aid                             172
8-7    Comparison of DPE and "Constant Property" Simulations              174

8A-1    Simulations with School Tax Rate Endogenous           179
8A-2    Simulations with Property Value Endogenous            180
8A-3    Evaluative Statistics for Endogenous Simulations      181

## Preface

The precise origins of this work, how and when we committed ourselves to writing a book on public school finance, are not clear. Certainly it happened at the Center for Educational Policy Research at the Harvard Graduate School of Education. David K. Cohen, the center's director, supported this work with inordinate patience, providing the initial Massachusetts data, office space, facilities, computer time, and salaries. We hope this book is some recompense to him and the center's sponsors.

Since those early days, Michelson moved to the Harvard Center for Law and Education, where Terry Villareal helped organize the files, arrange the bibliography, and type several chapters. Michelson is now Senior Economist at the Center for Community Economic Development in Cambridge. Grubb moved to the Child and Government Project at the University of California, Berkeley, where Mary Norton, Barbara Lewis, and Susan Gabbs undertook the typing chore. That project also provided additional computer time for the simulations in Chapter 8, for which we are grateful.

Finally, we have less technical credits to give, for the personal and professional support required to get from the beginning to the end of this process. We list them alphabetically. They are (largely) innocent of any faults: Charles Benson, Arthur Blake, Martin Feldstein, J. Harold Flannery, Thomas Flygare, Erica Black Grubb, C. Brent Harold, Christopher Jencks, Helen Ladd, Minnie Lawlers, Kadimah and Mark A. Michelson, W.T. Parmenter, Ralph Pochoda, David Stern, Carole and Michael A. Stewart, Mark Zanger.

**Part I
The Existence and Origins of
School Finance Inequality**

# 1 Equality and School Finance

No period since the first two decades of this century has seen such widespread concern over education and such a prolonged period of public argument, legislation, court action, and even some change as the present time. The peculiar role education plays in our conception of society is responsible for the breadth of interest in education. It is commonly viewed not only as the source of training for later occupation but also as the vehicle of economic mobility—the reason for our supposed classlessness. Education is believed not only to transmit our national culture and heritage but also to instill a set of individual values consistent with maintenance of society. It is weighted with a history which views it, like the frontier, as the arena of opportunity, where merit and hard work reap their rewards. We continue to demand that education lead the country in resolving such complex problems as segregation (both racial and class), poverty, and technical inefficiency. Small wonder, then, that schools receive so much attention in times of crisis and that debates over educational policy reflect the deepest differences within our society.

But the demands placed on education change rapidly. The launching of Sputnik in 1957 resulted in a determination to "catch up" through science education. In the mid-1960s, with the civil rights movement, we "discovered" the second-class status of blacks, prompting an evaluation of the role of education in alleviating both poverty and discrimination. The emphasis shifted from development of a technological elite to Great Society programs for the economically and educationally poor. By the end of the sixties, evaluations of large-scale programs raised doubts that compensatory education was compensating; and soon a controversy arose over the *possible* efficacy of such programs, a controversy still very much alive in the early 1970s. At present numerous proposals for reorganizing public schooling compete for attention, including community control of schools, "free" or alternative schools, voucher plans, greater control by higher levels of government, and no schools at all. What unites these proposals is only that they are all, in one dimension or another, radical—they either promise or threaten to thoroughly transform public schooling. In less than two decades, we have moved from specific goal-oriented elitist demands on education through compensatory education to the present stage of sweeping proposals for structural change.

In the process, the number and complexity of issues surrounding education have increased. One of these issues—the one behind this book—is the nature of inequality in education. As a society, we now have a clearer idea that the results

3

of education are unequal, in a nonrandom way. We have a better idea of how educational processes and implicit rules favor middle-class, white children. We are more conscious of the kinds of deprivations with which children begin school, and why certain aspects of family background constitute deprivations relative to the workings of schools. We are beginning to ask schools to provide remedial action where necessary (and possible); but we can also see that some *failure* is the fault of the way *success* is defined. We are conscious that inequalities in resource availability parallel other kinds of inequities. Along with new demands has come a reexamination of previous public education: a new educational history is being written, one which provides a better understanding of how various kinds of inequities developed, persisted, and were reinforced despite an ideal and rhetoric of equality.

Finally, the last two decades have seen a change in tactics. The reforms of the Sputnik era depended on infusions of federal aid, too small to have noticeable impact but important as "seed money," combined with educational leadership and calls to action from the federal government. Most important, perhaps, was the guarantee of jobs for the new engineering corps. If schools would produce them, government and aerospace industry would employ them. Compensatory education *seemed* similar: it was legislated, funded, and recognized. Unfortunately, there was no increase in the rewards for success, no jobs for the newly "compensated" except those they could take away from others. Federal legislation may have been an effective vehicle for special training combined with postschool demand, but it did not prove effective in promoting *equality* by almost any definition.

Beginning with the 1954 *Brown* v. *Board of Education* decision of the U.S. Supreme Court, and increasing since then, educational reformers have looked to the courts as the equalizing institution the legislatures were not. The unifying theme of the past four years has been the argument that the Fourteenth Amendment of the Constitution guarantees "equal protection" to all citizens within a state, and that inequities in education amount to a denial of equal protection.[1]

Because the courts are generally thought capable of handling only obvious inequities, many of the cases argue for greater equality of resources—usually financial resources rather than real resources such as teachers, books, and so forth—either among districts within states or within districts.[2] The first such case at the state level to receive a favorable decision was *Serrano* v. *Priest*, where the Supreme Court of California found that "the public school financing system denies children equal protection of the laws because it produces substantial disparities among school districts in the amount of revenue available for education."[3] Similar favorable opinions followed in Minnesota, Texas, and New Jersey. The Texas opinion was subsequently overturned by the Supreme Court,[4] but this denial is not likely to end equal protection litigation and consequent pressure on state legislatures. A number of equal protection suits

have been based on state constitutions rather than (or as well as) the federal
Constitution, and hence—whatever the influence of the Supreme Court decision
in *Rodriguez*—the possibility remains that state courts will interpret their state
constitutions independently. Indeed, the New Jersey State Supreme Court
decided in favor of the original plaintiffs after the final *Rodriguez* decision and
included a lengthy explanation of why they could do so.[5] Other post-*Rodriguez*
victories include *Hollins* v. *Shofstall* in Arizona and *Thompson* v. *Engel King* in
Idaho.

Complaints have also been brought to the courts concerning within-district
inequities. These include the now famous *Hobson* v. *Hansen* in Washington,
D.C.; a complaint filed against the San Francisco Unified School District by
members of the Mexican-American community; and one filed by blacks in
Chicago. In Detroit, the allocation of teachers as well as funds was at issue,
and plaintiffs have won at lower levels.[6] These cases all argue against excessive
or patterned inequalities in school expenditures, when the pattern is not compensatory.[7] However, despite the similarity between the cases at the state level
and those seeking to eliminate patterned inequalities among educational units—
districts and schools respectively—the difference between the types of cases is
more than one of the level of government involved. At the district level, the
principle that all pupils should be equitably treated has been generally accepted,
while the analogous principle with respect to districts within one state has
received legal support in only a few states. Suits at the state level affect large
numbers of districts at one blow, whereas litigation at the district level requires
district by district suits.

### The Importance of School Revenues

In this book we will be primarily concerned with inequities in school
finance—specifically, available revenues among different districts within states.
The focus on revenues may seem a step backwards, as a good deal of educational
research since 1966 has been concerned with equality of *output*, and "real"
rather than monetary inputs, for example, teachers and books rather than
dollars.[8] Hence our emphasis on revenues requires some justification.

In the first place, to the extent that legislative solutions to inequities are
sought, the issue has always been one of money. At the state level, the political
pressures appear to respond to the distribution of dollars, and the application
of political power by representatives of wealthy districts has limited attempts
to make revenue distributions more equal. (See Chapters 2 and 5.) Legislatures
can set standards according to reasonable (i.e., not unconstitutional) whims.
Courts, however, try to justify their actions by rigorous logic, as opposed to
popular demand, and must keep in mind the consequences of setting precedents.
Revenue flows may not be the best items to equalize, but they can be measured

accurately and can be observed systematically, quickly (as opposed to lifetime returns, say), and without much equivocation. This explains the reliance of judicial arguments on flows of money.

A third reason for reticence about so-called real equalities is the possibility of constraining the operation of schools. It is not clear what the appropriate level—or mix of levels—of control should be. Parents have legitimate desires that the schools reflect their values. Teachers have legitimate desires to bring to children values differing from those of their parents. The state has an interest in seeing that certain modes of thought and behavior, and perhaps certain skills, are learned. Some people who argue for strict equality implicitly argue for a predominance of state interest. It is conceivable that if these people were to consider the structural implications of their arguments—that is, which interests should predominate, and how the system therefore would have to be structured—they would prefer dollar equality with the state's interest in school content de-emphasized.

## Concepts of Equality

For the sake of argument, let us assume that schooling is a production process with a known, measurable, and common output. Since the production of that output might vary according to the nature of the raw materials (students), we have four possible standards of equality:

1. Equality of revenues or expenditures per pupil
2. Equality of inputs (teachers with specified characteristics, buildings, heat, etc.)
3. Equality of real resources (teachers able to communicate with students equally, buildings relevant to the students' lives, etc.)
4. Equality of outputs (test scores, ability to get specified jobs, etc.)

Equal financial flows might not lead to equality in inputs, resources, or outputs.[9] The price of an input differs among communities and even among schools because of price variations and because of the supply of teachers. For example, white upper-middle-class suburbs will find teachers with given characteristics demanding less pay than teachers in central cities or rural areas.[10] Thus with the same finances, inputs would vary even if they were intended to be the same.

If inputs were equalized, they might not operate as we would want. Should every school have a greenhouse—even country schools in the South? Some people would argue that every school, not just schools with Spanish-speaking children, should have Spanish-speaking teachers. But is this true also of Portuguese, American Indian, French? Presumably we really care about resources, not inputs.

But how do we determine what is a resource? The traditional solution is to structure decision making to be as close to the problem as possible. The determination of what is a resource for the particular children, following this organization, would be made at the school level. But then how can people at the school level determine if there is equality of resources *among* schools? If we have appropriate resources, we are unlikely to be able to observe equality, for the determination of one precludes the determination of the other.

Finally, we have the call for equal outputs. But what price are we willing to pay for this equality? Is every child to be equal in all output measures, or are groups of children to be equal? If groups are not equal, to which children do we pay additional attention? Are they to be equal in their averages only, or also in the intragroup distributions? Should the school be held accountable for the failure of the postschool society to reward all skills equally?

The impossibility of following along these lines should be obvious. Indeed, they are fruitless on more fundamental grounds. We reject the assumptions necessary to make these arguments: Schools should *not* produce a fixed set of outputs in order to satisfy a fetish for equality. From the child's point of view, there may be nothing desirable about being fitted into the state's concept of output equality. The crucial question in education should not be how to turn out students who are similar in "important" ways, but how to assume some fair treatment by society in access to resources while in school.

We have not even considered the *technical* problems in nonrevenue equality measures, because they pale before the logical ones. But should one hold steadfastly to a view of equality we have rejected, he is bound to show how it can be achieved. There is no agreement on "educational production functions" even where the same output measure is used. Jencks (124) finds no indication that relationships are stable among cities, and Michelson attempted to reproduce his own results in (170) with comparable data from another city to no avail.[11] Although there is—at least conceptually—a production relationship between inputs and outputs, we cannot foresee agreement as to the nature of this relation.

The overall technical problem, then, is that any standard of equalization with respect to resources *or* outputs requires a fully developed and estimated educational production function. Should the function differ among kinds of children, then defining even *resource equality* becomes problematic. (See Hanushek [101]). The use of standards with respect to inputs other than revenues also raises technical problems which have not yet been solved: a price index is necessary to measure differences in input costs among districts, including the cost differences due to teacher preferences, land and construction, even transportation. Strictly speaking, construction of a price index would also require an educational production function if it is to be pricing resources (as opposed to inputs) and if production functions vary among districts. Complex indexes do exist (as in the current Texas school finance law, for example), and may be necessary for dealing with problems of large cities, areas with large

numbers of disadvantaged students, or extremely small districts.[12]  Given that
indexing is itself such a problem, indexing in terms other than dollars seems
beyond public acceptability.


### The Relationship between Inputs
### and Outcomes

We have presented a number of logical and technical reasons, as well as
reasons having to do with the justifiability of standards of equality, for focusing
on school resources in terms of revenues or expenditures.  However, a second
challenge to the importance of resources must be answered:  If school inputs
make little difference to variations in school outputs, equalizing revenues will
accomplish nothing in terms of the outcomes of schooling.[13]

In the first place, this argument requires a specification of what the outcomes of schooling are.  All of its supporters cite evidence from the Equal
Educational Opportunity Survey; hence they must assume that schooling works
principally to instill cognitive skills in children, as the only output measures
analyzed in the Coleman report and subsequent reanalyses were achievement
test scores.  Even here, however, the report did not find that school resources
had *no* effect.  Consistently, a number of teacher characteristics, including
verbal score and years of schooling, have proved significant in explaining variations in achievement test scores.  And while these variables did not prove over-
whelmingly important, given the gross disparities characterizing the present
allocation of educational resources, the Coleman results indicate that equalization would produce some differences in achievement test scores.[14]

In addition, the notion that schools function primarily to instill cognitive
abilities has come under increasing attack, beginning with the Coleman report
itself:  given that schools appear to make much less difference to achievement
test scores than had been expected, it may be that their primary impact on
students has nothing to do with cognitive abilities.  A number of studies directed
by Berg (20) reinforce this doubt.  He found, in samples of rather narrowly
defined jobs, that years of schooling were, if anything, *negatively* related to productivity on the job.  In the same vein, several inquiries have indicated that,
while years of schooling may be related to earnings, it is not the cognitive
content of schooling that is relevant to job performance.  Gintis (82) has argued,
from both data on earnings and the sociological literature, that the years of
schooling variable, which is so clearly related to income, captures not the effects
of cognitive skills learned in school, but another dimension of schooling—the
extent to which schools inculcate the personality traits and attitudes necessary
for successful work performance.[15]  Similarly, investigating a white-collar and a
blue-collar work setting, Edwards (73) found that supervisor ratings, which
correlated highly with promotions and earnings, were related less to years of

schooling than to three measures of personality traits—the ability to follow rules, dependability, and internalization of workplace norms. A Department of Labor survey indicated that about 63 percent of workers with less than three years of college did not use their formal training, whether from school or a specific job training program. Only 12 percent mentioned formal training as the most important method of learning the skills required on the job.[16] Finally, adherents of the dual labor-market theory stress that behavioral norms distinguish workers in secondary jobs—badly paid, unstable jobs with poor working conditions and little chance for advancement or salary increases—from those who hold primary jobs.[17] Hence, while the evidence that schools work primarily to instill personality traits and values rather than cognitive abilities may be unconvincing to some, there is sufficient evidence to constitute a serious counterhypothesis to the view that schools instill cognitive skills valuable in the labor market.[18]

School expenditures might therefore matter a great deal to the outcomes of education. The less crowded classrooms of wealthier school districts permit less authoritarian relations. Such schools can more readily encourage the facility for independent inquiry and self-paced, self-motivated work—character traits which serve one well in college and in professional and managerial jobs. More crowded schools are likely to inculcate the patterns of obedience and regimented acceptance required in most lower-level blue-collar and white-collar jobs.[19] Secondly, some of the most important lessons taught in schools are transmitted through the structure of schooling and classroom method rather than through curriculum content, including the appropriateness of regularity and punctuality, the legitimacy of hierarchical relations, and the necessity of working for external rewards.[20] In a society in which so much is conditioned on socioeconomic status, schooling is one of the first and most pervasive examples in a child's life that inequities are ubiquitous and apparently the normal state of the world. If children perceive that the implements of education depend on parental income and community wealth, they may come to see this mechanism of distribution as the fair one—just as individuals come to see schooling as a fair mechanism for distributing the social goods of society.[21] And insofar as schools provide environments which signal to children the importance of education, children from low-income families with poor facilities will tend to regard education as unimportant,[22] in contrast to children in new, well-equipped schools where the educational system is a source of community pride.[23] In sum, the quality of school facilities may provide, irrespective of the impact they have on cognitive abilities, the first mechanisms of the "cooling-out" process, the procedure by which the aspirations of lower-class children are systematically lowered.[24]

The argument that school resources may seriously affect the noncognitive traits passed on by schools concentrates—as does the argument of cognitive skill transmission—on the outputs of schools. However, it is close to another argument which relates not to the results of schooling but to the actual time spent in school.

The horrendous conditions which can prevail in schools with inadequate resources have been thoroughly documented.[25]  It seems unjust indeed to provide some children with swimming pools and the range of activities of the wealthiest suburban schools while other children receive inadequate shelter and lighting.[26]  Perhaps the productive value of schooling is not the sole criterion by which it should be judged.

The final argument for equalization of revenues is simply that greater equality in the provision of important public goods and services is desirable—particularly in the case of schooling, where the doctrine of equality of educational opportunity has so proved such a persuasive slogan.[27]  If our society is ever to divorce the provision of essential goods and services—housing, medical care, adequate food, education—from the wealth of recipients, then narrowing the disparities in school resources is a necessary first step, if only as a symbol to adults and an indication to children that some commodities should not be conditioned on income.

### Arguing for Equality

The arguments in favor of equalizing expenditures across schools and districts can therefore be divided into those about the productivity of educational resources, all of which start from the importance of providing equality of educational opportunity to all children, and simple moral arguments.[28]  Some opponents of equalization contend that the productivity arguments have been mooted by recent social scientific evidence.  We have tried to cast doubt on both the content and the assumptions of this view.  One might argue, given some uncertainty about the productivity of school resources, that the standard of equality of educational opportunity implies that the harm to society of unequal school resource allocation in the event resources *are* productive is far larger than the cost of equal allocation if resources prove unproductive.  In other words, there should be a presumption that inequities in funding lead to unequal educations, and uncertainty about the productivity of schooling should lead to equalization of school resources.[29]

But beyond this, the evidence used to debate the productivity argument—the use of statistical analysis—is of a particular and not universally accepted sort.  The lack of acceptance of this evidence by various courts is more than a refusal to acknowledge or understand social science procedures.  Rather, it utilizes a different kind of evidence of the effectiveness of schools,[30] one based more on observation of the pervasiveness of schools' influence on personal and subjective evaluations, and related more to the long history of descriptive studies[31] than to the manipulation of numbers.[32]  Given the incompatibility of the two kinds of evidence, we suspect that alignments on the issue of equalization of school resources are, and will continue to be, based largely on simple moral arguments.

### Levels of Resource Inequalities

In Chapter 3 we will document what should be obvious from casual observation—that inequalities in educational expenditures exist among states, among
districts within states, and among schools within districts. This study will concentrate largely on the second of these sources, interdistrict inequalities. It is
worthwhile outlining briefly why intrastate inequalities are both the subject
of our analysis and the object of much of the current legal and judicial concern.
Both interstate and intrastate disparities are caused largely by differences in
wealth. It seems logical that the federal government could act as an agent of
equalization among the states, and states could serve the same function in the
intrastate case. The federal government could add to state revenues so as to
equalize among states, but it is not bound to do so by any interpretation of the
Constitution. It has so far appeared unable or unwilling to spend the amounts
which interstate equalization would require.

Our efforts will be misplaced, however, if interdistrict inequalities are small
relative to interstate or intradistrict inequalities. This seems not to be the case.[33]
We will document in Chapter 4 that interstate inequalities in total revenue among
states are somewhat larger than inequalities within the states chosen for analysis,
although our sample of states is biased toward those with smaller within-state
variation. Katzman concluded that the magnitude of inequality for the two
levels is about the same,[34] and given the bias in our sample, we agree with his
conclusion. Measuring inequalities within districts is much more difficult. What
data there is suggests that within-district inequality is smaller than that within
states.[35] Although the data on which to base any conclusion is weak, it appears
that intrastate inequality is as large as any other source, and efforts to diminish
it are therefore important.

### Succeeding Chapters

In our view, analysis that has as an objective some statement or proposal
about the future must have a historical grounding. Institutions evolve, and only
in seeing the forces behind that evolution can one reasonably evaluate possible
further evolution. In Chapter 2, then, we offer a brief history of public education in the United States, with emphasis on the public finance of schools. We
have found that many analysts underrate the importance of the forces we delin-
eate, feeling that new legislation or some court decision will rectify all problems.
We strongly disagree, and even though the statistical analysis in later chapters
does not directly utilize the historical analysis, our *interpretation* of the statistical analysis will do so (in Chapter 9).

In Part II we analyze the distribution of school funds. This requires an
explanation of what a *distribution* is, how funds are currently distributed, what

*redistribution* is and how it might be measured. Redistribution is not an obvious concept, and measuring it is not straightforward. We demonstrate a fallacy in most studies of redistribution which have not been based on a behavioral model, and we discuss what kinds of estimates would derive from a behavioral approach to redistribution problems.

In Part III we describe and estimate a behavioral model of intrastate public school finance. This is a technically complicated estimation which many readers will not want to follow in fine detail. We trust that we will have made clear in Part II why such a model is necessary in order to investigate the role of the state in redistributing school funds. Finally, in Chapter 8, we utilize the statistical model to simulate the effects of alternative state actions in Massachusetts. We conclude with a summary opinion (Chapter 9), considering the historical and the statistical analyses, on what kinds of state formulations we think are best, and why even the best equalization schemes must in some absolute sense "fail."

Part II essentially describes the *results* of a process which involves individuals, collectives (school districts), state action, and responses to that action. Part III investigates the behavioral responses of local districts to state actions which may be seen by districts as *exogenous*, or predetermined at any point in time and beyond local control. Part III is therefore about the *process* which generates the results described in Part II. But state actions are not exogenous. They are the result of prior behavior, political influences, and compromises. That is partly what Chapter 2 is about, but what is missing is a more rigorous current political analysis, indicating which private interests are favored in state legislation, and how these interests predominate. Except for that (serious) omission, we intend to describe the process, the results, and some of the underlying forces in public school finance.

### Notes

1. See Wise (279) and Coons, Clune, and Sugarman (52) for development of the equal protection argument, as well as discussions of how far the argument can be applied. For some of the early debate on the issue, see the articles in Daly (60).
2. The restriction of the various suits to issues of resource inequalities rather than inequities in the outcomes of schooling was reinforced by the denial of two early suits, *McInnis* v. *Shapiro* and *Burruss* v. *Wilkerson*, essentially on the grounds that the courts could not—not yet, at any rate—handle issues as complex and unresolved as the outcomes of schooling.
3. The *Serrano* decision has been reprinted in the *Harvard Educational Review*, November 1971, and in "Selected Court Decisions Relating to Equal Educational Opportunity," U.S. Government Printing Office.

4. *San Antonio Independent School District* v. *Rodriguez*.
5. Supreme Court of New Jersey, A-58 September Term 1972, decision by Justice Weintraub, April 3, 1973 (typescript).
6. *Hobson* v. *Hansen, Mission Coalition, et al.* v. *San Francisco Unified School District, Brown, Cortez, et al.* v. *Board of Education of the City of Chicago, Bradley* v. *Milliken*. The most recent *Hobson* decision is the most elaborate judicial response yet. Rather than mandating a legislative authority to fulfill a relatively vague criterion in its allocation, it set out a specific rule: teacher expenditures per pupil could not deviate in the Washington, D.C. elementary schools by more than 5 percent of the mean expenditures on these teachers for the district. The mandate then went directly to the executive authority (the school board and superintendent) to put this rule into effect. The school board hired consultants to reallocate teachers and issued a report declaring the system in compliance by the fall of 1971.
7. A logical extension of those cases is that all public services, not just education, should be equalized under these criteria. See *Hawkins* v. *Town of Shaw,* wherein street services and lighting are required to be the same in all parts of town.
8. This trend was largely sparked by the Coleman report (51), which indicated that school inputs could not predict school outputs, as reflected in achievement test scores. For a review of this literature, see Averch et al. (7).
9. The distinction between inputs and resources might be confusing. Consider two schools staffed with "identical" teachers who speak only English. If the pupils in one school speak only Spanish, the *inputs* are the same in both schools but the *resources* (the specific inputs needed to perform productive functions) would be different. For a more detailed explanation and investigation of the "resourceness" of different inputs for different children, see Michelson (170). The U.S. Supreme Court has ruled that identical inputs are insufficient if they are shown to be unequal resources (in *Lau* v. *Nichols*).
10. See Owen (200), Toder (258), Levin (153).
11. Purely technical problems of current educational production functions include the lack of longitudinal data, the lack of learning models, the use of overly simple additive linear specifications, least-squares bias, sample bias, errors in variables, the unmeasurability of some critical factors, and an exclusive focus on achievement test scores.
12. Large cities may find attracting resources difficult (Owen [200]), or may find other prices extremely high (Listokin [157], B. Levin [151], Callahan, Wilkin, and Sillerman [43]). Many state formulations now recognize diseconomies of extremely small scale, but we are not convinced that these exist. See Bussard (42), Michelson (171).
13. See, for example, Moynihan (186) and Finn and Lenkowsky (76), and Cohen (50). This argument has gained some support from Jencks et al. (125), who

have been widely and erroneously cited as saying that "schools make no difference." In fact, the only original material relevant to this argument presented by Jencks is a rather simple and badly specified wage equation (Appendix B), from which he concludes that equalizing years of schooling in the population would not equalize earnings very much. This result is due to the wide variation in earnings for individuals with similar years of schooling, a well-known point which few would dispute. But schooling is still critical to the probability of earning a given level of income, as has been conceded by Jencks (125). Properly interpreted, the book does not call for the abandonment of efforts to decrease unequal inequalities in schooling as much as it calls for additional mechanisms to narrow the income distribution more directly.

14. Coleman et al. (51); Mosteller and Moynihan (185); Bowles (29); Michelson (170), Hanushek (101), H. Levin (152) and (153), Boardman (27), Winkler (277). See Guthrie et al. (98) in conjunction with the review by Rivlin (220). See the review by Ribich (218) for an attempt to draw a conclusion, and Averch (7) for details of many studies.

15. For similar arguments, see Parsons (202) and Dreeben (69). For similar results from training after school, see the review by Goldstein (84) and see especially Schiller (228).

16. U.S. Department of Labor (264).

17. See especially Piore (208). Within the primary market, a distinction may be made between *routinized* or lower-tier workers and *creative* or upper-tier workers, with the two kinds of jobs again distinguished largely by the personality traits and attitudes required for successful work. See Piore (207) and Gordon (85) and (86).

18. In addition, the history of schooling supports this counterhypothesis. For overviews, see Chapter 2 and Bowles (30). See also Katz's (140) contention that the assumption of schools instilling noncognitive traits would be the most fruitful for historians of education.

19. For similar views, see Bowles (30), Friedenburg (80). The notion that schools largely train for docility has received widespread attention from critics of schools; see Silberman (240).

20. See especially Dreeben (69).

21. For a general analysis of the role of schooling in legitimizing the distribution of income and status, see Bowles and Gintis (33). See also Sennett and Cobb (232), Ch. 3.

22. See *Robinson* v. *Cahill*, in *Selected Court Decisions*, p. 546-547.

23. Class-related differences in attitudes toward schools have been described by Hyman (117) and Toby (257).

24. For general discussions of cooling-out see Clark (48) and Karabel (135).

25. See Kozol (148), Herndon (109), Kohl (146), Silberman (240).

26. See also Jencks et al. (125), pp. 256-257.

27. The concept of equal educational opportunity has also proved rather mal-
    leable, adapting to the larger requirements imposed on the educational
    system. See Grubb and Lazerson (94) or Cohen and Lazerson (49) for an
    analysis of the shift in the content of the phrase during the vocational
    education movement, shortly after 1900.
28. For more elaborate discussion, see Cohen (50).
29. This principle has been enunciated in *Hobson* v. *Hansen,* and in Justice
    Marshall's dissent in the Supreme Court's decision in *San Antonio Inde-
    pendent School District* v. *Rodriquez.*
30. See, for example, the discussion in *Serrano* v. *Priest.* The Supreme Court's
    reversal of *Rodriquez* simply noted the controversial nature of the Coleman-
    type evidence, and did not use it in any important way to buttress its
    rejection of education as a fundamental interest. But in his dissent, Justice
    Marshall, after noting the disagreement over the effect of expenditures on
    school quality, proceeded to use another basis for claiming why expendi-
    tures betoken school quality: "It is difficult to believe that if the children
    of Texas had free choice, they would choose to be educated with fewer
    resources, and hence with more antiquated plants, less experienced teachers,
    and a less diversified curriculum."
        In New Jersey, the superior court recognized the existence of contro-
    versy. It then proceeded to stress those statistical findings favorable to the
    efficacy of school resources, but more particularly those experiments (in
    Hartford, Washington D.C., and Jersey City) supporting the efficacy of
    schooling. *Robinson* v. *Cahill,* in *Selected Court Decision*, pp. 545-47.
    The Supreme Court of New Jersey affirmed this position.
31. For example, Lynd and Lynd (159), Hollingshead (113).
32. For additional comments on the weaknesses of the "numbers game," see
    Michelson's (173) review of Jencks et al. (125).
33. In theory we could decompose the variation of expenditures by school
    into among-state, within-state, and within-district variation in order to
    determine the relative magnitude of each source of inequality. Such an
    approach would necessitate data on the average expenditure per pupil for
    each state, district, and school in the country. Even analysis of variance
    for interstate and intrastate variance would require an overwhelming amount
    of data. Approximations to analysis of variance by using either incomplete
    samples of states or incomplete samples of districts within states were judged
    to be unreliable.
34. Katzman (141), Ch. 5, especially Table 5.1.
35. The average coefficient of variation (standard deviation divided by the mean)
    of expenditure per pupil for Atlanta, Boston, and Chicago is 0.14, while the
    coefficient of variation of intra-state inequality reported is 0.22-0.26
    (Katzman [141], Tables 5.1 and 5.8).

# 2

## School Financing Patterns and the Functions of Schooling: An Historical Analysis

We start from a concern with inequalities in the provision of resources to schools. In order to assess the possibilities for changing the current patterns of school financing, we need to know how those patterns developed, and more specifically whether they have been complementary or antagonistic to the more basic purposes of schooling. An analysis of the functions of schooling and the patterns of financing should enable us to understand the persistence of inequality in the provision of resources.

The lack of such an analysis previously may come from the tendency of social scientists to analyze schooling in terms of their own academic specialties. Economists explore the contributions of education to productivity and growth and view education as an investment with a determinable rate of return. Sociologists investigate the function of education in stabilizing society and inculcating societal norms. Political scientists analyze schools as a source of jobs, and school boards as bases of political power. Psychologists discuss psychological and cognitive development in relation to formal schooling and shape the kinds of curricula generally available.[1] While this is an inevitable result of academic specialization, it does produce a series of partial analyses, and more particularly tends to divorce current educational practices and institutions from their histories. As a result, we lose sight of motivations for education which are not economic (or sociological or political or psychological) but which were crucial in the development of education. Hence this separation works to diminish our understanding of the purposes and possibilities of education. Although we may not totally avoid this separation ourselves, we will begin with an outline of the creation and spread of public education in the United States to provide the necessary framework for the analysis which follows. After briefly characterizing schooling in the colonial era, we will focus on the two periods of great change in educational institutions—the mid-nineteenth century and the Progressive era—on the assumption that during periods of crisis and change the most essential elements of schooling can best be isolated. The second section of this chapter will describe the development of the present system of school finance, showing how the financing of public education has been supportive of other functions of schooling. This is not a surprising finding, of course; however, this investigation does fit in with current reinterpretations of the history of education and lends added weight to some of this new work.[2]

The history of education is complex, and we can hardly investigate most of the subtleties and ambiguities inherent in the material of this chapter. For example, we will not attempt to assess the motives of conventional educators or reformers, nor assess whether knowing these motives would be interesting or important. We will describe tendencies which have strengthened over time, but which have never been universally applicable. Finally, we will not extensively substantiate arguments we have made in detail elsewhere.

### The Purposes of Education

Most nonliterate or "traditional" societies transmit both general and vocational information to succeeding generations, and allocate labor, without the institution presumed to perform both of these functions in modern societies: schools. There are a number of explanations for the development of this institution. The most obvious are that literacy and the scope of knowledge places increased requirements on individuals, that informal learning is more difficult and schooling more effective in societies with *disembodied* economies,[3] that required skills change from generation to generation, and that with technical change the ability to adapt to change is more valuable than any particular skill. Thus society requires institutions within which knowledge is stored (libraries), expanded (research), utilized (development), and transmitted (schools and training programs). Younger members of society are engaged in learning communication skills and the rudiments of advanced technology. This description emphasizes the shift from traditional mechanisms of allocating labor to allocation through market forces, and the role which education plays in preparing individuals for the labor market and future occupations.

This might be an acceptable description of the functioning of public schools were there not compelling reasons to question its completeness. We will discover that education in the United States was not closely bound to the nature of occupations and the labor market until the beginning of this century, and that prior to that time other motives—largely, the noncognitive content of schooling—shaped the development of public schools. In particular, the first model contains no mechanisms which channel individual behavior into societally desired behavior. In an alternative explanation of modern education, a major difference between modern and traditional or preliterate societies is that status and power are not now legally inherited and are not based on traditional relations (such as the attachment of a tribe to its chief) but are based on production relations and the wealth and status resulting from one's position in the system of production. The most important mechanism for allocating positions in the productive system is formal education, in which children complete a set of seemingly desirable requirements and are so certified. The certification is then used independently of the background of individuals to select among candidates for a particular position. Wealth and status are inherited only insofar as children replicate the productive characteristics of their parents.[4]

Under this second model, schools function to establish, maintain, and legit-imize the class structure. Schools exemplify a set of rules which operate to induce objectively determinable characteristics in people, characteristics then used to select individuals into positions of class and status. In the process, schools establish a reward structure congruent with societal norms. Addition-ally, schools may be called upon to establish the propriety of these rules so that the workings and the outcome of education are accepted even by those who do not benefit from them. The rules must be applied fairly: Many institutions in our society are constrained by ideals of democracy and equality of oppor-tunity. When it is determined that outcomes have been overtly manipulated, most people object to the results. But where outcomes are the product of biased rules applied without overt favoritism, many people appear satisfied. Equality of *process* is important, despite inequality of outcomes, in the Ameri-can democratic ideal.

Increasingly over time, education has tended not only to establish classes, but to *preserve* them from generation to generation. The education system has done this while appearing to be eminently fair, and educational reforms were constantly evaluated by the criterion of democratic operation. But the "right" people—the children of those with higher class and status—have always benefited the most from schools. Education has functioned to manipulate outcomes *covertly,* both by setting the rules and by changing them when necessary, so that certain groups within society would benefit from them consistently, yet in seeming consonance with "equality of educational opportunity." [5]

One might question whether schools must in fact discriminate in order to favor certain classes of children. If schools merely succeed in mantaining the rank order of skills acquired elsewhere, and these skills are then employed to select the leaders of society, this would be sufficient to preserve class structure. Current research findings are consistent with this possibility. [6] This presents the likelihood that, like many social systems, the school system in its stratifica-tion function is redundant. Many facets are not strictly necessary, and many inequalities in its processes might be rectified without markedly equalizing outcomes such as the distribution of income or status. This implies that, to some extent, the functioning of education to manipulate outcomes and the existence of resource disparities may be unimportant, since other mechanisms exist which also insure that outcomes will be consistently biased in favor of certain groups. But, although schools may not be strictly necessary to preserve class structure, neither has their development been haphazard. In a society pervaded by inequalities, schools have increasingly come to be important mechanisms for transmitting many of those inequalities from one generation to the next, and for justifying the pattern of inequalities as the result of a fair, rational process. For the purposes of studying schooling in this country, it seems to us more important to understand how schools have come to function in these ways than to calculate the independent effect of schooling on stratification.

### Education in the Colonial Era

Development of the school system in the Massachusetts Bay Colony and the state of Massachusetts is better documented than most school systems. Many states designed their systems after Massachusetts, just as that colony's original education statutes followed the Elizabethan laws of the earliest years of the seventeenth century, and these laws in turn had their roots in the Reformation. Indeed, the religious character of public education continued until the early nineteenth century: "The Bible was put into the hands of the people to be for each one an individual guide and help, and at least an education sufficient to read and understand it was a necessary corollary."[7] The Massachusetts General Court, in issuing the first law in the colonies requiring the establishment of schools, made clear the ideological basis of the action. "It being one chief point of that older deluder, Satan, to keep men from the knowledge of the scriptures, . . ."[8] the state required (1) that townships of at least 50 households establish an elementary school which would focus on biblical training, and (2) every town of at least 100 households must establish a grammar school able to prepare the children for university entrance. This "Old Deluder" law of 1647 had been preceded by a 1642 statute in which the court instructed the town leaders "to take account from time to time of their parents and masters of their children concerning their calling and employment of their children, especially of their ability to read and understand the principles of religion and the capital laws of the country."[9]

Thus the religious basis of education—education for morality—co-existed with the need for a citizenry able to read, understand, and act according to law. At least one interpreter saw this latter function as predominant:

> They [the General Court] knew that an industrious child was a squared stone fit to be builded into the edifice they were rearing, so they would have the children put to work. They called illiteracy barbarism, and therefore, not for the Church's sake nor for the child's sake, but for the sake of the commonwealth, they insisted on universal education.[10]

Whether moral or more Machiavellian reasons underlay the law, it was certainly not designed to liberate the children from the bonds of society, but to bind the children to society. No mention is made of the acquisition of skills, save those required for admission to the university.

The university at issue was Harvard University, which had been established by the court in 1636. Harvard functioned initially to train ministers and lawyers. Since these were among the most powerful men, it served to maintain an elite class, though by means of objective entrance examinations which the average student could not hope to pass.[11] The privileged students, moreover, did not necessarily acquire skills in production or trade, or more basic skills which might be required to operate successfully in a labor market among upper-class progeny. At this time there was no such market, and the educational content served only to set standards for the populace and identify the elite.[12]

It is impossible to describe education in the colonial era very precisely, because a uniform system of schools did not yet exist. Education was carried on in a variety of dame schools, private academies, public schools, and church-supported schools. Yet we can discern two important threads running through the picture of early Massachusetts education. One is that the basic education of children—even those who could not afford it—was a sound investment in terms of maintaining society. The school could supplement the home as a transmitter of morals and culture,[13] and society would function more smoothly from having its children adhere to societally determined norms. The second aspect of education appears to contradict the first: Education began to identify classes. In the colonial era this function of education is only barely discernible. Success in commerce or agriculture was more important than education in defining elite groups, and education had very little importance in labor markets. But insofar as higher education was important, it served to identify members of the upper class.

Public schools attended by the masses would serve the first function, transmitting to children a mode of adaptive behavior and uncritical thought, but they could not simultaneously serve the second. This contradiction was resolved by creating a dual educational system. Primary schools were local and locally financed. Grammar schools which would prepare students for entry to Harvard were required only in reasonably large towns. Poorer families could not afford to send their children to such a school—afford in the sense of not needing the child's labor for support of the family. Thus a low level of schooling was established for many, but a higher level was established for the few. Stratification occurred both among schools—from residential segregation and local control—and between levels of schooling.

### The Early Reform Era

In the early nineteenth century the economic value of education was appreciated in two ways. As Lester Ward expressed one aspect, "from an economic point of view, an uneducated class is an expensive class."[14] This updates a theme from earlier times: The state benefits from education in that it creates a working class out of an indolent class, a law-abiding class out of a lawless class. A second economic benefit is the direct output created by the now educated, hence employed, person. As Horace Mann emphasized:

The greatest of all the arts in political economy is to change a

consumer into a producer; and the next greatest is to increase the
producer's producing power—an end to be directly attained by
increasing his intelligence.[15]

With the benefits of public education recognized, the next logical step was
to increase its scope. Particularly after 1830, the concept of universal public
education spread, and public systems of education increasingly replaced the
variety of schools which dominated education in the early years of the century.[16]
The emphasis was on a *system* of education, one which presented the same moral
structure and culture to all citizens. Public education became systematized and
bureaucratized in form.[17]  The education provided was, at least ideally, available
to all—hence the label "common school education"—and justified in democratic
and egalitarian terms.

The facts, however, tended to be somewhat different from the rhetoric.
Even from the beginning of the mid-eighteenth century, reform had tended to
come in such a way as to alienate lower-class parents from schools. The values
embodied in schools were those of the ruling middle and upper classes.[18]  Hence,
not only was access to education—at least, the highest level of education, the
high school—difficult for the children of the poor, but so was its content and
style. A particularly vivid example involved the vote to abolish the high school
in Beverly, Massachusetts in 1860. The "wealthy and prominent citizens"
supported the school "as the harbinger of manufacturing and urban growth,"
and on the basis of the state benefit arguments advanced above. The opponents
consisted of an alliance between those who had no children (and were not per-
suaded that they would benefit as citizens of a better society), and "the least
affluent citizens who felt that the high school would not benefit their children."[19]
Education was far from the sole prerequisite for success, but it now overtly
appeared to benefit the children from higher social strata. Public high school
would tax the poor and benefit the children of the merchant and white-collar rich.

In addition, education became increasingly identified with industry during
this period: "The school became the means of instilling in the population the
qualities necessary for success in industrial society."[20]  As industrialization progressed, industrial values became more important in society and in the moral
content of education. When Cubberley noted that "weeks, months, and even
years are spent in drilling on problems of a type no man in practical life ever
solves, and which can be of no use to anyone except a school teacher,"[21] he
accurately described a process which taught children not *how* to work, just *to*
work. The structure of classes and the bureaucratic form of education itself,
derived partly from bureaucracy in industry,[22] taught the importance of
punctuality, obediance, efficiency, and the efficacy of hierarchical and bureaucratic forms of organization. On the other hand, textbooks in the nineteenth
century actually inveighed against creative thinking. Intellectualism was an
elite characteristic and would therefore have to be preserved for elite groups

in the universities. For the masses, moral education and acceptance of one's place in moral society was the goal of schooling.[23]

By 1870, public education was far from completely developed. Formal schooling was not yet crucial to many occupations, and the Horatio Alger stories of the period stressed the importance of moral attributes rather than cognitive skills learned in schools.[24] However, the basic structure of education had been established. It was universal, free, and compulsory, but also bureaucratic, class-biased, and racist.[25] While some education was available to all, high schools (and universities) were largely reserved for children of middle- and upper-class parents. Hence something like a dual school system existed.

### The Progressive Era

By 1890 industrialization was generally complete or well under way, with the replacement of skilled labor by machines and unskilled labor.[26] Industrial values had begun to dominate society. Education internalized these values, and began to model itself after corporate capitalist enterprises, with the values of efficiency and order, the hierarchical relations of bureaucracies, and the duty to serve the economic order.[27] At the same time increasingly large numbers of children flooded into the high schools, especially the "children of the plain people,"[28] lower-class and working-class children. Immigrants had been flooding East Coast urban schools for several decades.

The response to all these forces was the vocational education movement. Spearheaded by businessmen who argued that it would increase productivity and restore international competitiveness, vocational education was also championed as superior in terms of "moral education," as capable of solving many of the societal problems which industrialization had brought and many of the problems important to educators (e.g., the high dropout rates, the necessity for individualizing instruction, the demand for greater equality of educational opportunity). Vocational education was the panacea of the moment, and support for it was strong enough to overcome political obstacles to federal aid. With the establishment of vocational education came the destruction of the common school ideology, the notion that all students in high schools were to receive the same education. It was replaced by differentiated curricula and ability-grouping or tracking. Mechanisms were developed to administer education which were consistent with the drive for efficiency, rationality, objectivity, and strict hierarchical orderings of jobs. These included testing, vocational guidance offices, and extensive surveys of vocational requirements and opportunities.

There are no indications that vocational education made any difference to job performance, except insofar as it furthered "industrial intelligence," the non-cognitive requirements for industrial jobs such as punctuality, obedience, and so forth. Nor did it solve any of the other problems which it was supposed to. But, in the face of increased enrollments in high schools, it did provide the mechanisms and rationale for the differentiation of education. Education continued as a dual system, with a tendency to channel middle- and upper-class children into academic tracks and lower- and working-class children into vocational tracks and, the lowest of the low, a "general" track. Since this was happening when formal education was becoming a prerequisite for many jobs, one's occupation (and hence one's position in society) tended to depend more on schooling than it previously had.[29]

This is not to argue that education was or is a perfect mechanism of transmitting status from generation to generation. However, we can recognize in the vocational education movement the further development of two functions of public education which appear throughout its history. First, education served to prepare the masses of people for their roles in the economy—in the nineteenth and early twentieth centuries a corporate-capitalist industrial economy—and to teach them the cultural standards and personality norms necessary both to individual survival in society and by extension to the survival of society. Second, education served as one of the important mechanisms to select middle- and upper-middle-class children into the next generation's privileged classes.[30] Education has also appeared as an "objective" process, and surrounded itself with the trappings of objectivity. Hence, the results of education are taken as fair, and failure to rise in society is a personal failure, not a systemic failure.[31] The mechanisms which produced inequalities in the results—e.g., the necessity of working which prevented attendance, low scores on "objective" tests of mental ability—were seen as not under the control of the educational system, so the system saw itself as providing equal educational opportunity. The emphasis was on developing a fair *process*. The fact that the *outcomes* were neither fair nor equal attracted relatively less attention.

### The Structure of Public Education and the Development of School Finance

Public education developed with the state always playing a role—although at first only regulatory and permissive. In 1683, Massachusetts decreed that towns with 500 or more families were required to support two grammar and two writing schools. Control existed at an even more decentralized level than the town. Towns in Massachusetts were usually divided into "districts" which derived their revenue from towns but had complete control over its expenditure. This system of districts had generally superseded the earlier township system by the middle of the eighteenth century and became sanctioned by a series of laws around 1800. The district system appears to have been analogous to present proposals for community control. The system spread from Massachusetts to the other New England states, and thence to other northern states. However, one of the strong tendencies throughout the nineteenth century was the increasing bureaucratization of education, including the centralization of control for reasons of efficiency and coordination of policy.[32] In Massachusetts the district system came under fire as early as 1824. It was gradually replaced by the older system of control by towns, although it was not finally abolished until 1882.[33]

Another aspect of centralization was increasing control by the state. In the early years of the eighteenth century the state began to supervise the running of schools, first by establishing that they be inspected—initially by ministers, a residue of the earliest religious schooling, and later by a public body established for the purposes of inspection. State boards of education began to be established at the beginning of the nineteenth century and gradually gained power to certify teachers, establish standards with respect to buildings, curricula, days of school, books, and so forth.[34] However, states did not take over the finance of education, at least not in the North. Massachusetts was an extreme example. Despite the establishment of state aid funds as early as 1834, state revenues accounted for only a small portion of total revenue—1.6 percent in 1895, and 2.8 percent as late as 1915. But as Table 2-1 indicates, this pattern of reliance on local revenue was typical of northern states prior to 1900.

One reason for the continued dominance of local finance despite increased state power over minimum standards of education was the notion of local autonomy. In the Northeast, where public education was firmly established before state control, there was ready opposition to attempts to encroach on the prerogatives of local school districts. And, rightly or wrongly, state finance had been seen as leading to greater state control.[35] Local autonomy itself, of course, meant stratification by social class as transportation networks developed and social classes came to live in different political jurisdictions.

However, this model of firmly established local districts preventing extensive state finance before 1900 did not hold in the South. As Table 2-1 shows, state support of education overwhelmed local support in the Southern states, with the exceptions of Florida and Arkansas. After the Civil War, education in the Southern states was established on a state basis—with state financing—by Reconstruction governments under the control of Northern interests. An important purpose of public education was to serve as the transmitter of Northern culture and morals, to bring "the conquered white people into ideological harmony with the victors."[36] Hence Southern states, in contrast to those in the North, started from a system of state financing. The initial levels of educational financing proved inadequate, especially as literacy tests for voting (designed to disenfranchise blacks) prompted whites to call for more education for themselves and as industrialization progressed. Although state financing did provide some of the revenue necessary for educational expansion, most states turned to increased amounts of county and local taxes because of the fear that the state would support black schools, and fear that the Fourteenth Amendment would require

**Table 2-1**
**Percentages of Public School Revenue Derived from Federal and State Sources, 1890-1930**

| | 1890 | 1895 | 1900 | 1905 | 1910 | 1915 | 1920 | 1925 | 1930 |
|---|---|---|---|---|---|---|---|---|---|
| *North Atlantic* | | | | | | | | | |
| Connecticut | 19.9 | 17.3 | 15.9 | 18.4 | 14.0 | 13.5 | 12.3 | 9.5 | 8.1 |
| Delaware | 26.1 | 24.0 | 24.0 | 32.0 | 32.7 | 46.2 | 35.3 | 81.5 | 87.9 |
| Maine | 30.9 | 30.8 | 29.2 | 29.1 | 36.5 | 50.0 | 35.6 | 27.0 | 28.6 |
| Maryland | 34.4 | 28.6 | 26.5 | 35.1 | 39.2 | 32.8 | 41.6 | 20.7 | 17.7 |
| Massachusetts | 3.4 | 1.6 | 1.2 | 2.1 | 2.0 | 1.8 | 12.3 | 9.4 | 9.5 |
| New Hampshire | 9.8 | 11.4 | 3.9 | 4.6 | 7.0 | 7.4 | 8.7 | 11.1 | 9.0 |
| New Jersey | 62.3 | 48.8 | 40.6 | 32.9 | 17.6 | 46.6 | 35.6 | 22.5 | 21.2 |
| New York | 19.8 | 18.3 | 10.9 | 71.3 | 9.0 | 15.3 | 30.1 | 7.1 | 16.6 |
| Pennsylvania | 10.6 | 26.4 | 22.0 | 16.2 | 15.6 | 10.1 | 15.9 | 14.8 | 13.9 |
| Rhode Island | 13.1 | 9.5 | 9.4 | 8.7 | 8.6 | 6.3 | 5.2 | 5.5 | 8.6 |
| Vermont | 9.5 | 16.0 | 15.7 | 15.7 | 19.8 | 20.8 | 33.1 | 20.5 | 12.2 |
| *Southeast* | | | | | | | | | |
| Alabama | 67.7 | 80.6 | 82.3 | 65.6 | 74.1 | 52.7 | 51.3 | 33.2 | 40.8 |
| Arkansas | 48.9 | 33.4 | 31.1 | 29.1 | 35.3 | 34.1 | 23.7 | 35.5 | 33.7 |
| Florida | 22.6 | 18.5 | 18.3 | 21.8 | 13.5 | 10.6 | 7.2 | 5.6 | 22.8 |
| Georgia | 56.5 | 72.9 | 64.4 | 66.4 | 53.0 | 44.8 | 43.5 | 32.7 | 35.6 |
| Kentucky | 59.3 | 54.6 | 52.6 | 62.3 | 53.0 | 45.3 | 37.1 | 29.3 | 26.1 |
| Louisiana | 37.2 | 24.3 | 30.0 | 28.6 | 25.3 | 24.1 | 24.5 | 21.0 | 26.9 |
| Mississippi | 44.3 | 81.9 | 59.4 | 77.3 | 55.2 | 51.6 | 52.1 | 27.4 | 33.5 |
| North Carolina | 77.4 | 83.2 | 82.9 | 71.3 | 9.0 | 15.3 | 30.1 | 7.1 | 16.6 |
| South Carolina | 82.7 | 79.7 | 65.5 | 61.4 | 3.9 | 9.2 | 15.8 | 26.4 | 25.5 |
| Tennessee | 81.7 | 87.8 | 7.2 | 19.7 | 15.9 | 19.2 | 17.8 | 21.7 | 24.7 |
| Texas | 79.9 | 73.7 | 75.0 | 66.3 | 57.2 | 44.1 | 54.0 | 37.8 | 42.6 |
| Virginia | 52.7 | 53.4 | 50.4 | 46.4 | 39.1 | 31.8 | 36.7 | 27.9 | 27.9 |
| West Virginia | 28.2 | 21.5 | 20.2 | 21.9 | 19.0 | 12.1 | 6.4 | 7.4 | 8.3 |
| *Great Lakes and Plains* | | | | | | | | | |
| Illinois | 14.3 | 10.4 | 10.2 | 7.9 | 5.2 | 9.7 | 8.7 | 6.9 | 5.3 |
| Indiana | 36.9 | 31.5 | 29.2 | 21.1 | 21.0 | 16.9 | 10.6 | 10.3 | 5.5 |
| Iowa | 3.9 | 2.8 | 1.4 | 8.0 | 7.5 | 8.3 | 1.5 | 3.8 | 4.3 |
| Kansas | 7.2 | 9.2 | 9.4 | 7.9 | 6.1 | 3.5 | 2.3 | 1.4 | 1.7 |
| Michigan | 14.0 | 16.3 | 15.6 | 23.9 | 41.1 | 28.3 | 17.1 | 20.5 | 18.2 |
| Minnesota | 18.1 | 24.9 | 22.7 | 21.1 | 20.8 | 28.0 | 19.5 | 18.8 | 20.6 |
| Missouri | 18.9 | 24.1 | 20.8 | 17.6 | 19.4 | 15.2 | 11.9 | 6.6 | 10.6 |
| Nebraska | 19.2 | 13.6 | 17.4 | 12.7 | 8.9 | 8.5 | 6.6 | 3.8 | 5.4 |
| North Dakota | 21.1 | 31.0 | 30.7 | 13.9 | 20.5 | 17.9 | 12.1 | 21.4 | 11.1 |
| Ohio | 19.0 | 16.0 | 15.2 | 11.5 | 10.2 | 9.0 | 7.3 | 4.8 | 4.1 |
| South Dakota | 14.8 | 10.9 | 13.7 | 18.2 | 14.9 | 13.1 | 16.6 | 9.9 | 10.1 |
| Wisconsin | 19.5 | 16.3 | 13.3 | 17.3 | 15.8 | 20.6 | 15.6 | 11.0 | 17.0 |
| *West and Southwest* | | | | | | | | | |
| Arizona | 1.0 | 78.8 | 4.0 | 8.7 | 7.4 | 24.6 | 18.7 | 25.2 | 19.6 |
| California | 51.6 | 51.0 | 48.7 | 45.7 | 28.1 | 25.5 | 20.4 | 20.8 | 25.6 |
| Colorado | 5.2 | 4.7 | 4.0 | 4.4 | 2.3 | 31.6 | 9.6 | 4.0 | 3.2 |
| Idaho | – | 4.5 | 40.4 | 10.5 | 14.0 | 12.6 | 9.7 | 8.0 | 7.7 |
| Montana | – | – | – | 47.6 | 6.7 | 56.1 | 9.9 | 7.8 | 14.1 |
| Nevada | 35.0 | 56.4 | 55.5 | 51.8 | 35.0 | 37.7 | 26.6 | 23.3 | 19.0 |
| New Mexico | – | – | 91.5 | 60.0 | 7.8 | 30.1 | 17.6 | 18.3 | 21.8 |
| Oklahoma | – | 36.8 | 18.1 | 16.6 | 15.8 | 15.3 | 7.5 | 10.3 | 10.6 |
| Oregon | 16.4 | 15.6 | 12.4 | 11.9 | 6.9 | 6.7 | 4.8 | 16.9 | 2.3 |
| Utah | 47.3 | 32.8 | 28.2 | 24.4 | 26.8 | 20.8 | 31.5 | 37.8 | 33.6 |
| Washington | – | 8.8 | 43.8 | 49.2 | 28.4 | 22.4 | 18.1 | 27.2 | 28.9 |
| Wyoming | – | – | 14.8 | 21.6 | 19.5 | 38.4 | 24.3 | 34.1 | 27.1 |

Source: Paul Mort, *State Support for Public Education* (Washington: American Council on Education, 1933), p. 26. Reprinted with permission of the American Council on Education.

state funds to be equitably disbursed.[37]  Hence support of education in the
South became decreasingly state-dominated after 1900, although local revenues
never became as important as they were in the rest of the country.[38]

### State and Local Finance in the
### Twentieth Century[39]

At the turn of the century, several educators noted that reliance on local
finance had led to considerable inequalities among school districts.[40]  The
consensus was that when this country was predominantly agricultural, wealth
was evenly spread and local financing resulted in relatively equal ability to
support education.  But as industrialization shifted the source of wealth to
industry in place of agriculture, and urbanization produced concentrations
of wealth, abilities to support education began to differ greatly.  The generally
accepted answer to this problem was to increase state support, first by flat
grants (e.g., grants per capita or per pupil), and increasingly via foundation
plans.[41]  Table 2-2 demonstrates the changing composition of total revenue
over time.  The goal in any case was greater equality of revenues for public
education.

Ellwood Cubberley first ennunciated in 1905 the principles of state aid
which have dominated thinking on the subject throughout this century: State

Table 2-2
**Local, State, and Federal Revenue as Percentages of Total Revenue**

|           | *Federal* | *State* | *Local* |
|-----------|-----------|---------|---------|
| 1889-1890 | (0)       | 23.8    | (76.2)  |
| 1899-1900 | (0)       | 19.9    | (80.9)  |
| 1909-1910 | (0)       | 17.0    | (83.0)  |
| 1919-1920 | 0.3       | 16.5    | 83.2    |
| 1929-1930 | 0.4       | 16.9    | 82.7    |
| 1939-1940 | 1.8       | 30.3    | 68.0    |
| 1949-1950 | 2.9       | 39.8    | 57.3    |
| 1959-1960 | 4.4       | 39.1    | 56.5    |
| 1963-1964 | 4.4       | 39.3    | 56.3    |
| 1965-1966 | 7.9       | 39.1    | 53.0    |
| 1968-1969 | 7.3       | 40.7    | 52.0    |

Sources:  1890–1910: *Biennial Survey of Education,* 1920-1922, p. 15 (federal and
local figures are approximated); 1920–1966: *Digest of Education Statistics,* 1968,
Table 67, p. 56; 1968-1969: NEA, *Estimates of School Statistics,* 1968–69.

aid should be distributed "in definite relation to the needs of the community and to the efforts which it makes to provide good schools and to secure the attendance of children at them." He conceived of ultimately replacing local districts with a state system of schools.[42] However, the largest part of *School Funds and Their Apportionment* is a minute analysis of the different variables which might be used in state aid formulas, a perfect example of concentration on a process seemingly fair, yet rewarding children differentially according to characteristics of their parents. Similarly, the authors of the foundation plan stated that:

> In its extreme form the interpretation [of equalization of educational opportunity or equalization of school support] is somewhat as follows: The state should insure equal educational facilities to every child within its borders at a uniform effort throughout the state in terms of the burden of taxation; the tax burden of education should throughout the state be in relation to tax-paying ability, and the provision for schools should be uniform in relation to the educable population desiring education.[43]

Phrased this way, the philosophy of the foundation plan seemed to call for nothing short of freeing educational revenues from dependence on local wealth and making them a function of local tax effort—precisely as embodied in the percentage equalizing plan and as restated in the concept of "district power equalizing."[44] However, Strayer and Haig proceeded to qualify their statement:

> Most of the supporters of this proposition, however, would not preclude any particular community from offering at its own expense a particularly rich and costly educational program. They would insist that there be an adequate minimum offered everywhere, the expense of which should be considered a prior claim on the state's economic resources.[45]

Instead of providing the mechanisms for achieving substantial equalization, therefore, foundation plans merely provided a minimum (or foundation) level of support. Local districts were free to add local revenues to this minimum level. They were in fact encouraged to do so, a principle which was further developed and justified by Mort as the "efficiency principle."[46] The result was that although state support of education increased after 1920, inequalities among school districts remained large. Especially when compared to the amount of rhetoric supporting equalization of school resource distribution, the impact of foundation plans seems weak indeed.

In 1961 a third type of state aid plan—percentage equalizing—was proposed,[47] and was adopted by eight states in the 1960s. In its pure form, percentage equalization is designed to eliminate one of the primary causes of inequalities in school resources—the dependence of local tax revenues on the local property tax base. Under percentage equalizing, school revenues (exclusive of federal aid) are a function of the local tax effort for education, but not of local property value. However, adoption of percentage equalizing plans has—at least so far—made relatively little difference to inequalities at the district level. For one thing, the small amounts of state aid distributed according to percentage equalizing plans means that it can have relatively little effect.[48] Perhaps more importantly, the experience of the last decade indicates the ease with which the equalizing intentions of percentage equalizing formulas can be undermined by state legislatures.[49] As in previous periods, the 1960s saw considerable pressure for greater equalization and revision of state aid programs,[50] but with relatively little equalization coming from state legislatures.

There has been some reduction in intrastate inequalities in this century,[51] but the current controversy over school financing and the resulting court challenges attest to the inadequacy of progress. There are three important points to be summarized from the history of state aid to local school districts.[52] The first is that the generally accepted state-financing principles of today were formulated as early as 1922, including the "progressive" ones which have been seriously considered only in the past decade or so.[53] As in most aspects of education, we find ourselves grappling again with old problems because the previous solutions have not worked as well as their designers had hoped. Second, the commitment to equalization of revenues has always been tempered by other principles which have weakened the equalization effects of state aid—among them the stimulation of additional local revenue for schooling, the maintenance of "lighthouse districts" of purportedly special excellence, the maintenance of local control, and the provision of across-the-board property tax relief.[54] Third, concern over inequalities in the provision of school resources has manifested itself—from the efforts of Cubberley to the most recent ones of Coons, Clune, and Sugarman—in formulas designed to alleviate inequalities. The search has been for a mechanism or process of passing from one distribution of school resources to another distribution, the process required to be fair and justifiable according to current standards.[55] Often, therefore, the emphasis of writers on school finance has been that of evaluating alternative variables to be used in formulas, measuring different kinds of needs and ability to pay, devising formulas which balance several principles or goals of state intervention against each other, and otherwise attending to the minutiae of devising aid formulas. The fact that gross inequities in educational resources have persisted has sometimes been forgotten in the process: "reforming zeal [has been] dissipated in confrontation with minutiae."[56]

But the overwhelming point of the history of school finance is the congruence between the inequalities in resources provided to schools and the functions of schooling in reproducing the class structure from one generation to the next.

Because school resources are so closely linked to inequalities in income and wealth, the present mechanisms of financing schools provide an initial source of class bias in the provision of schooling. This is true no matter what function of the school one thinks is most important. In the realm of teaching cognitive skills, additional resources can buy additional teacher characteristics which may be productive of higher achievement scores,[57] reinforcing the tendency of such teachers to migrate to schools and districts where white, middle-class children predominate.[58] In the realm of noncognitive traits, lower expenditures per pupil force the crowded classrooms and the lack of physical equipment contributing to the authoritarian classroom relations and the general unpleasantness of surroundings that characterize lower- and working-class schools.[59] Finally, the facile identification of school quality with easily perceived expenditures levels reinforces the class-biased use of school background as a credential, particularly important in terms of access to college.[60]

The congruity between the distribution of school resources and the class-stratification function of schools helps explain the strength of political and legal opposition toward attempts to equalize school resources.[61] Such efforts do not represent only self-interest on the part of those who stand to lose from the abolition of the current system of school financing. They represent in addition the efforts of the educational institution to preserve one aspect of its class-differentiation function,[62] couched in the same arguments about local control and the rights of individuals and communities to allocate resources as they see fit which have marked much of the opposition to equalization of school resources in this century.

### Aid Versus Control

In the debates over the extension of state and federal aid, the fear of control was important in defeating attempts at support of education by higher levels of government.[63] In print, educators feared control over educational policy, the *kind* of education offered—for example, the way in which teachers taught, the books used, and so forth.[64] However, even by 1900 education differed very little from district to district. A national professional organization (the National Educational Association), educators with national reputations, the existence of several widely read educational publications, normal schools for teachers, state boards of education, regional accrediting institutions, and the tendency for school districts to copy the methods of other districts[65] were all forces leading to homogeneity of teaching methods, curricula, organizational forms, teacher certification processes, and so forth. There were exceptions,[66] but their rarity underscores the approximate uniformity of public education within states at any one time.[67] In addition, state control prior to 1920 was achieved in the non-Southern states *without* state financing. States had legal authority over schools, and they exercised control by establishing minimum standards. Since states did have legal authority, state financing was not a prerequisite for state control.[68] The fears of educators over increased state control must be interpreted as sincere, but it is questionable whether increased state aid itself would have brought about significant changes in educational structure or greater state control. The vehemence of the discussion over state finance and local autonomy implies that autonomy has been important to educators independently of whether state control would change the operation of schools or not. If autonomy is an end in itself, then protests against state financing were sincerely motivated. However, the *functional* significance of local control has been more to maintain inequalities than to assure that local schools would be free to educate children as they saw fit.

It is considerably more certain that increased state aid would have seriously limited the ability of local districts to maintain greatly unequal expenditures.[69] In addition, state aid programs always introduce the possibility that wealthy districts will support education in poor districts. We are suggesting that the public arguments may have been about control over educational policy (Strayer's interna), but the most important issues in increasing state aid have concerned the maintenance of advantage and the problem of redistribution of resources (Strayer's externa).

If local control had little functional importance at the turn of the century, it has even less now. Particularly since the end of World War II, the methods and content of public education have been increasingly standardized across the nation, both by the mechanisms noted above, by the growth of national tests, and by programs administered by the federal government.[70] These nationalizing influences are independent of sources of funding for elementary and secondary education. Increasingly, therefore, it appears that the locus of control is independent of the source of revenue.[71]

Finally, cross-section evidence that state control is not closely tied to the extent of state funding has been collected by Levin et al. (151, Ch. 5.) They found little relation between the percentage of revenues derived from the state and the extent of state control, as measured by scores on eleven dimensions of control. Instead, they found—as argued above—that state finance laws provided the real limitations on local autonomy.

We therefore assume that finance and control are separable, at least at the state level we are emphasizing.[72] This may only be because of a lack of variety in public "education." Whether state support for schools could be relied upon if districts seriously challenged the prevailing concept of education (as might be the case for community-controlled schools or "free" schools) is debatable. That is, it may be that increased state support of schools has not resulted in increased state control because control was already in reliable hands, with local educators generally following established and accepted models of what education should be.

Not only total state finance, but also the other extreme of administrative autonomy—finance by the individual school—has been opposed by the National Education Association. By resolution adopted by their Representative Assembly, the NEA opposes the "so-called 'voucher plan' " without distinguishing among plans or considering their provisions.[73]  If the NEA genuinely feared that such plans "could lead to racial, economic, and social isolation of children" they would have passed a resolution favoring "metropolitan" school systems. Fear that vouchers would "weaken or destroy the public school system" are more credible and must lead us to examine what aspects of that system the NEA wishes most of all to preserve. Surely our historic sketch has been deficient in not recognizing struggles for power within the educational establishment. But if fear of state control provides opposition to state finance, fear of parental control must provide opposition to vouchers. Within the larger forces outlined above, public education is also an institution with a large budget—over 50 percent of local government expenditures are for schools—which inevitably engenders political battles for control. Even if control of funds is the driving force behind opposition to educational reforms, the results in terms of the curriculum, both overt and covert, are still biased as we have described them.

In the following chapters, we will analyze school finance separately from school policies because the control of schools (either financial or political) has meant little to the standards by which they operate. Instead, these standards have been determined by the larger requirements of our society and the restrictions imposed by the public nature of education.


### Conclusions


We have argued that one of the important functions of education has been to serve as an objective mechanism selecting children of middle-class parents into the middle class of the next generation. This process, while not strictly necessary for transmission of upper-class status, also legitimizes direct wealth transfers. Dual school systems have evolved: At first high schools were not simply successors to elementary schools, but were designed for children of the middle and upper class. Later came mechanisms for differentiating curricula within high schools, associated mostly with the vocational education movement. At all times the structure of educational finance reinforced the function of schooling in reproducing the class structure. In the earliest example, the abolition of the district system in Massachusetts and elsewhere precluded control over schools by lower-class groups and hindered the redistribution of educational resources from wealthy sections of a town to poorer sections. In the model we have taken as representative of non-Southern states, towns and cities developed school systems with relatively little state financing and used the importance of local autonomy as an argument against the expansion of state financing. Even when interdistrict inequalities were perceived and decried as undemocratic, the programs of state aid which developed did little to decrease them. Local financing dominated public education, and the resulting correlation between community wealth and educational expenditures served as another mechanism for differentiating the education of lower-class children from that of middle-class children—admittedly an imperfect mechanism, but one whose bias is unmistakable.

In the Southern model, state school systems were created after the Civil War, but local financing began to supplant state financing in an effort to prevent distributing resources to black schools. In the South maintaining inequality concerned differentiating the education of whites from that of blacks, and this was accomplished through the establishment of separate school systems. Local financing was thus not as important in the South as in the rest of the country, and school districts remained relatively large.

### Notes

1. See, for example, Bloom's review of the state of education research (26), which required compartmentalization similar to that described here.
2. For two reviews of recent histories, see Lazerson (150) and Kaestle (132).
3. A *disembodied* economy is one where production is not integrated with daily life, where work and leisure are mutually exclusive, both in time and space. See Polanyi (212) and (213).
4. Needless to say, wealth can be inherited and position may be inherited in a small number of cases. But this is quantitatively unimportant compared to other mechanisms of preserving status from generation to generation. See Michelson (173).
5. For similar arguments about schooling and its history, see Bowles (30) and Bowles and Gintis (33).
6. See, for example, Coleman et al. (51), Mosteller and Moynihan (185), and the review of this literature in Averch et al. (7).
7. Jackson (120), p. 7.
8. Jackson (120), p. 16; from Shurtleff (237), vol. II, p. 203.
9. Jackson (120), pp. 8-9. We quote from Jackson because the original records are difficult to read and utilize an archaic grammar which is given here in "translation."
10. Martin (166), p. 9.
11. Reading knowledge of Greek and Latin was the only overt requirement for Harvard admission, though financial ability was obviously required also. See Quincy (215).
12. "Of the five social classes identifiable in Massachusetts Bay, the most important was an 'upper' class composed of men of wealth and education . . . " Haskins (106).

13. A decline in both religion and family ties among native-born progeny of the early Puritans has been asserted, as by Bailyn (10). See also Dunn (70), Greven (88), and Powell (214). We do not want to imply that school was the only replacement for the church and family, but that it was the state's response to a real problem. See Cremin (55).

14. Vassar (267), vol. II, *1860 to the Present*, p. 131; quotation from Lester Ward, *Dynamic Sociology*, 1883.

15. Vassar (267), vol. I, p. 236; quotation from Horace Mann, *Education and Prosperity*, 1848.

16. Katz (136) and (140); Weber (270).

17. Katz (138), especially section 4, and (139); Kaestle (133).

18. Katz (137); Weber (270).

19. Katz (137), p. 85.

20. Katz (137), p. 43.

21. Cubberley (58), p. 406.

22. Katz (139).

23. Tyack (260), p. 182.

24. Perkinson (204).

25. Katz (139). The South lagged behind the rest of the country by thirty to forty years (Harlan [102]), but still followed the model which northern schools had set earlier. The earliest protest against the subtle racism in the ordinary school curriculum which we have encountered is in Horace Mann's 11th Report as Massachusetts' Commissioner of Education, 1848.

26. Stone (245).

27. See Callahan (44), Cohen and Lazerson (49), Grubb and Lazerson (95), and Katz (138).

28. The phrase is cited in Krug (149), Ch. 8.

29. For the development of these arguments, see Grubb and Lazerson (94) or (95).

30. The fact that the mechanism was not perfect is important. The ability of a few lower-class children to attain the highest level of education and socio-economic status is crucial to demonstrating that the educational system is "fair."

31. For recent documentation of this attitude, see Sennett and Cobb (232).

32. See especially Katz (139).

33. Webster (271), Ch. 4.

34. Webster (271), Chs. 5-9.

35. See the discussion in G.N. Strayer, Jr. (246), Ch. 1, in Fairlie (74), Jackson (121), and Webster (271), and the annotated sources in Educational Finance Inquiry Commission (72), pp. 19-24.

36. Harlan (102), p. 3; see also Bond (28), Ch. 6.

37. Harlan (102); Bond (28), especially Ch. 9, Ch. 13.

38. We might surmise that in non-Southern states there are greater inequalities *among* districts, while in the South, inequalities *within* districts (particularly between predominantly black and predominantly white schools) are greater.
39. For a description of earlier state financing plans, see Burke (39), Ch. 16, 17.
40. Cubberley (59), Harris (103), Strayer (247), and Swift (251).
41. See especially Strayer and Haig (248) and Mort (184). See also the description of the history of different forms of state aid in Coons, Clune, and Sugarman (52), who emphasize the discrepancy between the rhetoric of proposals for state aid and the actual results, Benson (17), Ch. 6, Johns (126), and Jones (131), Ch. 1.
42. Cubberley (59), p. 4.
43. Strayer and Haig (249), p. 173.
44. Benson (16), Coons, Clune, and Sugarman (52).
45. Strayer and Haig (248), p. 173.
46. Mort (184), pp. 36-39.
47. Benson (16). Actually, Benson has presented percentage equalizing in two rather distinct forms. In the pure form, a district may be required to transfer locally raised revenue to the state, when the "reimbursement percentage" $(1 - m \cdot P_i/\overline{P})$—from the percentage equalizing formula $S_i = (1 - m \cdot P_i/\overline{P}) \cdot (S_i + L_i)$—is negative. $P$ represents property value, $S$ is state revenue and $L$ is local revenue. This will happen whenever $P_i > \overline{P}/m$—i.e., when a district is relatively wealthy. In a second form, which Benson labels a "resource equalizer" (in [17], pp. 90-92), the reimbursement percentage is not allowed to fall below zero. In effect, this is the form which every state adopting some form of percentage equalizing has used, since none of them (except, at the moment, Maine) permit the reimbursement percentage to go below zero. In contrast to percentage equalizing, which seeks to make the distribution of revenues independent of the local property tax base, a resource equalizer is a device for assuring a minimum yield per mill of local tax rate. The formula is precisely equivalent to $S_i - (P^* - P_i)t_i$, where $P^*$ is the minimum yield per mill of the local tax rate $t_i$, and is equivalent to $\overline{P}/m$ from the percentage equalizing formula. For a fuller discussion of these formulas, see Chapter 5. For appropriate interpretations of the effects of these formulas on local school districts, see Chapter 8.
48. Of the states which distributed some aid through variants of percentage equalizing plans as of 1968-69—Maine, Massachusetts, Rhode Island, New York, Pennsylvania, Wisconsin, Iowa, and Utah—aid distributed through the percentage equalizing formula amounted, as a percentage of total school revenues, to 3, 13, 28, 44, 32, 20, 21, and 3 percent respectively. Only in New York, therefore, was a substantial amount of aid distributed through this plan. More recently, a number of states have revised their state aid programs, partly in response to the cases mentioned in Chapter 1. For descriptions of new state finance laws, see Grubb (91).

49. Massachusetts is a particularly egregious example. Starting from the form of percentage equalizing as suggested by Charles Benson (see Weinberg [272]), the legislature imposed various floors, ceilings, and other restrictions on the original formula, all of which had the effect of weakening the equalizing provisions of the formula. See Daniere (61) for documentation of the effects of these changes. In Chapter 5 we will return to the problem of how formulas are manipulated so as to undermine their equalizing effects. In addition, we will estimate in Chapter 8 how small the equalizing effects of the modified percentage equalizing formula in Massachusetts really are.

50. For documentation of changes in state aid plans, compare Johns (126), Munse (189), and earlier government documents cited therein.

51. See the Gini coefficients by states for 1940 and 1960 in Harrison and McLoone (104), Table 18, p. 86.

52. It should be noted that the history of federal aid is, like that of state aid for schooling, a history of unsuccessful attempts to solve major problems. As early as 1870, general federal aid to education was proposed to solve problems which were acknowledged by educators to be important, including inequities in the provision of education. The Hoar bill of 1870 failed for many of the same reasons that have doomed all subsequent attempts to provide general-purpose federal aid, among these the argument that federal support would lead to federal control. See Tiedt (256), especially Ch. 2, and the annotated bibliography in Norton (195), especially pp. 80-82. As Table 2-2 indicates, federal revenues for education have increased relatively, but as the result of a series of uncoordinated programs with specific purposes rather than comprehensive and general plans of aid.

53. The principles underlying percentage equalizing formulas were outlined by Updegraff (261) in 1922. State assumption of all educational financing was mentioned by Cubberley in 1906 and espoused more strongly by Morrison (182) in 1930. Finally, as noted earlier, the value assumptions of percentage equalizing or "power equalizing" were first enunciated by Strayer and Haig (248) in 1923, even though they advocated foundation plans.

54. For a recent statement of such desiderata, see NEFP (192), Chapter 1.

55. In Chapter 4 we will evaluate the success, in terms of equalizing resources among districts, of focusing on the passage of equalizing formulas rather than increased state aid.

56. Coons, Clune and Sugarman (52), p. 65. A particularly good recent example of this phenomenon is the work of the National Educational Finance Project, which spent the bulk of $2 million generating such minutiae. See the review of the NEFP by Grubb (89).

57. Coleman et al. (51); Mosteller and Moynihan (185); Bowles (29); Hanushek (101).

58. Owen (200).

59. Silberman (240), Gintis (82).
60. Friedenberg (81), Kozol (148), Herndon (109), Kohl (146). For another discussion of the social relations of the classroom, see Bowles (31).
61. We will attempt to document the manifestation of political power in Chapter 5, although the lack of political histories of school financing makes this task difficult indeed. Legal opposition to court-mandated equalization of resources has included *amici curiae* briefs filed for the defendants in various *Serrano*-type suits by wealthy school districts. For the critical *Rodriguez* case, the list of *amici curiae* included Beverly Hills, Bloomfield Hills, Dearborn, and Grosse Pointe, Michigan.
62. We find it difficult to explain the presence of no fewer than thirty state attorneys general among the *amici curiae* for the defendants in the *Rodriquez* case in any other way.
63. During the period of initial concern over the development of state programs of state aid, from 1906 to the middle 1920s, the rejection of centralization of finance was a standard part of every treatise on school finance. The importance of local control was also supported from time to time by one "example" of the evils of state support: A number of writers mentioned that in the early 1800s Connecticut had almost ruined its system of public education by allowing local concern and support for education to dwindle. See, e.g., Swift (252) and (253). However, no substantiation of this example was ever offered, nor have we been able to trace its validity.
64. In discussing justifications for state control, George D. Strayer, Jr. (246) used the European distinction between the *interna* of education—educational policy—and the *externa*, the financial provisions, certification of teachers, and the other arrangements necessary to the existence of education. Strayer felt, as did most educators, that state control over the *externa* was justified (especially in terms of centralization of education), but that control over *interna* belonged to the local district.
65. Tyack (259).
66. See, for example, Katz (136).
67. Even considerable differences among states—especially between Southern and non-Southern states, as Bond (28) documents—appear to have been differences in degree of development of school systems rather than real differences in the desirata governing public education.
68. Bailey et al. ([9], pp. 7-11) discuss the tension between the legal fact of state control and the historically rooted belief in the importance of local control.
69. We offer evidence in Chapter 5 that the equalizing effect of state aid is largely a function of the amount of state aid and relatively independent of the manner in which aid is distributed.
70. The papers in Campbell and Bunnell (45) investigate the effects of the National Science Foundation, the National Merit Scholarship Program,

the National Defense Education Act, and the College Entrance Examination Board on high schools. The editors conclude (pp. 125-6) that there has been a real shift in decision making away from the local and state levels, not as a result of legal provisions (as in the case of state control) or of decreased state and local finance, but because of national programs which tend to set standards for local educational efforts. They predict that nationalizing forces will grow stronger, and casual observation suggests that this has happened.

71. Note, for example, Marshall's dissent from the majority opinion in the Supreme Court's *Rodriguez* decision. He stressed state control over local districts through state laws; additionally, he argued that local control of finance as a mechanism of choosing the level of educational offering is "wholly inappropriate" because of the relative poverty of many school districts. See also White's dissent, and see Coons, Clune, and Sugarman (52).

    The majority's defense of local control in the *Rodriquez* case is instructive. Powell's opinion cites the same history of emphasis on local control (in footnote 109) which we have attacked above. In support of the existence of local control, the opinion offers a list of educational activities which are clearly and completely left to the local districts (footnote 108). Of all the activities cited, it is difficult to see how they could be affected by state rather than local funding—except, in the sense stressed by Justices Marshall and White, that "the power to decide whether to offer a kindergarten program . . . or vocational training program . . . or a program of special education for the handicapped" is likely to be an empty power for poor districts.

72. The case of federal aid and federal control may be rather different. Since the federal government had no legal jurisdiction over schools prior to the 1954 *Brown* case, federal aid was the only overt mechanism of federal influence. The Smith-Hughes Act, for example, served to stimulate vocational education and provided for enforcement of the government's intent through the Federal Board for Vocational Education and the threat of withholding grants for vocational education. The *Brown* case provided the legal basis for federal control in the sphere of desegregation, but federal control is greatly facilitated by the existence of federal aid and the threat of withholding aid, as the desegregation efforts of the past few years indicate. Both proponents of federal aid and federal officials have denied that they want increased federal control (Munger and Fenno [187], pp. 47-48.) Murphy (190) has documented that, at least in the case of Title I, greater aid does not lead to greater control. However, this does not contradict the possibility of a link between aid and control at the federal level. Federal aid for specific purposes does not appear to provide greater control via control over expenditure of that aid, but rather provides a lever for enforcing other federal goals (such as those mandated by federal courts).

73. NEA Resolution 72-2, June 1973, in NEA Handbook, 1973, pp. 27-28.

**Part II
Existing Distributions and
Mechanisms of Redistribution**

# 3

### Distribution and
### Redistribution — A Primer

Part II provides the conceptual and factual basis for the econometric work of Part III. In Part II we will describe existing inequalities in resources, current mechanisms of state aid to education, and the ways in which theoretical formulations are circumscribed in practice. Part III will analyze existing inequalities by simulating the effects of changes in the institutional rules regulating school finance.

In this chapter we investigate concepts of distribution and redistribution. While parts of this analysis may appear self-evident, it illustrates some complexities of redistribution mechanisms that often go unnoticed and provides a framework for understanding the model to be presented in Chapter 7. Chapter 4 then describes existing inequalities in school resources and the sources of these inequalities, while Chapter 5 details existing mechanisms intended to moderate gross inequalities in the distribution of school resources.

### Concepts of Distribution and Redistribution

A distribution is a description of who has how much of something. Although we might focus on the distribution of real inputs to the schooling process—teachers with specified credentials, books, and so forth—we chose not to do so for reasons given in Chapter 1. In this volume we are concerned with revenues and expenditures in public schools, over the period of one school year. So that the size of the school, district, or state will not affect the analysis, revenues and expenditures are defined in per pupil terms.

Distributions can be described in several ways. One method is given in Table 3-1 for a complete sample of Massachusetts school districts. Districts have been ranked from low revenue to high revenue per pupil and divided into ten equal-sized groups (by number of pupils). Both the number of pupils and revenues are expressed in percentage terms. The bottom 10 percent of pupils received only 7.52 percent of total school revenues in the state, while the top 10 percent received 13.68 percent, almost twice as much. We can cumulate the percentages to form the curve—a Lorenz curve—in Figure 3-1. In a completely equal distribution, the bottom 10 percent of pupils would receive 10 percent of total revenues, as would every other 10 percent of pupils, and the Lorenz curve would be the 45° line. Hence the further away from this line the Lorenz curve is, the more unequal is the distribution. The area between the Lorenz curve and the 45 degree line is then a measure of inequality, the Gini coefficient.[1]

Implicitly, the concept of redistribution involves a comparison of two distributions. In the case of schools—where state or federal governments may seek to manipulate distributions in order to achieve greater equality, to increase total revenues, or to change the burden of taxes—the redistribution caused by state programs consists of the difference between the distribution of school revenues before and after manipulation by the state.

However, the differences due to redistribution may take either of two distinct forms. In the first case, the distribution is made more equal (or less equal), but the rank order of members of the population remains the same. Suppose, for example, that school funds were redistributed so that the bottom decile in Table 3-1 received 8 percent of the funds, the additional funds coming from the top decile. The same children would be in the bottom and the top deciles as before; only the difference between them would have changed. The Lorenz curve in Figure 3-1 would lie closer to the 45° line. In the second case, only the rank order of the population changes, not the shape of the distribution. If school funds in Massachusetts were redistributed so that those children formerly in the bottom decile received 13.7 percent of the state's school revenues, and the top children received 7.5 percent of the funds, these two groups of children would have switched places in the distribution, but Table 3-1 (and Figure 3-1) would still describe the distribution of school funds.

In most instances where there are two polar cases, the world lies somewhere

**Table 3-1**
**Distribution of Expenditures per Pupil Using District Averages,
351 Districts, Massachusetts, 1968-69**

| Percentage of pupils | Percentage of Expenditure |
|---|---|
| Lowest 10% | 7.52% |
| Second 10% | 8.39% |
| Third 10% | 8.82% |
| Fourth 10% | 9.32% |
| Fifth 10% | 9.71% |
| Sixth 10% | 10.11% |
| Seventh 10% | 10.40% |
| Eighth 10% | 10.69% |
| Ninth 10% | 11.35% |
| Top 10% | 13.68% |

Source: Data cited in Chapter 5.

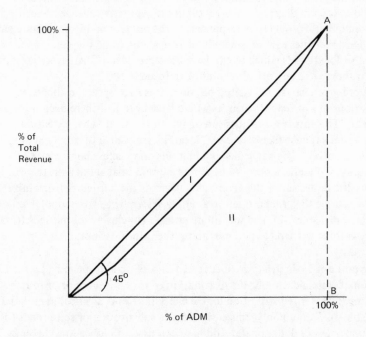

**Figure 3-1.** Distribution of Expenditures per Pupil Using District
          Averages, Massachusetts, 1968-69.

between them. Fortunately for the simplicity of our analysis, however, government redistributions rarely affect rank order. This general rule applies to welfare, unemployment benefits, and other cash flows, to Medicaid and other flows
of income in kind, and to all taxes.[2] It appears to be rigidly applicable to school
financing. Some reversals do occur among schools within districts under Title I
of the Elementary and Secondary Education Act of 1965 (ESEA). But among
districts, our prime concern, this is not so.[3] Hence we will ignore possible
changes in the rank order of the population as school funds are redistributed
among districts and concentrate on changes in the shape of the distributions
themselves.

*Patterns of Redistribution*

*Redistribution* involves a comparison of two distributions, before and after
a change. When the change stimulates a reaction–a behavioral response–it is
often difficult to observe the prior situation.[4]   Particularly in school finance, we
can observe the fiscal decisions of school boards in the light of their expectations
regarding state and federal aid. Indeed, in Massachusetts, where state revenue is

based on the *prior* year's expenditures by the school district, the amount of
state aid is known, except for the possibility of legislative change. Because one
can assume that districts have responded to the amount and form of state aid,
actual local revenues cannot generally be considered to be the same as the
amount of local funds which would have been provided if there were no state
aid or if there were any other amount of state aid.

In order to analyze redistribution, then, it is necessary to estimate what
the distributions of school revenues would have been had there been no external funds. This involves the question of substitution: to what extent do
external funds reduce (substitute for) local funds, instead of simply adding
to total resources. The particular assumptions one makes about what the
distribution would have been in the absence of external aid delimit the conclusions one draws about the extent and effect of the current redistributive
scheme. To see this, we have set up a simple system with five school districts
(presented in Table 3-2), and we will investigate conclusions about redistribution from three extreme hypotheses about the prior distribution.

**Hypothesis 1.** Districts are unaffected in total school spending by the
program of state aid; that is, the distribution of total revenues prior to redistribution and after redistribution look exactly the same, as in columns 4 and
5 of Table 3-2. Commonly, this is viewed as a substitution of state funds for
local funds. Every dollar of state aid has been used to reduce local taxes in
all five districts. In this case, the state has no control over the distribution
of educational resources, since complete substitution results in identical
distributions prior to, and subsequent to, state aid.

**Hypothesis 2.** The second hypothesis assumes there is no substitution.
After all, many states discourage substitution, and the largest source of
federal aid, Title I of ESEA, forbids it, although not necessarily successfully.[5]
Under this hypothesis, districts use every dollar of state aid to add to local
revenues, so that the observed amount of school resources in each district is
simply the sum of local revenues and state aid. Local taxation reflects local
desires for education, with state aid seen as a windfall unconnected with
either local or state taxes. In this case, the state does have some control over
revenue distribution, since it succeeds in establishing a somewhat more equal
distribution of educational resources (column 4 in place of column 6, with the
Gini coefficient reduced from .264 to .152).

**Hypothesis 3.** The final hypothesis assumes that citizens are conscious
of the state taxes they pay. Districts are assumed to reflect desires for education by the taxes they levy, both state and local, and the distribution of
revenues in the absence of state aid would be the sum of state and local taxes
for education (column 7).[6] In this case the redistributive power of the state

**Table 3-2**
**Hypothetical School Finance Data**

| District | (1) Observed Taxes per Pupil Local | (2) Observed Taxes per Pupil State | (3) Observed State Aid per Pupil | (4) Observed District Revenue per Pupil | (5) District Revenue per Pupil Prior to State Aid Hypothesis 1 | (6) District Revenue per Pupil Prior to State Aid Hypothesis 2 | (7) District Revenue per Pupil Prior to State Aid Hypothesis 3 |
|---|---|---|---|---|---|---|---|
| A | 200 | 50 | 250 | 450 | 450 | 200 | 250 |
| B | 300 | 100 | 200 | 500 | 500 | 300 | 400 |
| C | 400 | 150 | 150 | 550 | 550 | 400 | 550 |
| D | 550 | 250 | 150 | 700 | 700 | 550 | 800 |
| E | 800 | 350 | 150 | 950 | 950 | 800 | 1150 |
| Gini coefficient: | | | | .152 | .152 | .264 | .308 |

Note: Administrative costs are assumed to come out of general state revenues; federal aid is ignored.

aid program is even stronger than in hypothesis 2. (The Gini coefficient is reduced from .308 to .152). The additional distributive power derives from the fact that state taxes and state aid are not the same in each district. A and B receive more aid than they pay in taxes, and they use this difference to increase total resources for schools. Districts D and E receive less in aid than they pay in taxes, and this difference reduces revenues available to them for education. If each district received from the state exactly what it paid in state taxes, this hypothesis would amount to hypothesis 1, with each district simply substituting state aid for local revenue.[7]

### School and Nonschool Services

One method of evaluating state aid programs, then, is to consider how they affect the extent of inequality among distributions of educational resources, as by comparing columns 4, 5, 6, and 7 of Table 3-2. To describe the change in the degree of inequality among school districts it is necessary to know which of the three hypotheses holds—or, since we might not expect one model to apply to all districts within a state, what combination of these three hypotheses can be used to characterize school district behavior.

Another kind of redistribution also occurs, one which can be understood only if we consider the changes in the distribution of revenues for nonschool purposes implicit in Table 3-2. Assume that school revenues are spent on school services while other revenues are spent for nonschool goods and services which can be either private or public.[8] The most basic redistribution, in any system of public education, is one from nonschool to school services. If a district totally finances its own schools, this redistribution is easily described. However, a state aid program will change the extent of this redistribution, depending on which of the three assumptions illustrated in Table 3-2 is assumed.

Under hypothesis 1 we find no change in the distribution of school revenues. But districts A and B receive more in state aid than they pay in state taxes. Since this aid is not used to increase school services but substitutes for local tax revenues, it must be used for nonschool services (both public and private). Hence there is redistribution from nonschool services in districts D and E to nonschool services in A and B through the mechanism of state aid to schools.

Under hypothesis 2, with a zero substitution effect, the state coerces an increase in school revenues—that is, a redistribution from nonschool to school services—in every district. However, the *net* redistribution—state aid minus state taxes—is positive only in districts A and B, and negative in districts C, D, and E. Hence there is a net redistribution from nonschool services in C, D, and E (wealthy districts) to school services in A and B (poorer districts).

Under hypothesis 3, there is redistribution from nonschool to school services only in districts A and B. The decrease in school services in districts D and E equals the state revenue transferred away from them and to the poorer districts. Hence there is a redistribution from school services in wealthy districts to school services in poor districts.

Of course, more complex patterns of assumed behavior will change the nature of our finding regarding redistribution. For example, if our analysis of district D follows the assumptions of hypothesis 3, while that of district B follows the assumptions of hypothesis 1, then we find a redistribution from school services in D to nonschool services in B. Other possibilities for mixed behavior are numerous, and some of the more likely will be discussed in Chapter 7.

This discussion of the redistributive impact of state aid programs makes explicit the source and destination of all revenues, and the importance of accurately describing school district behavioral response to the state and federal aid system. If we can adequately estimate the prior distribution of school funds, then this analysis enables us to evaluate programs of intergovernmental aid. It is clear, for example, why many governments want to discourage substitution: the redistribution of funds for nonschool services is not the province of school aid programs. The redistributive patterns under hypotheses 2 and 3 may also be objectionable under certain conditions: redistribution from nonschool services in some districts to school services in others (hypothesis 2) is acceptable only if the first group of districts does not suffer from a lack of nonschool services (e.g., if they are neither poor nor suffer from "municipal overburden"), and redistribution of school services from some districts to others (hypothesis 3) is unacceptable if all districts are judged to have inadequate levels of school support compared to support for nonschool—especially private—goods and services.

Judgments about the equity and appropriateness of redistribution may be clarified if we think in terms of the people for whom services are rendered rather than the institutions which render them. Schools are presumably designed to provide services to children. The state also establishes systems of redistribution among adults, both by tax and transfer (as Social Security, unemployment, and welfare) and goods in kind (employment service, surplus food, subsidized transit, emergency health care, etc.). It also redistributes income specifically toward children (as in Aid to Families with Dependent Children) as well as providing services directly (schools). Conceptually, the state has determined how much of its income it will spend on children. It distributes or expends these funds through various agencies, including the family.

Public school finance must involve children. It may distribute funds from one set of children to another or from adults to children. Transfer of funds from one set of adults to another (as under hypothesis 1), except where the receiving adults act as an expending agency for children, is not the function of public school finance. As long as children are involved, arguments about proper school finance may proceed. But this is not the mechanism by which the state should reward "deserving" adults. Seeing this distinction will help the reader understand our terse dismissal of attempts to alleviate "municipal overburden" through school taxes in Chapter 9.

### Other Aspects of Redistribution

The discussion of redistribution should also clarify the role of the tax structure. In Table 3-2 the tax system is assumed to be progressive: wealthy districts (D and E) pay more in taxes per pupil than poor districts (A and B). Under each hypothesis, the redistribution among school and nonschool services and among districts caused by the introduction of the state aid program depends on the pattern of state aid minus state taxes and can therefore be changed simply by changing the allocation of state tax burdens among districts, without changing the allocation of state school aid. In particular, as previously noted, if state taxes are structured so that each district receives in state aid precisely the amount taxed away by the state, then hypothesis 3 reduces to hypothesis 1. The redistribution from adults in wealthy districts to adults in poorer districts under hypothesis 1 disappears, and the redistribution from adults in wealthy districts to children in poorer districts under hypothesis 2 disappears. If the combined tax-aid program is regressive with respect to districts,[9] then there is obviously redistribution from poor to rich districts. Whether it is from poor adults or children to rich adults or children depends on which hypothesis is adopted regarding the alternative uses of the redistributed funds.

Finally, Table 3-2 illustrates that state aid may affect not only the distribution of revenues for education, but also the total amount. Under hypothesis 2, state aid increases total revenues, while it does not affect the total under hypotheses 1 and 3. One of the dominant worries throughout the history of state aid has been the fear that total resources flowing to education would be reduced because apathy would reduce support by local school districts.[10] Mort's "efficiency principle," the use of mandatory levels of local taxes to qualify for state aid, the use of local contributions in foundations plans, and the development of incentive structures in percentage equalizing formulas are all methods of preventing local taxation from falling in response to state aid. The effect of greater state aid on total revenues has often been expressed in terms of a tradeoff between equality and quality of education.[11] The fear of this tradeoff is consistent with the efforts in the history of school finance to provide minimum acceptable levels of education rather than to pursue equality single-mindedly.[12] While one must admit the theoretical possibility that state aid programs designed to equalize among districts would reduce total resources available to education, there is no necessity for this to be true: the state could assume total control of finance and set a level of funding higher than the previous level. Furthermore, the empirical results of Part III will refute this theory.

## Conclusions

Redistribution can be a complex subject, partly because there are a number of different phenomena described by the term *redistribution* and partly because we seldom observe the distribution prior to redistribution. We have offered three simple hypotheses about unobserved prior distributions in order to outline the various possibilities. However, the nature of school district behavior is an empirical problem, one which can only be resolved by developing models describing behavior. The development of such a model will occupy Part III.

Although the theoretical concepts of this chapter compare taxes with expenditures, it is difficult in an empirical model to consider the tax side of the question. For one thing, the incidence of taxes has always been calculated for individuals. To our knowledge there are no studies which attempt to estimate the burden of state taxes by community. There are good reasons for this. Any study of tax incidence must rely on assumptions about tax shifting—for example, the extent to which taxes on businesses are paid by owners of the businesses, consumers of products, or workers in the form of lower wages. While these assumptions are problematic at the national and state levels, they become even more so at the community level because of the extent of tax shifting to nonresidents.[13] Secondly, there is some reason to doubt the importance of tax incidence by community. Since individuals pay state taxes, there is no obvious mechanism of collective consciousness about the amount of state taxes paid by the residents of a school district. Because of the lack of incidence data, it will be impossible to distinguish between hypotheses 2 and 3 in the empirical work of Part III. Without knowledge of the distribution of state tax burdens by community, hypothesis 3 simply looks like a case of behavior intermediate between hypotheses 1 and 2. Similarly, the rest of the discussion in this section will deal only tangentially with tax structures.

So far we have relied on a hypothetical distribution of school revenues to clarify several theoretical points. In the next chapter we will explore measures of inequality and descriptions of the current distributions of school revenues and expenditures, both among states and among districts within states. Finally, we have as yet said very little about the specific forms which state efforts have taken to remedy inequality, despite our earlier concern with the history of state aid. The third chapter of this part will briefly summarize the most important mechanisms of redistribution which states currently use.

## Notes

1. Referring to Figure 3-1, the Gini coefficient is defined as the area labeled I divided by the area under the 45 degree line, or I plus area II. This statistic is zero in the case of perfect equality and approaches one with greater inequality.

2. One of the difficulties with "reforms" of welfare which would continue to
   subsidize families after they obtain employment is that government transfers *would* affect the rank order, and much of the public finds this
   unacceptable.
3. Rank order statistics were computed for the districts within the six New
   England states from the data cited in Table 4-3. Both Kendall's tau and
   Spearman rank-order correlation coefficients were positive and significant
   at the 0.001 level for each state when local revenue was compared with
   local plus state revenue, with local plus federal revenue, and with total
   revenue. Hence neither state nor federal revenue significantly alters the
   rank order established by the distribution of local revenue.
4. It was to avoid the behavioral implications of redistribution that Samuelson
   (227) suggested an "instantaneous lump-sum tax" which would have to be
   levied on people according to rules which they were unable to figure out.
   Besides being contrary to any tax system a democracy would allow, it
   would still have behavioral implications, since people would have to prepare for the possibility of a high levy (by excess saving or insurance)
   which is seen by them as a random phenomenon. In short, it is simply
   impossible for the government to redistribute funds in a way which does
   not influence the distribution from which they are redistributing.
5. *ESEA Title I Program Guide No. 44*, Guideline 7.1, March 18, 1968. For
   a report indicating lack of success in preventing "supplanting" of state and
   local funds, see Martin and McClure (167).
6. Although districts have no control over the amounts of state taxes they
   pay, they are assumed to be conscious of them and to adjust their local
   taxes accordingly in the event of a state aid program. That is, each district
   perceives that a certain amount can be allocated to educational purposes,
   and the sum of state and local taxes for education will equal this amount.
7. The formula for hypothesis 3 is $SA + L_{post} = L_{prior} + (SA - ST)$, where
   $L_{post}$ and $L_{prior}$ refer to local revenue posterior and prior to the state aid
   program respectively, $SA$ is state aid, and $ST$ represents state taxes. If
   $SA = ST$, then this reduces to $SA + L_{post} = L_{prior}$, which is the formula
   for hypothesis 1. Hypothesis 2 can be represented by the formula
   $SA + L_{post} = L_{prior} + SA$, or $L_{post} = L_{prior}$.
8. This statement is not as innocuous as it seems. In the first place, it has
   been charged that school expenditures do not always result in school
   services, especially that increases in school expenditures take the form of
   higher salaries and more waste rather than greater amounts of real inputs.
   Secondly, many services are produced in or out of schools only for reasons
   of history and convention: public libraries, private tutoring, family outings,
   municipal theater and music, are all nonschool services, but might well be
   performed in schools and are complementary to the functions of schooling.
   See Chapter 6 for further discussion, along with Benson (15) and Grubb
   and Michelson (96).

9. This might happen if aid were a flat grant based on the number of teachers, and revenue were raised by sales tax.

10. The genesis of this fear appears to have been the experience of Connecticut in the early nineteenth century. Connecticut adopted a program with high levels of state financing, and local contributions for education decreased. The Connecticut schools were universally perceived as mediocre and lethargic, and the reason was felt to be that when school districts did not have to support education through taxation, their interest in maintaining good schools would diminish. The "experiment" was condemned by many educators as a catastrophe and was used as a warning against high levels of state financing, despite the lack of evidence that the financing mechanism was at fault.

11. Phrasing the tradeoff in terms of equality and quality (rather than total revenues) hints at self-interest on the part of those who want to prevent substantial redistribution and to maintain wealth-based advantages. Given the doubts induced by the Coleman report and its progeny, this argument is no longer as strong as it once was.

12. Proponents of minimum levels are still active; see, for example, Michelman (169).

13. That is, at the community level problems of tax importing and exporting become critical. See McLure (160) for a discussion and some estimates at the state level. Only one study that we know of, that of Grubb (92), has attempted to calculate tax incidence for one community. He was generally unsuccessful in accounting for tax imports and exports.

# 4

## The Extent and Source of Revenue Inequalities

Public schools are supported by three levels of government: local, state, and federal.[1] The percentage of support coming from these three sources varies greatly. In 1972 state funds contributed 6.5 percent to the total in New Hampshire, and almost 74.1 percent in Alaska, and individual districts could be found which were even more extreme.[2] Table 4-1 illustrates the regional variations in the extent of state support: New England is the lowest state support area, and the Southeast is the highest. As documented in Chapter 2, this difference has a historical basis. Low state support in the Northeast reflects the early emphasis on local financing and control which also resulted in a relatively large number of school districts. In the South, total state financing was instituted during Reconstruction. Although the local share subsequently grew—under pressures to improve schools and to spend as little as possible on schools for blacks—local finance never predominated. Finally, the federal share is obviously small in comparison to the state and local shares.

We intend to demonstrate three points. First, significant inequalities in public school revenues exist at all levels of government—among states, among districts within states, and among schools within districts. Second, inequality among districts is the result of inequalities in the local component of total revenue, state and Federal revenue decreasing inequality only moderately. Third, the reduction in inequality caused by state aid programs is due more to the amount of state aid than to the structure of state aid formulas.[3]

### Interstate Inequalities

We begin by comparing the average expenditure per pupil among states, neglecting for the moment resource variations *within* each of the states. In 1968-69 receipts from local, state, and federal sources averaged $1,346 in New York, while Alabama the average district received $461. As both casual observation and simple statistical evidence indicates, variations in revenues available among states are due largely to variations in income and wealth.[4] Table 4-2 presents Gini coefficients calculated among the fifty states, for various years.[5]

It is virtually impossible to attach meaning to the Gini coefficient of local revenues alone. States vary in their conception of state school funds as basic or supplementary: New Hampshire's state program is miserly compared with Delaware's, for example. Our inability to observe the true prior distribution of

**Table 4-1**
**Percentage Distribution of Funds for Public Elementary and**
**Secondary Education, 1971-72**

|                | Federal | State | Local |
|----------------|---------|-------|-------|
| New England    | 5.2     | 24.1  | 70.7  |
| Mideast        | 6.1     | 40.3  | 53.6  |
| Great Lakes    | 5.4     | 36.2  | 58.4  |
| Plains         | 6.5     | 35.0  | 58.6  |
| Southeast      | 14.9    | 51.6  | 33.6  |
| Southwest      | 11.6    | 46.7  | 41.8  |
| Rocky Mountain | 9.3     | 34.0  | 56.7  |
| Far West       | 6.8     | 37.0  | 56.1  |
| United States  | 8.0     | 40.2  | 51.8  |

Source: NEA, *Estimates of School Statistics, 1972-73,* Research Report
1972-R12, Table 9, p. 32.

local funds—that which would have occurred without state programs—is of
obvious importance here. Thus we cannot draw the apparent conclusion that
state support is strongly equalizing (comparing "state plus local" with "local").
In addition, poor states tend to have high levels of state support, so that local
revenues in poor states are systematically lower relative to local revenues in
wealthy states than the combined state plus local revenues.[6] However, as a
tentative conclusion, assuming that substitution of state for local funds does
not approach 100 percent, it appears that state aid is at least somewhat
equalizing.

Federal aid results in a slightly greater equality among states. Since
federal aid is small, and to a large extent supplemental, the observed effect
is probably not an artifact of the data. This equalization results not because
it is the intent of federal aid to equalize among states, but simply because
the distribution of federal aid per pupil is more equal than the distribution
of state plus local revenue.

The data also suggest that interstate inequality has declined slightly over
time. It is impossible to be very precise about comparing two Gini coefficients
since they are ordinal measures. However, we can make some gross comparisons. The fall in the Gini for local plus state revenue (from 0.1620 to 0.1460)
accounts for the drop in the Gini for total revenue (from 0.1510 to 0.1348);
hence it appears that greater equality over time has not been due to the
increased amount of federal aid.[7] Nor does it appear that state revenue has
become more of an equalizer over time. The distribution of school revenues
among states was more equal in 1968-69 than in 1955-56 primarily because

**Table 4-2**
**Gini Coefficients Reflecting Interstate Inequalities**

|                            | 1955-56 | 1959-60 | 1966-67 | 1967-68 | 1968-69 |
|----------------------------|---------|---------|---------|---------|---------|
| Local Revenue[a]           | 0.2473  | 0.2515  | 0.2234  | 0.2231  | 0.2327  |
| Local plus State Revenue   | 0.1620  | 0.1795  | 0.1418  | 0.1485  | 0.1460  |
| Local plus Federal Revenue | 0.2291  | 0.2413  | N.C.[b] | N.C.    | N.C.    |
| Total Revenue              | 0.1510  | 0.1527  | 0.1275  | 0.1336  | 0.1348  |

[a]Includes county revenues.

[b]Not computed.

Sources: 1955-56: U.S. Office of Education, Biennial Survey of Education, 1954-56, *Statistics of State School Systems*. 1959-60: U.S. Office of Education, *Digest of Educational Statistics, 1962*. 1966-67, 1967-68, 1968-69: NEA, *Estimates of School Statistics*, for 1966-67, 1967-68, 1968-69. NEA data was used because of the unavailability of Office of Education data on ADA for years more recent than 1965-66. See Deitch (64) for a discussion of some of the differences between Office of Education and NEA data.

more local funds were raised in poorer states in the later year relative to districts in rich states.

## Intrastate Inequalities

Turning to inequalities among districts with states, Table 4-3 presents Gini coefficients by sources of revenue for fifteen states.[8] Before analyzing the results, one comment on the general magnitude of the Gini coefficients is in order. Economists are accustomed to Gini coefficients in the range of 0.30 to 0.40, since the distribution of income among families in this country has remained relatively constant since World War II at around 0.35 (e.g., Miller [180], Schultz [230]). In comparison, the Ginis of Tables 4-2 and 4-3 appear small, even trivial. If the Gini describing the distribution of income were to be as low as 0.05, we might well ignore the problem of income inequities which has been the target of so much attention in the past. However, there are several reasons why the Ginis presented do not describe a negligible problem. First, they describe *per pupil* expenditures. Although a difference between two districts of $100 per pupil makes only a small difference in a Gini coefficient, it makes a considerable difference when multiplied over a class of 30 (resulting in a difference of $3000 per class) or in a school of 1,500 (giving the school in the richer district an advantage of $150,000). Secondly, Gini coefficients conceal serious disparities between those at the top and those at the bottom: The richest

**Table 4-3**
**Gini Coefficients Measuring Intrastate Inequalities**

| | Local Revenue | Local + State Revenue | Local + Federal Revenue | Total Revenue | Current Expenditures |
|---|---|---|---|---|---|
| Maine (338 districts) | 0.1673 | 0.0827 | 0.1482 | 0.0714 | 0.0714 |
| New Hampshire (234 districts) | 0.1409 | 0.1107 | 0.1151 | 0.0849 | 0.0849 |
| Vermont (253 districts) | 0.1796 | 0.0919 | 0.1524 | 0.0803 | 0.0803 |
| Massachusetts (160 districts) | 0.1190 | 0.0929 | 0.1096 | 0.0882 | N.C.[c] |
| (351 districts) | 0.1408 | 0.0965 | 0.1260 | 0.0907 | 0.0908 |
| Connecticut (169 districts) | 0.1364 | 0.0997 | 0.1287 | 0.0962 | 0.0965 |
| Rhode Island (39 districts) | 0.0899 | 0.0655 | 0.0760 | 0.0546 | 0.0547 |
| Maryland (24 counties) | 0.1267 | 0.0583 | 0.1034 | 0.0499 | 0.0528 |
| South Carolina (93 districts) | 0.2067 | 0.0845 | 0.1209 | 0.0686 | 0.0623 |
| (46 counties) | 0.1838 | 0.0738 | 0.0969 | 0.0548 | 0.0502 |
| Florida (67 districts) | 0.1918 | 0.0692 | 0.1570 | 0.0653 | 0.1131 |

| | | | | | |
|---|---|---|---|---|---|
| Alabama (120 districts) | 0.3148[b] | 0.0672 | 0.1529 | 0.0686 | N.C. |
| Louisiana (66 districts) | 0.2689 | 0.0792 | 0.2101[a] | 0.0561 | 0.0446 |
| Mississippi (148 districts) | 0.2801 | 0.1442 | 0.2398 | 0.1551 | 0.1804 |
| Nevada (17 counties) | 0.0555[b] | 0.0305 | 0.0392 | 0.0295 | 0.0278 |
| Oregon (36 counties) | 0.0814[b] | 0.0635 | 0.0746 | 0.0590 | N.C. |
| Utah (40 districts) | 0.2349 | 0.0522 | 0.1989 | 0.0552 | 0.0518 |

[a]Local plus Title I revenue.
[b]Includes county revenue.
[c]Not computed.

Sources: For Massachusetts (160 districts) and South Carolina, data used and cited in Chapter 9. For the six New England states, data generously provided by Stephen Weiss of the Federal Reserve Bank of Boston, and described fully in Weiss (274). Maryland: data taken from "Background Information," prepared for the Commission to Study the State's Role in Financing Education by the Department of Fiscal Services, Annapolis, Maryland, 1970. Florida: data from Report of the Commissioner of Education, 1968-69. Alabama: Department of Education, "One Hundred Twentieth Annual Report, 1970: Statistical and Financial Data for 1969-70". Louisiana: Department of Education, "One Hundred Twentieth Annual Report for the Session 1968-69." Mississippi: Department of Education, "Rankings of Mississippi School Districts, 1969-70" and "Current Expenditures per Pupil by School Districts and Related Information." Nevada: Superintendent of Public Instruction, "Interim Report of Selected Data, July 1, 1968 to June 30, 1969 Inclusive." Oregon: data (not in book form) supplied by the Oregon Department of Education. Utah: "Thirty-eighth Report of the Superintendent of Public Instruction of the State of Utah for the Biennial Period Ending June 30, 1970." For Alabama, Mississippi, and Oregon, data pertain to the year 1969-70; for all other states, data refers to 1968-69. Gini coefficients were calculated by the method of triangles.

district in Mississippi spent $825 per pupil, the poorest $321. In Nevada, the extremes were $1,679 and $707, despite the low Gini. The extremes for total revenue among 160 Massachusetts districts were $1428 and $553. These examples could be extended. (Coons, Clune, and Sugarman [52] give additional cases.) Such examples, while extreme, are crucial to our notion of the unfairness of existing distribution.

More importantly, these figures exclude within-district variation, which may be considerable. Since preconceptions about Gini coefficients generally come from income distributions, we can look at the distribution of average family income in 159 Massachusetts districts. The Gini coefficient of family income among school districts is 0.058, *smaller* than the measure of resource disparities. If the family income distribution in Massachusetts is in fact around 0.30-0.40, then a great deal of that inequality lies within school districts; but then, so may there be a great deal of inequality in school resource distribution within districts. All in all, the Ginis presented in this chapter are not by any means trivial, but are evidence of substantial inequities.[9]

The most obvious conclusion to be drawn from Table 4-3 is that the source of inequality in total revenues is, without exception, local revenue. State revenue, Title I aid, and total federal aid all tend to equalize the distribution of revenues available. State revenue equalizes more than federal revenue, although we have not determined by how much or how it does so. It seems possible that the type of state aid plan does not determine the extent of equalization by state aid. Those states—such as Connecticut, South Carolina, and Oregon—which have flat-grant programs equalize the distribution of resources as much or more than those which intend to produce equalization with more sophisticated formulas (especially Massachusetts and Rhode Island). Finally, the degree of equalization appears to depend on the amount of state aid: equalization is considerably greater in the South where state aid is relatively more important.[10] From this data, we might surmise that the extent of equalization depends more on the amount of intergovernmental aid than on the way in which that aid is distributed. We will formally test this hypothesis below.

In general, we note that the inequality in the distribution of total revenues is greater *among* districts in Northern states, where there are more (and more homogeneous) school districts, than in the South. We might suspect that that inequality is greater *within* districts in the South than in the North for two reasons. One is the greater homogeneity of Northern districts. The tendency to finance by counties rather than towns and cities in the South means that school boards may not be as responsive to voter pressure and may inadvertently or purposefully find it easier to allocate funds unequally within districts than in Northern towns. The second reason is that the long history of racially segregated schools provides both a tendency and a justification for unequal allocation of funds within districts. The testing of this hypothesis is a project beyond our present resources.

### The Equalizing Power of State and
### Federal Aid

As one way of testing the hypothesis that equalization is due to the amount rather than the form of state (and federal) aid, we can ask what possible reductions in the Gini coefficients could be achieved, given the existing amounts of state and federal aid. A careful answer to this question would involve a statistical model (such as that presented in Part III) to predict how total revenue would adjust to changes in the structure of intergovernmental aid. However, we will start with a simple, extreme assumption. This will enable us to derive some initial answers to the above question and to illustrate an important point: even a small amount of intergovernmental aid may produce a significant reduction in inequality *if* it is distributed appropriately.

Let us assume that the amounts of revenue from different sources are independent of each other, so that changing the distribution of state and federal aid would leave the distribution of local revenue unchanged (hypothesis 2 of the previous chapter). If we consider interstate inequalities first, we can derive a hypothetical Gini coefficient to reflect the distribution of the given amount of federal funds, but minimizing inequality: the federal government is assumed to distribute the current dollar amount of aid only to the poorest states. This would bring a large number of states to a minimum level of total revenue per pupil, while the remaining states would receive no federal aid at all. The hypothetical Gini coefficient of total revenue distributed in this way (for 1968-69) is 0.086, compared with the actual coefficient of 0.135 from Table 4-2. The difference in the two coefficients indicates that the equalizing effect among states of the small amount of federal aid, under these assumptions, could be quite large.

Similarly, coefficients can be calculated for districts within states to reflect current amounts of state aid, federal aid, and federal and state aid, hypothetically distributed so as to minimize Gini coefficients (Table 4-4). Again, the equalization impact of intergovernmental funds could be considerably stronger than it is, even in states (such as New Hampshire) which rely to a great extent on local revenue.[11]

It should be emphasized, however, that the data in Table 4-4 are not descriptive of real possibilities for reforming school finance. The hypothetical distributions of state aid require that the majority of districts receive no state aid whatsoever, and that they do not increase local funds in reaction. The political feasibility of such a state aid program appears rather remote, especially since new state aid formulas often have "save harmless" clauses written into them to insure that no district will get less state aid under a new program than under the old one.[12] The hypothetical distributions of federal aid ignore the fact that equalization, either among states or among districts, has never been one of the important goals of federal aid to education. However, we have

Table 4-4
Gini Coefficients for Hypothetical Distributions of State and Federal Aid,
for Selected States

|  | Total Revenue (actual) | Total Revenue, Hypothetical State Aid | Total Revenue, Hypothetical Federal Aid | Total Revenue, Hypothetical State and Federal Aid |
|---|---|---|---|---|
| Rhode Island | 0.055 | 0.000 | 0.015 | 0.000 |
| Massachusetts (351 districts) | 0.088 | 0.029 | 0.048 | 0.020 |
| New Hampshire | 0.085 | 0.051 | 0.048 | 0.034 |
| South Carolina (93 districts) | 0.069 | 0.000 | 0.005 | 0.000 |
| Maryland | 0.050 | 0.000 | 0.011 | 0.000 |

Source: Data as given for Table 4-3.

illustrated that under some theoretical conditions the existing amounts of intergovernmental aid could be considerably more equalizing than they now are.


### The Equalizing Power of State and Federal
### Aid—A Statistical Test

In contrast to the theoretical exercise with the form of state and federal aid,
we look now at its amount. We can test the hypothesis that intrastate equalization is due to the amount rather than the form of state aid using the data for
1959-60 collected by Harrison and McLoone (104).[13] This data provides
several measures of intrastate inequality for each of the states except Hawaii
that can be used as the dependent variables in simple cross-section regression
equations. We can then include among the independent variables those we
suspect of influencing intrastate inequality. Two of these should reflect the
relative importance of state financing for a particular state and the form which
the distribution of state aid takes. Hence we will include the percentage of
school revenues from state sources, and the percentage of state aid disbursed
through equalizing formulas. Although the latter is a crude measure of the
structure of distribution mechanisms, it is difficult to think of any variable
which could capture the variability and complexity of formulas throughout
the country. In 1959-60, equalizing formulas were almost exclusively foundation programs, and nonequalizing formulas were all flat grants. Because a
greater number of school districts may permit greater inequities among districts
(as opposed to inequities within districts), the number of districts may be an

important explanatory variable. Finally, property valuation and income may affect the extent of inequality from state to state, education being a superior consumption good.

The regression results are presented in Table 4-5.[14] As hypothesized, a greater percentage of state aid implies less interdistrict inequality, and partial correlation coefficients indicate that this variable is important. In contrast, the effect of greater reliance on equalization formulas is uncertain and, in any case, much less significant. Greater numbers of districts lead to greater inequality as expected. Finally, the negative effect of median expenditure and property valuation per pupil and the positive effect of income per pupil are generally significant.

Unexpectedly, the regression for the Gini coefficient is the weakest of the five. We have no sure explanation for this. However, in general, the figures in Table 4-5 corroborate our hypothesis: the amount of state aid is an important factor in the equalization brought about by state support for schools, but the state aid formula is relatively unimportant. Since it seems that the level of state funding is a major contributor to equality of district school revenues despite formula manipulations, since the formulas we have hypothesized go far beyond any we have observed, and since the average level of state support is well below that observed in some states, we must conclude that increasing state support is a much more reasonable direction in which to look for equalization than is finding the optimal state aid formula.

### Intradistrict Inequalities

As we move to lower levels of government, the data requirements for precisely describing the extent of inequities grow. At the intrastate level, ideally we would have collected data on every individual district in the country. To study intradistrict inequalities, complete data on the resources allocated to all schools within a large number of "representative" school districts would be desirable. Because of data and time limitations, therefore, our documentation is often sketchier than we would have liked. In this section we will not present original data analyses to document the existence of inequalities, but will rely on separate instances documented by other researchers.

The differences between inequalities at the district level and those previously analyzed should be obvious. State and federal governments confront unequal local revenue, and theoretically if not politically these governments could eliminate or alleviate that inequality. But these levels of government do not act to alleviate interschool inequalities.[15] Whereas interdistrict and interstate inequities arise from reliance on local financing and the market forces which tend to create homogeneous communities, interschool inequities within districts must be due to deliberate policies of resource allocation. There may

## Table 4-5
### Regression Results Explaining Intrastate Inequality in Expenditures per Pupil, Forty-Nine States, 1959-60

| Dependent Variable | Intercept | % State | % Equal | DIST | PROP | Income | MED |
|---|---|---|---|---|---|---|---|
| 1. Range | 1189 | -9.071 | -1.153 | 0.566 | -0.0288 | 0.124 | 0.0392 |
| SEE = 685.9 | | (0.200)[a] | (0.063) | (0.504) | (0.248) | (0.332) | (0.067) |
| $R^2 = 0.509$ | | | | | | | |
| 2. Range/MED | 0.396 | -0.00195 | 0.0000415 | 0.0000758 | -0.0000053 | 0.0000053 | |
| SEE = 0.0991 | | (0.292) | (0.016) | (0.477) | (0.320) | (0.148) | |
| $R^2 = 0.595$ | | | | | | | |
| 3. R7525 | 1.493 | -0.00201 | -0.000148 | 0.000106 | -0.0000053 | 0.0000236 | -0.0000345 |
| SEE = 0.1256 | | (0.240) | (0.044) | (0.515) | (0.249) | (0.344) | (0.318) |
| $R^2 = 0.452$ | | | | | | | |
| 4. R9802 | 2.834 | -0.00668 | -0.000772 | 0.000500 | -0.0000147 | 0.0000471 | -0.107 |
| SEE = 0.4253 | | (0.236) | (0.068) | (0.643) | (0.206) | (0.211) | (0.283) |
| $R^2 = 0.565$ | | | | | | | |

5. GINI
$SEE = 0.0326$

$R^2 = 0.250$

| | | | | | | | |
|---|---|---|---|---|---|---|---|
| 0.0690 | 0.000119 | 0.000128 | 0.0000087 | 0.0000012 | 0.0000089 | -0.0000092 |
| | (0.056) | (0.145) | (0.186) | (0.225) | (0.468) | (0.312) |

[a]Figures in parentheses are partial correlation coefficients. T-statistics are not given because the observations constitute the universe of multi-district states, not a sample.

Sources: RANGE (difference in expenditure per classroom unit from the 25th to the 75th percentile) and R7525 (ratio of per classroom expenditure at the 75th percentile to expenditure at the 25th percentile) from Harrison and McLoone (104), Table 6, p. 70; R9802 (ratio of per classroom expenditure at the 98th percentile to expenditure at the second percentile) from ibid., Table 7, p. 71; GINI (the Gini coefficient of expenditure per classroom unit) from ibid., Table 18, p. 86; % State (percentage of revenues from state sources) from NEA *Estimates of School Statistics*, 1959-60, Table 11, p. 28; % Equal (percentage of state aid distributed through equalizing formulas) from Munse (188), Table 8, p. 12; DIST (number of public school systems) from Harrison and McLoone (104), Table 41, p. 125; PROP (property valuation per pupil) from ibid., Table 30, p. 105.

be seemingly "fair" policies which result in "unfair" resource allocation:  the
most common example is allowing experienced teachers to choose in which
school they wish to teach, resulting in the most experienced (and highest paid)
teachers concentrated in white middle-class schools.[16]  Some seemingly unfair
allocations may be reasonable, such as the allocation of more dollars per pupil
to vocational schools with higher costs for materials and to smaller schools
with presumed diseconomies of scale.[17]  Other allocations may appear to be,
and be, unfair.[18]

The extent and even the definition of intradistrict inequities are complex
issues to which we cannot possibly do justice.  However, there is some evidence
that points not only to intradistrict inequities but to real (and presumably inten-
tional) discrimination.  We will review some of that evidence here.

Katzman (141) concluded that the strongest correlate of pupil expenditures in Boston elementary schools was a measure of voting participation, perhaps indicating that school board members (elected at large) were sensitive to
voting patterns to the extent that they rewarded the faithful.  However, he also
reports a positive relationship between expenditures and Irish origin, and
between expenditures and percentage nonwhite.  More recently the Boston
Finance Commission found "serious inequities and inequalities" in per pupil
funding of Boston's "mini-districts."  Schools in Roxbury, the black section,
were *above* average in general, but in Dorchester, a working-class white and
black neighborhood, they were below average.  The Boston picture shows great
inequalities from no obvious overriding rationale.[19]  A recent study of Philadelphia also found no discriminatory pattern in the allocation of noncompen-
satory items, looking at blacks and Spanish versus whites, and disadvantaged
versus nondisadvantaged.[20]  In contrast, using a sample of nine cities, Owen
(200) demonstrated that schools in black and poor neighborhoods received
lower expenditures per pupil, largely because of teacher allocation mechanisms.
Levin et al. (151) demonstrated for a sample of districts greater resources
flowing to schools in wealthy neighborhoods because of teacher transfer
policies, and to schools in poor areas because of federal aid for compensatory
education.

A complaint in San Francisco charged that "the Spanish-speaking ('Latino')
schools of the Mission have the lowest instructional expenditure per pupil in
any part of San Francisco," citing the following figures:[21]

| Per Pupil | Latinos | Rest of City |
|---|---|---|
| Instructional | $513 | $592 |
| Total | $588 | $677 |

A Chicago complaint is similar:[22]

The disparities among elementary schools in the Chicago School

System operate systematically to discriminate against non-Caucasian students and students from families of low or moderate income or dependent economic status. Elementary schools with a predominant enrollment of non-Caucasian students generally receive smaller per-pupil expenditures and budget appropriations than schools with a predominant enrollment of Caucasian students.

Complainants presented the following data:[23]

| Per Pupil | Predominantly White | Mixed | Predominantly Nonwhite |
|---|---|---|---|
| Instructional Expenditures | $459 | $405 | $413 |
| Total Appropriations | $552 | $485 | $491 |

Detroit has allocated school resources in favor of the wealthy and white in the past.[24] In a many-faceted case involving the allocation of teachers by races as well as (and perhaps more importantly) an underappropriation of funds to black children, the fiscal 1970 figures have been presented to the court.[25]

| Schools with K-6 Only[a] | Percentage Black | | |
|---|---|---|---|
| | 0-10 | Above 10 and Less than 90 | 90-100 |
| Per Pupil Cost, Certified Teachers | $417 | $354 | $360 |
| Per Pupil Cost, All Teachers | $432 | $374 | $380 |
| Per Pupil Cost, Total Personnel | $495 | $427 | $430 |
| Number of Schools | 27 | 34 | 91 |

| Schools with K-7, K-8, or K-9[a] | Percentage Black | | |
|---|---|---|---|
| | 0-10 | Above 10 and Less than 90 | 90-100 |
| Per Pupil Cost, Certified Teachers | $401 | $377 | $349 |
| Per Pupil Cost, All Teachers | $415 | $391 | $368 |
| Per Pupil Cost, Total Personnel | $478 | $450 | $427 |
| Number of Schools | 32 | 26 | 18 |

[a]A few schools were eliminated due to incomplete or inaccurate data. All figures are averages per school weighted by school enrollment.

In Washington, D.C., the favored area is specified by geography, the area west of Rock Creek Park being substantially whiter and wealthier than any other area of the city. The area known as Anacostia is also geographically divided from the center of the district and is known as a poor black area. Plaintiffs and defendants jointly agreed on the following figures:[26]

| Per Pupil | West of Rock Creek Park | Citywide | East of Anacostia River |
|---|---|---|---|
| Teacher Costs, including Kindergarten | $622 | $497 | $445 |
| Teacher Costs, excluding Kindergarten | $654 | $532 | $477 |

Per pupil expenditures in New York City (in 1968) favored the minority schools:

| | |
|---|---|
| 90 percent or more black or Puerto Rican | $769.57 |
| 90 percent or more white or Oriental | $649.85 |

Nonetheless, Paul Ritterband (219) accuses the board of education of racial bias in resource allocation. He refers to educational "production function" literature and to his own path coefficients as evidence for the proposition that pupil-teacher ratios are unrelated to pupil performance, within the ranges found, but teacher qualifications (as reflected in their salaries) are. Teacher salaries in the white schools average $10,143, and in black schools, $8721. Increasing class size by one would release $36 per pupil on the average, Ritterband calculates, representing resources available for remediation. "The Board of Education's response to failure is not only educationally irrelevant, but is administered prejudically. Since the Board of Education spends more per pupil in schools which have a low level of achievement, the expenditure per Puerto Rican child should be greater than the expenditure per black child since Puerto Rican achievement is lower."[27] In fact, blacks receive more funds than Puerto Ricans.

Our conclusions are not detailed, since the data of this section refers to a miniscule sample of districts. It is clear, however, that considerable intradistrict differentials exist, and that some (though not all) of them are discriminatory, the results of political processes which favor wealth and whiteness.

## Conclusions

In this chapter we have presented evidence that inequalities in educational resources exist at all levels of government: interstate, interdistrict, and inter-school. Of course this does not complete a catalogue of differences in educational resources which might be investigated. We have omitted intraschool differences due to tracking, the effect of private schools on the educational resources which might be investigated. We have omitted intraschool differences due to tracking, the effect of private schools on the educational opportunities available to different children, education provided formally and informally by parents, and so forth. However, within the relatively narrow focus of this section, we have identified the important sources of inequality. The first culprit is dependence on local financing, which sets the pattern for inequalities at all levels. State and federal aid do tend to reduce resource inequalities, both among states and within states, although not as much as might be possible with a different distribution of current funds. However, the effective equalizing power of state aid is due almost entirely to the level of state funding and not to the form of state aid formulas.

This much is cold statistics. However, the results in this chapter are con-sistent with the historical view developed in Chapter 2. Given that one of the purposes of education has been to transmit socioeconomic status from genera-tion to generation via the differentiation of schools, we would expect the following. To the extent that there has been a strong history or rhetoric of equal treatment of citizens by governmental units, there will be a proliferation of units, and resource disparities will be found *among* units. This is the case in the Northeast, for example. Where equal treatment has never been a govern-mental obligation, then disparities may exist *within* rather than among units; and we have found interdistrict revenue disparities to be less severe in the South. The importance of local financing, in this historical view, has been to create a mechanism whereby inequalities in resource availabilities were both institutionalized and also justified by the prevailing dogma of local control and noninterference in matters judged to be of local concern only. The *process* of revenue distribution is rationalized by an appeal to "fairness," but the *result* is simply ignored. The rhetoric of equality is weak compared with the rhetoric of individual or group preferences. The rhetoric of *process* equality allows groups to choose to be unequal, cloaking that choice under the name "freedom." These are powerful forces which will not be undone by a simple formula mani-pulation.

In either the Northern or the Southern model, equalization of school resource disparities has been left to the states. But the political process is the mechanism of such equalization, and politics is at the same time a vehicle for favoritism and for the expression of power—either economic power or purely political power. Hence the political systems equalize the disparities created by local financing only incompletely. In the following chapter we will investigate the nature of the mechanisms of state and federal aid, with a view to illustrating how the political (or judicial) process reacts to perceived problems—in this case, the problem of resource inequalities.

## Notes

1. There are only a few exceptions to this. In some states, counties raise substantial amounts of revenue in addition to local districts. Of the states analyzed in Table 4-3, this is true of Nevada, Alabama, and Oregon. Hawaii and Alaska have virtually no local school funds.
2. This omits the special case of Hawaii, which is peculiar in that the entire state comprises one district with six subdistricts, with the result that almost all revenue—88.7 percent—comes from the state. The federal share in Alaska is understated (hence the state's share is overstated) by omission of Bureau of Indian Affairs funds supporting schools for natives.
3. Levin et al. (151) have also presented data in support of the latter two assertions.
4. See Deitch (64), O'Brien (197), Fisher (78) and (79), Renshaw (217), Shapiro (235), Sacks and Harris (225).
5. To understand the tables in this chapter, it is sufficient to know that a Gini coefficient indicates relative equality the closer it approaches zero. The calculation of the Gini coefficient is described in Note 1 of Chapter 3. While Gini coefficients necessarily have some drawbacks, since they compress a vector of information into one number, they are better than the alternatives.

Both Berke et al. (21) and the National Educational Finance Project (128) used correlation coefficients to measure the distributional impact of intergovernmental aid. But equalization is a relative concept, whereas correlation coefficients are measures of absolute amounts and therefore cannot accurately reflect equalization effects. For example, Berke et al. find a negative but "inconsequential" correlation between local revenue per pupil and federal aid, "thus indicating that federal aid assists districts with less revenue for education as much as districts with greater funds for their schools" (p. 45). But this really proves nothing about whether federal aid has produced more equal revenues or not.

A constant amount of federal aid per pupil for each district would result in a zero correlation coefficient (since the correlation between any variable and a constant is zero), but would decrease inequality. This can be most simply seen by considering two districts. $(R_1 + F)/(R_2 + F)$ approaches one as F (federal aid) becomes large relative to $R_1$ and $R_2$ (other revenue), and approaches 1 even faster to the extent that F substitutes for $R_1$ and $R_2$.

6. For example, average local revenue is low in Mississippi, both because Mississippi is poor (state plus local revenue is low also), and because Mississippi is a high state aid state. From the data cited in Table 4-5, the correlation between %STATE and MED is −.196.

7. As a percentage of total school revenues, federal revenue peaked in fiscal 1968 and has declined steadily since.

8. The choice of states was dictated by data availability and time limitations. States which had both elementary and secondary school districts were avoided because of the difficulty of combining or comparing the two kinds of districts. States with large numbers of districts were avoided because of the data burden involved. The Office of Education collects district data for all the states every ten years, with a view to documenting the extent of intrastate inequalities. (For data for 1959-60, see Harrison and McLoone [104]; for 1949-50, see Hutchins and Munse [116]; for 1939-40, see Norton and Lawler [194].) Unfortunately Harrison and McLoone proceeded in terms of expenditures, used the classroom rather than the pupil as the unit of analysis, and collected data only on a stratified random sample of districts (rather than the complete sampling used here). For these reasons it is difficult to integrate their results with ours, but in general they confirm our results of less interdistrict variation in the South. (See their Chapter 2.) The U.S. Office of Education is currently collecting district data for 1969-70 for the continuation of this decennial series, but currently there are no banks of data on individual school districts suitable to our purposes.

9. The differences between the two sets of Gini coefficients given for South Carolina and Massachusetts need explanation. For South Carolina, the 93 districts were aggregated into 43 counties. and coefficients derived for both sets of data. Gini coefficients are lowered when data is aggregated, as inequalities are averaged away. For Massachusetts, 192 small rural districts were eliminated in deriving a sample of 159 for which a complete set of socioeconomic data could be obtained (see Chapter 7). Hence the two sets of Gini coefficients represent different samples, the smaller of which has some interdistrict variation removed.

10. That is, the apparent *reduction* in the Gini coefficient due to state aid is larger, although the distribution of total revenue is not necessarily more equal. There is, however, some tendency for the Southern states, with the exception of Mississippi, to have lower Gini coefficients for total revenue than the New England states. This provides some weak evidence that high-support states may be more successful than low-support states in promoting equality despite the form of state aid formula.

11. For a more complete discussion of these hypothetical Gini coefficients, see Michelson (176).

12. See the description of the legislative process leading to a new formula for state aid in Massachusetts, in Levine (155).

13. We have expressed some reservations about this data above. Particularly because the data is based on a sample of districts within the states rather than the universe of districts, regressions based on this data may not be very reliable. We therefore confine our analysis to hypothesis testing rather than concentrating on the magnitude of the resulting coefficients.

14. Several other specifications were tried, using different measures of property valuation, income, and district structure. The results given here appeared consistently in other specifications.

15. The courts, however, have accepted this role to some extent. See Wright's opinion in *Hobson* v. *Hansen II*.

16. See Owen (201), Levin et al. (151).

17. The burden of proof, however, must be on those who claim that the obvious measure is false. See Michelson (171).

18. Throughout we mean *fairness* to indicate that most people would agree with the decision rule whether they benefited from it or not.

19. See "FinCom Hits Unequal Pupil Funding," *Boston Globe*, June 29, 1973, p 3. Note that school officials, especially Business Manager Leo M. Burke, provided noninvidious explanations for many of the extreme figures produced by FinCom.

20. Summers and Wolfe (250).

21. *Mission Coalition* v. *San Francisco Unified School District*, plaintiffs' assertion of facts, December 9, 1970, p. 2. Year of data not specified, but presumably fiscal 1970.

22. *Brown, Cortez et al.* v. *Board of Education of the City of Chicago*, complaint, pp. 6-7.

23. From "Results of a Study of Patterns of Discrimination in Budget Allocations to Elementary Schools in the Chicago School District," report prepared at the Urban Systems Laboratory, MIT, under the supervision of H.W. Bruck, March 1971, and submitted as Exhibit 1 to the complaint; pp. 3-4.

24. See Sexton (233).

25. *Bradley* v. *Milliken*. Paul Smith, using data supplied by the Detroit School Department, made these calculations on behalf of the plaintiff at the Harvard Center for Law and Education.

26. "Second Joint Memorandum of Plaintiffs and Defendants," April 12, 1971, in *Hobson* v. *Hansen* II. Data for fiscal 1971.

27. Ritterband (219), p. 167.

28. From a linear regression, Ritterband calculates the equation EXP = $675.74 + 1.35B + 0.37PR$ where EXP is expenditures per pupil, B represents black children, PR represents Puerto Rican children, and the constant obviously represents the average expenditure in a 100 percent white school.

# 5

## The Structure of State Aid: Mechanisms of Redistribution

Unlike the interactive behavioral process which generates local revenue, most state and federal revenues for education come to districts through fixed formulas. Although the impact of a formula is not always obvious, the amount of funds flowing to a district at a particular time is.[1] The analysis of local revenue for education requires a model which simulates behavior—essentially, political behavior—of school districts. However, the political battles over state and federal revenues occur well in advance of its distribution, during the legislative process. Once a program of state or federal aid is established, revenue is disbursed according to formulas and guidelines which permit comparatively little overt manipulation.

There are several reasons for analyzing the formulas used to disburse state aid: to clarify the mechanisms by which redistribution of revenues take place, to understand the effect of state and federal intervention into what remains essentially a local enterprise, and to elucidate some of the biases and limitations of intergovernmental aid programs. We will concentrate on mechanisms of state aid only.[2] Since there exist comprehensive reviews of the technical aspects of state aid formulas elsewhere,[3] this chapter will concentrate on the applications of the various formulas in practice, on deviations from established formulas implying political forces at work, and on the little political analysis which exists. We will not discuss categorical grants since categorical aid is usually provided ad hoc on the basis of need and activity in the categorical area (construction, transportation, and so forth).[4]

### Basic State Aid Formulas

Increasing amounts of state aid over time, and the progression from flat grants to foundation programs to the limited use of plans modeled after the percentage equalizing formula, are evidence that states have seen themselves as responsible for at least minimum levels of educational resources and have been concerned about the inequalities generated by reliance on local financing. Yet this is hardly the only concern of state governments and may not be the prime concern. Other important goals of state finance have included property tax relief and stimulation of local spending. Despite the general trend toward "progressive" state aid formulations, modifications and exceptions circumscribe

71

their impact. This can best be seen by describing the state aid formulas as they are actually used, since some of the ways in which the equalizing effects of standard aid formulas are weakened are relatively subtle.[5]

The simplest as well as the earliest form[6] of state aid for general purposes is the flat grant, under which a state pays each district a certain amount per unit of instruction. More formally,

$$S_i = a \cdot B_i \tag{5.1}$$

where $S_i$ is state aid to district $i$, $B_i$ represents the units of instruction in district $i$, and $a$ is a dollar amount provided for each instruction unit. The unit of instruction used in the formula varies from state to state. Most commonly, the number of pupils, the number of teachers, or the number of classrooms is used. Districts are free to raise any amount of local revenue desired above the amount provided by the state. In 1971-72, eight states distributed substantial amounts of state aid through flat-grant formulas, and fourteen others had minimal flat-grant programs, essentially vestigial. Table 5-1 summarizes both the sources of school revenue by states and the kinds of formulas used in 1971-72.

A more sophisticated type of formula was developed during the 1920s to provide greater equalization of school resources. The foundation plan establishes a foundation or basic level of resources which each district is entitled to receive. However, instead of providing the whole of this amount (as under the flat grant), the local district is required to provide a share of the foundation amount, the share being proportional to its wealth. Typically, each district is required to tax itself at a certain rate, and the state covers the difference between the foundation level and the local share.

$$S_i = a \cdot B_i - k \cdot W_i \tag{5.2}$$

where $W_i$ is an index of local wealth, and $k$ is a parameter which determines the amount of the local share, given local wealth $W_i$. The foundation amount is $a \cdot B_i$, and the local share is $k \cdot W_i$. In 1971-72, thirty-four states used some form of the foundation plan.

Both of the formulas presented so far aim to ensure that each district will have a *minimum* amount of revenue, $a \cdot B_i$. In addition, the foundation plan equalizes revenues for education insofar as the state contribution is lower for wealthy than for poor districts. Neither one, however, is designed to ameliorate the unequal distribution of education resources produced by autonomous local districts. A formula designed to move in this direction is the percentage equalizing plan, which came into use during the 1960s, but only in six states—Iowa, Massachusetts, New York, Pennsylvania, Rhode Island, and Wisconsin.[7]

**Table 5-1**
**Sources of Revenue and Forms of State Aid, 1971-72**

| | Source of Revenue as a Percentage of Total Revenue, 1971-72 | | | Percentage of State Aid Disbursed through: | | | |
|---|---|---|---|---|---|---|---|
| | Federal | State | Local | Flat Grants | Foundation Plans | Percentage Equalizing Formulas | Categorical Aid |
| Connecticut | 2.7 | 22.4 | 75.0 | 82.3 | | | 17.7 |
| Maine | 9.7 | 33.4 | 56.9 | | 76.6ª | 11.4[b,f] | 12.0 |
| Massachusetts | 5.4 | 23.2 | 71.4 | | | 85.9[d] | 14.1 |
| New Hampshire | 5.8 | 6.5 | 87.7 | 20.3 | 28.3 | | 51.4[b] |
| Rhode Island | 9.0 | 35.3 | 55.7 | | | 83.9 | 16.1 |
| Vermont | 6.1 | 33.0 | 60.9 | | | 72.1 | 27.9[b] |
| Delaware | 7.8 | 69.6 | 22.6 | 74.3 | | | 25.7[b] |
| Maryland | 7.1 | 43.3 | 49.7 | | | | 59.5[b] |
| New Jersey | 4.6 | 25.4 | 70.0 | | | 55.9[d] | 44.1 |
| New York | 5.8 | 42.3 | 51.9 | | | 92.6ª | 7.4 |
| Pennsylvania | 6.5 | 47.0 | 46.5 | | | 76.8 | 23.2 |
| District of Columbia | 13.3 | 0 | 86.7 | | | | |
| Alabama | 18.1 | 62.4 | 19.5 | 5.4 | 88.4 | | 6.2 |
| Arkansas | 16.6 | 46.1 | 37.4 | | | | 12.0 |
| Florida | 11.3 | 52.9 | 35.9 | 6.9 | 84.3 | (f) | 8.8 |
| Georgia | 13.7 | 51.8 | 34.5 | | 79.9 | | 20.1 |
| Kentucky | 16.6 | 53.5 | 29.8 | | 98.8 | | .2 |
| Louisiana | 14.1 | 56.0 | 29.9 | | 86.3 | | 13.7 |
| Mississippi | 27.6 | 48.2 | 24.2 | 2.8 | 79.1 | | 18.1 |
| North Carolina | 15.9 | 62.6 | 21.5 | 90.5 | | | 9.5 |
| South Carolina | 18.0 | 55.0 | 27.0 | 77.6 | | | 22.4 |
| Tennessee | 14.0 | 44.4 | 41.5 | | 91.2 | | 8.8[b] |
| Virginia | 11.8 | 33.8 | 54.4 | 23.2 | 65.3 | | 11.5 |
| West Virginia | 13.0 | 54.9 | 32.0 | | 94.5ª | | 5.5 |
| Illinois | 6.8 | 37.8 | 55.4 | | 79.1 | (f) | 20.9 |
| Indiana | 5.4 | 31.5 | 63.1 | 13.9 | 77.1 | | 9.0 |
| Michigan | 3.8 | 44.5 | 51.7 | | 85.8 | (f) | 14.2 |
| Ohio | 6.2 | 30.5 | 63.3 | | 81.6 | | 19.4 |
| Wisconsin | 4.3 | 30.4 | 65.4 | 21.3 | | 46.8[f] | 31.9 |
| Iowa | 3.9 | 31.3 | 65.0 | 19.5 | | 54.4[c] | 26.1 |
| Kansas | 8.0 | 27.4 | 64.6 | | 86.8 | 6.7[f] | 6.5 |
| Minnesota | 4.7 | 48.4 | 46.7 | | 82.2 | | 17.8 |
| Missouri | 8.2 | 33.7 | 58.1 | | 81.4 | | 18.6 |
| Nebraska | 6.3 | 17.8 | 75.9 | 5.9 | 80.4ª | | 13.7 |
| North Dakota | 11.9 | 29.4 | 58.7 | 10.3 | 84.7 | | 5.0 |
| South Dakota | 12.5 | 15.1 | 72.3 | 15.0 | 78.7 | | 6.3 |
| Arizona | 9.4 | 40.1 | 50.5 | 88.1 | 8.2 | | 3.7 |
| New Mexico | 19.6 | 60.0 | 20.4 | 83.4 | | | 16.6 |
| Oklahoma | 10.8 | 44.5 | 44.7 | | 50.1ª | 37.4 | 12.5 |
| Texas | 11.3 | 47.0 | 41.7 | 32.0 | 65.5ª | | 2.5 |
| Colorado | 8.7 | 27.5 | 64.2 | | 85.9 | (f) | 14.1 |
| Idaho | 13.0 | 39.4 | 47.6 | | 99.2ª | | 0.8 |

**Table 5-1 (Continued)**

| | Source of Revenue as a Percentage of Total Revenue, 1971-72 | | | Percentage of State Aid Disbursed through: | | | |
| | Federal | State | Local | Flat Grants | Foundation Plans | Percentage Equalizing Formulas | Categorical Aid |
|---|---|---|---|---|---|---|---|
| Montana | 8.5 | 23.9 | 67.7 | 18.0 | 76.2 | (f) | 3.8 |
| Utah | 9.3 | 52.1 | 38.6 | 72.2[e] | | 9.8[f] | 18.0 |
| Wyoming | 10.6 | 33.8 | 55.6 | | 96.4[a] | | 3.6 |
| California | 6.8 | 36.7 | 56.5 | 41.2 | 38.6 | | 21.2 |
| Nevada | 8.2 | 39.4 | 52.4 | | 100.0[a] | | |
| Oregon | 4.5 | 19.9 | 75.6 | 70.2 | 13.7 | | 16.1 |
| Washington | 8.4 | 49.0 | 42.6 | | 64.5 | | 35.5 |
| Alaska | 15.5 | 74.1 | 10.4 | | 59.7 | | 40.3 |
| Hawaii | 8.4 | 88.7 | 2.9 | 100.0 | | | |

[a]Includes transportation, otherwise included under Categorical Aid.

[b]Includes construction and debt service, otherwise included in general aid formulas.

[c]Tax reduction funds based on local valuation and tax rates.

[d]Different formulas for general-purpose aid and construction aid.

[e]Since there is full recapture on a 16 mill tax, this part of state aid is effectively a flat grant with a state property tax.

[f]State has passed a bill since 1971-72 incorporating some version of percentage equalizing. See Grubb (91).

Sources: (Columns 1-3): NEA, *Estimates of School Statistics, 1972-73,* Table 9, p. 32; (Columns 4-7): Johns (129).

In its pure form, percentage equalizing is expressed:

$$S_i = \left( 1 - d \cdot \frac{W_i}{\overline{W}} \right) \cdot R_i \tag{5.3}$$

where $(1 - d \cdot W_i/\overline{W})$ is a fraction labeled the "reimbursement percentage" (negatively related to wealth $W_i$), $\overline{W}$ is the state average of the index of wealth, $d$ is a parameter which has a value between zero and one, and $R_i$ is the total educational revenue per pupil in district $i$. The major purpose of this formula is to free districts from dependence on local wealth. If local revenue per pupil is the product of a tax rate $t_i$ times the local wealth base $W_i$ (most commonly, property valuation), then total revenue (ignoring federal aid) is:

$$R_i = t_i \cdot W_i + S_i$$

$$= t_i \cdot W_i + \left( 1 - d \cdot \frac{W_i}{\overline{W}} \right) \cdot R_i \ .$$

or, after rearranging terms,

$$R_i = t_i \, \frac{\overline{W}}{d} \, . \tag{5.4}$$

Hence total (state plus local) revenue is a function of the local tax rate alone, but not of local wealth.

The general concept that total revenue should be a function of tax effort, not tax-raising ability, is currently recognized as "power equalizing."[8] Since $\overline{W}$ and $d$ are both constants, we can write a general linear form of power equalizing as:

$$R_i = t_i K \tag{5.5}$$

where $K$ is any figure set by the legislature or a delegated authority. Under a rigorous application of this formulation,

$$
\begin{aligned}
S_i &= R_i - t_i W_i \\
&= t_i \left( K - W_i \right)
\end{aligned}
\tag{5.6}
$$

which will be negative when district wealth $W_i$ is larger than the power equalizing constant $K$. The state would then collect from the district the excess of revenues raised over $t_i K$. An even more general form of power equalizing is:

$$R_i = f(t_i) \, .$$

That is, total revenue equals some (not necessarily linear) function of the local tax rate, which may be spelled out by a table of per pupil revenues given $t_i$, or by formula.[9]

New state legislation has tended to adopt the power equalizing approach, no doubt inspired by cases like *Serrano* v. *Priest* which, while not mandating this solution to presently unconstitutional school finance procedures, have lent credibility and prestige to it. Nine states in 1973 adopted a power equalizing school finance law, only four of which (Maine, Kansas, Wisconsin and Utah) had any previous experience with percentage equalizing.

### Formula Variations

The three basic formulas (considering percentage equalizing and district power equalizing equivalent) cover almost all of state aid distributed for general purposes. However, the variations in the actual formulas used are virtually endless, since the variables can be defined in various ways, and floors and ceilings can be imposed on the values the formulas generate.

For the definition of the unit of instruction, $B_i$, in the flat-grant formula and in foundation programs, most states use some measure of pupils: average daily attendance, average daily membership, or a census of school-age children. There has been long debate over which of these is most appropriate, considering incentive effects versus distributional effects. The use of average daily attendance may penalize districts with high absentee rates, which tend to be large, urban districts with high concentrations of children from poor families. Defining the unit of instruction as school-age or school-attending children favors those districts with large numbers of children in private school, covertly subsidizing these schools by relieving the tax burden of local parents.[10] In addition, some state aid programs use the number of teachers as the unit of instruction. This favors those districts which can afford to have a relatively higher teacher-pupil ratio, and the consideration of training and experience favors districts which either attempt to attract teachers with better qualifications through higher salaries or which attract these teachers because of community socioeconomic status, locational factors, and so forth.[11] The effect is to distribute larger sums to communities with relatively large amounts of local revenue and to middle-class suburbs, and smaller sums to rural areas.[12]

In many states, the parameter ($a$ or $d$) in state aid formulas is varied to reflect assumed cost differences. Secondary students are considered more costly than elementary students, and rural education is often considered more costly than urban due to diseconomies of small scale. Whether justified on those grounds or not, the distributional effects of giving rural school special consideration is to make revenues among districts more equal, since rural districts tend to be relatively poor.[13] Finally, two states (Maryland and Pennsylvania) provide special funds on the basis of population density, a mechanism for alleviating "municipal overburden."[14] Pennsylvania grants additional revenue to districts with a large number of poor families, and New York increases aid to districts with high tax rates. These variations tend to favor poor districts.

Of the states whose public school aid was based in 1971–72 on a foundation program or percentage equalizing formula, all used property valuation as the measure of wealth, $W_i$, although a few included taxable income and other local sources of nonproperty tax revenue. However, all states in 1971–72 imposed a restriction on the formulas in equations (5.2) and (5.3): If state aid is calculated to be less than zero, then it is set either at zero or at some minimum level. The provision of a floor effectively creates two formulas, one which applies to the majority of districts, and one which applies only to those districts which are wealthy enough that state aid would otherwise be negative. Since some wealthy districts thereby receive state funds, the distribution of state aid is less equalizing than it would be under strict application of the formula.

Essentially, there is a tradeoff in the foundation program between two alternatives which are both politically unpopular. As $k$ increases, the amount of revenue from state taxes necessary to support the foundation program decreases, but the likelihood increases that the formula will generate negative amounts of state aid for wealthy districts. A low $k$, on the other hand, avoids the possibility that the formula will require wealthy districts to pay the state, but it also requires larger amounts of revenue from state sources. The compromise in most cases has been to set $k$ high enough that for some districts the formula in equation (5.2) generates negative amounts of state aid, and then to place a floor on the amount of state aid distributed to each district.

Another possible change in the foundation grant formula is illustrated by the California program of state aid. California distributes most of its general purpose aid through a flat grant of $125 per pupil in ADA, supplemented by a foundation program enacted many years after the flat-grant program. In calculating the distribution of aid under the equalizing program, both the local contribution $k \cdot W_i$ and the $125 of basic aid is subtracted from the foundation amount of $a \cdot B_i$. The result is that less state aid is distributed than would be the case if basic aid were ignored in the computation under the equalizing program; and because there is a floor in the foundation program, state aid is less equalizing than it would be if the equalizing program had entirely superseded the system of flat grants.[15] Similar changes affect the foundation programs in Alabama, Nebraska, South Dakota, and Virginia.[16] One can infer that the pressures for larger amounts of state aid and a formula with equalizing provisions have been countered by opposing political pressures.

Similarly, those states using percentage equalizing formulas in 1971-72 imposed restrictions so that no districts would be required to remit revenues to the state as under a strict application of equation (5.3). In Rhode Island, a floor of 0.30 for the reimbursement percentage has been established. In New York, there is a ceiling on the reimbursement percentage of 0.90, a guaranteed minimum amount of state aid, and the reimbursement percentage is applied to total expenditures minus federal aid and other state aid. Massachusetts imposes a floor and a ceiling on reimbursable expenditures. New Jersey, Pennsylvania, Wisconsin, and Oklahoma all provide for minimum amounts of state aid.

Such restrictions represent, as in the case of foundation programs, a political solution to a mathematical tradeoff: If equation (5.6) is set so that no district state aid is non-negative, then it is necessary to set $K$ equal to $W_{max}$, the wealth of the richest district. Equation (5.5) becomes $t_i \cdot W_{max}$ and the state aid program equalizes fiscal capacity—the yield per mill of tax—at the level of the wealthiest district in the state. This would require a large flow of state taxes and disbursements, as we will indicate in Chapter 8. However, if $K$ is set smaller than $W_{max}$, some wealthy districts will have to pay some of their locally raised revenues to the state. This very visible transfer of local taxes to the state is often politically unacceptable. The establishment of

floors applying either to the reimbursement percentage or to the amount of
state aid per district permits state taxes and disbursements to remain relatively
low while assuring the political support of wealthy districts. The price paid
in this compromise is the decreased equalization effect of the state aid program.[17]

The percentage equalizing formula, which in original intent equalizes completely except for differences in local "effort," can be manipulated in several
other subtle ways that almost vitiate its equalizing effect, as can be seen in the
case of Massachusetts.[18] The intent of the experts who drafted the original
proposal for the revision of the Massachusetts school aid program was to offer
a "pure" percentage equalizing formula, the form of equation (5.3).[19] However, this formula was modified in three ways which proved to restrict its
equalizing potential severely.

First, the reimbursement percentage, $P$, where $P = 1 - d \cdot W_i/\overline{W}$, cannot be
lower than 0.15 or higher than 0.75. The ceiling affects only one district, but
the floor applies to 84 districts (out of 351), including 57 districts which would
have a negative reimbursement percentage under application of the pure formula.[20] This restriction provides these wealthy districts with state aid which
they would not otherwise have, and thereby lessens the equalizing effect of the
state aid program.

Second, state aid is reduced if federal aid exceeds a certain level.[21] The
effect of this restriction is that the state effectively "taxes" away part of federal
aid received by districts, and this part increases as federal aid increases relative
to total revenue. It is also larger the poorer is the district.[22]

Third, if $L_i$ exceeds 110 percent of the state average or is less than 80 percent
of the state average, this floor and ceiling figure is used in calculating state aid.
While the total effect of this restriction on the equalizing effect of the formula
is unclear, it does restrict the incentive effect of the percentage equalizing formula. In addition, state aid to communities is prorated according to the availability of funds for the state aid program, with state aid reduced by the same
percentage in each community. To the extent that the original formulation is
equalizing, the loss from prorating state aid is disequalizing.[23]

### State Aid in Practice

The Massachusetts situation is probably not atypical.[24] Yet despite formula
manipulations designed to reduce the equalizing impact of state aid from its theoretical limits, that aid is equalizing, as the data in Tables 4-3 and the regressions
in Table 4-5 indicate. As long as the distribution of state aid is more equal than
the distribution of local revenue would have been without that aid, then state aid
will tend to make the distribution of total revenue more equal.[25] The evidence
presented in the previous chapter implies that increasing state aid would have a

greater equalizing effect than would improving the formulas used, allowing all other political realities to be what they are. The description of the actual state aid formulas used indicates why this is so: the equalizing effects of formulas are relatively easy to compromise, with the result that the equalizing effect of any state aid program may be little greater than that of a flat-grant program.[26]

Given the purposes and the history of state aid programs, it is difficult to envision a program which would not tend to equalize the distribution of total school resources to some extent. Both political and ideological forces assure that state aid distributions will not be so biased in favor of wealthy districts that they will promote inequality.[27] Yet the same political forces constrain the equalizing effect of formulas. Both formula manipulations and increases in state aid have been enacted in the past seventy years in the name of equalization. The evidence suggests to us that an increased level of state aid is the less corruptible route toward equalization.

This conclusion is in some opposition to current trends in thinking about possible solutions to school finance problems, especially as stimulated by *Serrano* and other cases. There are two ways to evaluate the probable success of district power equalizing (DPE). One is to evaluate whether it would be likely to satisfy a court mandate, such as in *Serrano*. In Part 3 of this book, we will present a model and simulations in an attempt to address this issue. The second kind of evaluation is to judge whether, apart from the mandate of *Serrano*, district power equalizing could have a great impact on equalization among districts. The fate of percentage equalizing plans in Massachusetts, Rhode Island, New York, Iowa, and Utah casts some doubt on the ability of district power equalizing to come through the legislative process unscathed. Like other formula manipulations, its intent seems doomed to partial failure. Effort might better be spent pressing for larger amounts of state aid under current formulations, since the effect can be more easily estimated and, in most cases, will be unequivocably equalizing.

Indeed, the increase in the anticipated state share has been overlooked in much of the discussion about school finance legislation of 1973. All of the eleven new acts include substantial increases in state disbursements. The California and North Dakota bills approximately double state aid. In Wisconsin, state aid will increase by nearly 50 percent. Maine intends to increase state revenue from 31 percent to 51 percent of the total. Florida has increased its state appropriations by 19 percent.[28]

There are two reasons to believe that, despite the romance with new formulas and new names, most of the equalizing will come from this increased state aid. First, four of the new acts (those of Florida, Maine, Montana, and Utah) actually distribute little of the state contribution under power equalizing provisions. As noted above, a flat grant is equalizing, and—as the simulations in Chapter 8 will demonstrate—potentially more equalizing when combined with a DPE provision than is a pure DPE formula. Second, the new legislation includes measures of "need" far more relevant and equalizing than the presumed secondary-primary or rural-urban cost disparities. Colorado, Illinois, Utah, and Wisconsin will distribute aid for "compensatory education," while Colorado and Michigan consider aspects of municipal overburden, and Florida adjusts for price differences among districts. These enactments demonstrate that, contrary to some fears, there is sufficient flexibility at the state level to consider educational need within equalizing formulations.[29]

A potentially equalizing mechanism included in new finance bills is an attempt to limit the range of permissible behavior by districts. All new legislation includes ceilings on the expenditures or local tax rates. This is the first recognition that local district behavior can defeat state attempts at inducements toward equality. However, in every state except Wisconsin the ceiling can be overriden by district referendum, which makes unequalizing behavior more cumbersome, but still possible.

### State Taxes and the Distribution of State Tax Burdens

As illustrated in Chapter 3, it seems that we should know the distribution of state taxes if we are to assess the overall redistributive effects of state aid to schools. While there exist no data, to our knowledge, on the distribution of tax burdens by community, we can look at the distribution of tax burden by income class. Local taxes are almost always regressive and state taxes often so. That is, people in higher income classes pay a smaller percentage of their incomes in taxes than do people with lower income. However, state taxes are *relatively* progressive; they are less regressive than local taxes. We can illustrate this by showing the ratio of state taxes (as a percentage of income) to local taxes (as a percentage of income). Betsy Levin et al. provide us with data showing state and local taxes as a percentage of household income for eight states.[30] In all cases the ratio increases continually over the eight income classes. In Figure 5-1 we show this ratio for three states, selected only because they are easily plotted on one scale. Local taxes declined from 7.1 percent of income in the lowest income category to 2.2 percent in the highest category in California, while state taxes are slightly progressive, increasing from 1.6 percent in the lowest income category to 2.5 percent in the highest. In Washington and New Hampshire state tax rates go down as income goes up, but the state tax is still *relatively* progressive (less regressive) than the local tax.

The importance of the relative tax rates is that as public school finance becomes more a state function, there is a redistribution in taxes as well as in revenues. Figure 5-1 shows that this redistribution can be considerable: the ratio of state to local taxes is five times at high incomes what it is at low incomes. Although we do not have a more precise measure of the redistributive effects from shifting from local to state taxes, at least the direction is the same as for

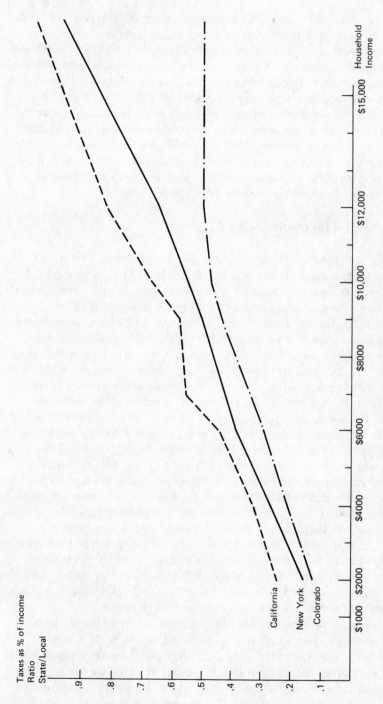

**Figure 5-1.** Ratio of State to Local Tax Burdens by Household Income, 1968–69

Source: Betsy Levin et al. (151) Tables II-12 and II-13

increases in state expenditures. Failing a restructuring of local taxes, we would support increased state support for education on tax grounds alone.

The tax-income relationship in a state is a function both of the proportion of taxes collected by various means, and also of state variations in tax definition. For example, a sales tax which includes food and clothing is considerably more regressive than one which exempts them. Similarly, some states have "admissions" taxes and other selective consumption taxes which might well be progressive. Some state income taxes are proportional after an exemption, while others have a progressive rate structure. However, it appears from the data of Levin et al. that the relative mix of taxes is more important than local variations in formulas in determining their overall progressivity—a conclusion parallel to that for the equalizing effect of state aid.[31]

### A Theory of Distribution Restated

Since state taxes are relatively progressive, any shift from local to state funding, revenue distributions held constant, is likely to redistribute income from rich to poor individuals, and by extension from wealthy to poor districts. However, while we can usually identify the incidence of total state taxes, as in Figure 5-1, we cannot usually identify a particular tax which supports state aid to education, the way we can identify the property tax as the source of local tax revenue in most cases.[32] There are two generally accepted normative arguments for linking government expenditures with specific taxes. The first is the case of benefit taxation, where government services have identifiable benefits to individual citizens, and taxes can be levied on the basis of such benefits. No one, however, claims that the property tax is, with respect to education, a benefit tax. Nor could this be claimed for any of the other taxes which support public education or, more generally, for any tax levied on parents which supports their children's education. The second reason for identification of a government service with a specific tax is political. If a specific tax can be identified as the revenue source for a government program, then citizens can choose, directly or indirectly, the tax level, hence the expenditure level they deem appropriate. Called "voter sovereignty," this power is most apparent when independent school districts vote on the level of taxes, or when citizens vote for a candidate pledged to specific tax levels. However, it is precisely the point of state aid to education that, in this case, citizen sovereignty should be ignored. Local financing results in an inequitable distribution of resources which the state intervenes to correct.

If one insists on analyzing school expenditures as redistributions from one community to another, there is no question that one needs to consider both taxes and expenditures. Our analysis in Chapter 3 described public school finance as a distribution of funds from nonschool to school services, or from adults to children. We asked whether state school funds were *in fact* going to children or to adults—whether districts were substituting state funds for local funds. We might still like to know whether state aid *re*distributes funds among adults, or merely taxes them from the state rather than the local level. This would depend on who pays state, who pays local taxes. But if we concentrate only on the question of whether and how funds are allocated to children, we need not be concerned with taxes at all. Children do not pay taxes.

Thus we are in the fortunate position of having an analysis which allows us to ignore that which we could not have done anyway. But the distinction between these two issues, between redistribution among adults and redistribution from adults to children, has more significance: it is our position that the state's responsibility to its child citizens should not be based on characteristics of the children's families. The problem of raising revenue to fulfill state obligations is serious. We see tax design and collection as poor from many points of view—expensive, biased in incidence, selectively avoidable—and we support some tax reform. But we think the issue of who pays, while necessary for many analyses of government behavior, is a separable issue when the beneficiaries as individuals cannot have paid at all. It is this principle, that state school finance is supposed to direct resources to children, not to taxpayers, which will govern our recommendations in Chapter 9, and governs our continued analysis of school expenditures without regard to where the funds come from.

### Notes

1. Formulas often require revision after some experience. The Massachusetts state aid formula was modified to include the previous year's state aid in "reimbursable expenditures" subsequent to the year from which our data is derived.
2. Federal programs have generated considerably more research and discussion than have state programs, especially in the area of political analysis of legislative battle, where almost nothing has been written on the state level. For descriptions of federal programs of aid to education, see Reischauer and Hartman (216), and Berke and Kirst (23).
3. See Benson (17) and Coons, Clune, and Sugarman (52).
4. Categorical grants are also formula based, of course, and are often means of channeling state funds to districts which would be ineligible under general "need" formulations.
5. This section draws initially on the latest compendium of information on state aid programs, that of Johns (129) for 1971-72. Similar compendia exist for 1968-69, 1966-67, 1962-63, 1969-70, 1957-58, 1953-54, and 1949-50. For update information see Stauffer (242) or Grubb (91).
6. See Chapter 2, or Coons, Clune, and Sugarman's (52, Ch. 1) analysis of the history of different forms of state formulas.
7. Utah provided a small amount of its state aid—about 6 percent—through such a formula as well, but converted to the similar "power equalizing" formulation in 1973.

8. Coons, Clune and Sugarman (52). As a comparison of equations (5.4) and (5.6) shows, percentage equalizing and district power equalizing are formally equivalent if federal revenues are ignored. They are slightly different if federal revenues are considered.

9. For examples of nonlinear formulas, see Benson et al. (18).

10. Utah has resolved this dilemma by averaging ADA and ADM.

11. See Owen (200), (201).

12. In South Carolina—where aid is distributed according to average daily attendance, but considers the training and experience of teachers—the correlation between state aid and local revenue is 0.21.

    However, even in this case state aid is equalizing, since it is distributed more equally than is local revenue. Similarly, Levin et al. (151, Ch. 2) show that the use of a personnel unit formula in Delaware results in a correlation of 0.30 between property valuation per pupil and state revenue per pupil, but state aid still has an equalizing effect on total revenues.

13. Levin et al. (151), NEFP (127). Bussard (42) has concluded in a review of the literature that diseconomies of scale have not been conclusively demonstrated, whatever other reasons may exist for consolidation of small, rural schools. See also the discussion of economies of scale in Chapter 6.

14. See the discussion of municipal overburden in Chapter 6, and the results pertaining to it in Chapter 7. New Jersey and New York laws previously contained similar provisions.

15. Without the floor, the California system would be

$$\frac{S_i}{B_i} = 125 + a - t \cdot \frac{W_i}{B_i} - 125 = a - t \cdot \frac{W_i}{B_i},$$

a pure foundation plan. But with the floor

$$a - t \cdot \frac{W_i}{B_i} - 125 \geqslant 0,$$

*some* wealthy districts are guaranteed a minimum of \$125 per pupil, where they would receive less under a pure foundation plan. Of the \$125 minimum, \$120 is mandated in the state constitution and hence difficult to change.

16. Alabama also relies on 1938 property valuation in its foundation program, resulting in more aid flowing to developing districts and less to those in economic decline. Prior to 1967, Massachusetts relied on 1948 property valuation, with similar results. Large cities in particular were penalized.

17. In Chapter 8 we will analyze the effects of such a compromise.

18. Most of the discussion about the Massachusetts formula draws on Daniere (61).

19. Those originally consulted about the revision included Charles Benson, generally regarded as the originator of the percentage equalizing formula in (16).

20. The data are Daniere's and apply to 1966-67.

21. If $S_i + F_i > 0.75 (L_i + F_i)$, where $F_i$ is federal revenue, then state aid is set so that $S_i + F_i = 0.75 (L_i + F_i)$. This restriction affects 12 of the 159 districts in the sample used in Chapter 7.

22. This Massachusetts provision may be in violation of the federal "impact aid" law, 20 U.S.C. Sec. 236 et seq. as amended. See *Douglas Independent School District No. 3* v. *Jorgenson*.

23. In the simplest terms, the relative equality between two school districts can be measured by

$$\frac{L_i + S_i}{L_j + S_j}$$

In the case where state aid is reduced by the percentage $(1 - q)$, where $q < 1$, then there is less equality if

$$\frac{L_i + qS_i}{L_j + qS_j} < \frac{L_i + S_i}{L_j + S_j} \quad , \text{with } L_i < L_j \ .$$

24. In a history of the passage of the Chapter 70 bill in Massachusetts, based largely on official records of legislative proceedings, Levine (155) was unable to isolate political mechanisms at work. The process which appeared to shape the final Chapter 70 bill was largely governed by ignorance of what the proposed formula would do, and partisan pressures associated with passage of a sales tax. It is hard to believe that legislative process is as random as portrayed there. Rather, it is likely that the real political battles take place behind closed doors, and that only exhaustive interviewing many years afterward could reveal the actual process.

    Research into the state politics of education has been relatively limited and is still more descriptive than analytic; but see Baily, Frost, Marsh, and Wood (9), Masters, Salisbury, and Eliot (168), Usdan (266), Iannacone (118), Wirt and Kirst (278), and Kirst (145).

25. Considering two districts with local revenue $L_1$ and $L_2$, with $L_1 < L_2$, and state aid in each district of $S$ per pupil, then the ratio

$$\frac{L_1 + S}{L_2 + S}$$

approaches one, indicating greater equality, as $S$ becomes large relative to $L_1$ and $L_2$. More generally,

$$\frac{L_1 + S_1}{L_2 + S_2}$$

will be larger than $L_1/L_2$ (closer to one, indicating greater equality) if $S_1/S_2 > L_1/L_2$ —that is as long as state aid is distributed more equally than local revenue is.

26. In Chapter 8 we will present simulations which indicate that the Massachusetts program has very little more effect on inequality among districts than would a flat-grant program with the same state aid.

27. Even in the case of distribution of aid by classroom units, considering teacher experience and training, which may result in state aid positively correlated with local revenue, the positive correlation is not likely to be strong enough to create greater inequality. This occurs in South Carolina, Delaware, and North Carolina, for example.

28. These figures must be approximate since all bills allow districts to react to the new set of incentives.

29. The criticisms are contained in Callahan, Wilken and Sillerman (43), Berke, Kelly and Callahan (22), Churgin, Ehrenberg and Grossi (47), and others. For a more technical rebuttal, see Grubb and Michelson (96).

30. Betsy Levin et al. (151), pp. 72 and 74. State tax rates are also given for Hawaii, which collects no local taxes for schooling.

31. There have been a number of recent attacks on the conventional wisdom that the property tax is regressive. One strand of the argument, due largely to Mieskowski (178) and (179), theoretically demonstrates that the property tax is borne by capital owners, not renters. However, the validity of this conclusion—even accepting the general equilibrium model in which the argument is couched—depends on the assumption that the supply of capital taxable by property taxes is inelastic. Since there is no evidence in support of this assumption, and numerous possible objections to it (as well as to the model of perfect competition), this argument stands as only an interesting but currently untested hypothesis.

A second argument, mentioned by Reischauer and Hartman (216), relying on Peterson (205), is that the tax on renters is progressive because "the ratio of value to rent for structures occupied by the poor is probably far lower than it is for buildings occupied by higher income groups," (p. 29) and because of patterns of housing demand. There are two critical weaknesses in taking Peterson's argument that far. In the first place, he relies for values of the income elasticity of housing demand on estimates from de Leeuw (66), which can be shown to be biased upward (see Maisel,

Burnham and Austin [163]). "Correct" elasticities imply a slightly *regressive* tax. But even more importantly for our purposes, Peterson explicitly ignores biased assessment practices and variations in tax rates among jurisdictions as sources of regressivity. Though there is no evidence on the relative importance of demand patterns, assessment practices, and tax rate variation in property tax incidence, the latter two factors appear sufficient to account for the property tax's assumed regressivity. It is precisely these sources of regressivity which would be eliminated with a shift from local to statewide property taxation. Thus an argument that a statewide property tax might be progressive does not imply that local district property taxation is progressive.

32. For example, although the passage of the current Chapter 70 aid bill in Massachusetts was linked with the passage of a state sales tax, the funds for state aid currently come from the general fund, and are in no way linked with revenues from the sales tax. See Pechman (203).

**Part III**
**Estimates of School District Behavior**

# 6 Elements of a Model of Public School Finance

In the previous chapters we have investigated some of the conceptual, historical, and political problems in the allocation of school resources. Implicit in much of this was the assumption that the process which generates disparities in school resources is well known. The function of Part 3, therefore, is to provide an analysis of this process, through the development of a statistical model which will serve two purposes: explanation of the process and prediction of the effects of changes in public policy.

In this chapter we look at the various elements which will make up an econometric model of public school finance. We will discuss the requisite variables, the specification of equations, estimating procedures, and the requirements for a sample of districts. The chapter serves a second function: in building toward the sets of equations presented in Chapter 7, we will refer extensively (in notes) to previous work in this field.[1] Thus the text serves as a straightforward exposition of a reasonably rigorous theoretical investigation, while the notes serve as an outline of the literature.

The specific variables will be defined and the equations estimated in Chapter 7. In Chapter 7 we also derive the actual values of the parameters discussed theoretically in Chapter 6. The specific estimations will bring out some features not stressed theoretically. In Chapter 8 we use our model of public school finance to simulate various alternative state aid formulas. We wish to know how different the current program is in its results—the distribution of total school revenue per pupil among districts—from other formulations that are widely discussed. Tables of simulation results will summarize the work of Chapter 8. In Chapter 9 we leave the technical manipulations and draw conclusions about alternative public school finance formulas.

## Variables

Our unit of observation is the school district. This is the level at which tax and spending decisions are made, so that "behavior" of a school district means the consequences for district tax and spending of changes in variables outside district control, including mechanisms of state and federal aid. We need to assume consistency in this behavior, but not necessarily welfare optimality: We will assume that district behavior is transitive (if A is preferred to B and B to C, then A will be preferred to C), consistent (if some wealth leads to some expenditures, more wealth leads to more expenditures), and "rational." Rationality here is a price concept: If the cost of schooling goes up, all else equal, the district at least does not spend more than before the cost increase, and probably spends less. We make no assumptions about the welfare of the residents, nor the process by which decisions are made. We assume only that decisions are made, and that they are responsive to the economic and social environment.

There are three major uses for the community's income: schooling, nonschooling public expenditures, and private saving and expenditure. Ignoring for now the psychological problem of the total tax rate, let us lump nonschooling and private expenditures together as alternative to schooling.[2] We will consider nonschool expenditures explicitly below. If there is no state matching aid or other special inducement to educational spending, then an additional dollar of school expenditure requires a dollar less of nonschool expenditure, given community income. If there is a state aid program based on local revenues—a matching grant program—the cost to the district of an additional dollar of school expenditure is less than a dollar of alternative expenditures. In Figure 6-1 we draw a budget line, familiar in economic analysis.[3] This represents the amount of dollars available for school expenditure (on the vertical axis), or on nonschool expenditure (horizontal axis). We assume that state aid includes some matching funds for schooling so that a given amount of community wealth is represented by more school than nonschool dollars. The state matching rate, $m$, increases the effective income of the district by lowering the price of one of the things it buys. We can represent this price $P$ by the expression $P = 1/(1 + m)$. That is, an additional dollar of total school resources will cost a district only $1/(1 + m)$ dollars in *local* revenue, given a matching rate $m$. A flat grant or foundation program, without a matching rate, directly increases the resources available to a community, shifting out the budget line (an income effect). For completeness we must consider and will want to study a sample in which we can observe both effects.

There is another conception of price variation which is more usual in demand analysis. If the costs of school inputs vary among districts—because of cost-of-living differences, economies of scale, labor market conditions, transportation and building requirements, and so forth—then we should expect the demand for schooling to vary inversely with such prices, all other factors equal. When expenditures or revenues are the subject of analysis, as in Figure 6-1, then such cost variations are not explicitly considered because expenditures are the product of prices and quantities of inputs. Only when the "quantity of schooling" is separately analyzed are costs explicitly considered. Nonetheless, this conception of price must be kept in mind and carefully distinguished from price variations which are due to matching rates. We will refer to this source of price variation as cost variation.

District decisions will be represented by the familiar "indifference curves" of utility analysis, which express district behavior without normative judgment.

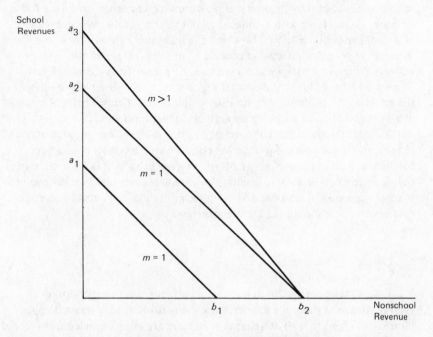

**Figure 6-1.**  District Budget Lines Showing Different State Matching Rates

These will be convex to the origin.  Any other shape would imply perverse
results, especially corner solutions in which the community either purchases
only schooling or abandons schools entirely.  By looking at budget lines and
these decisions, we can quickly isolate four effects we will want to account for
in any estimating model.

The matching rate $m$ may be a function of some characteristics of the district or may be uniform across all districts.  Similarly, of course, matching state
aid for nonschool expenditures will change the relative price of school funds.
In either case, different slopes of budget lines will reflect *relative* prices and
will affect district behavior.  We need also consider total budgets, the amounts
conceivably available for education expenditures in different districts. Budgets
and prices are measurable characteristics of the budget lines, but the behavior
we observe will be determined by the shape of the decision functions.  These
functions express a *revealed preference for schooling* indicating that different
districts with the same income and price structure may deliberately spend
different amounts on schools.  In analysis, these three elements—the shape
and location of budget lines, and the shape of decision curves—contain all
the information we have.  Decisions represent tangency points, expressing the
highest attainable utility given the budget constraint.

However, we may also observe *nontangencies*.  One way nontangencies would come about is by minimum expenditure requirements. In Figure 6-2 we show a budget line with a nonzero school matching rate and a desired level of school expenditures of $a_1$. However, if a minimum expenditure of $b$ is imposed on nonschool items, we observe $a_o$ of school expenditures. We are still observing district responses to income and price effects—school expenditure would be even lower if the matching rate were zero—but we also observe the effect of the minimum expenditure requirements. Central cities play a role in a metropolitan area requiring nonschool expenditures which are large relative to their total budgets. Similarly, we might observe the effects of population change, where the political process has not stabilized to a new population. Inertia is sometimes a tacit constraint on political behavior. Our model must therefore contain variables to account for four aspects of observed differences in school spending among districts: relative prices and costs, total budgets, preferences for schooling, and nontangencies.

*Local Expenditures*

It appears inappropriate to consider a particular year's expenditures as typical of expenditures in a district, since many districts have unusual expenditures from time to time. Capital expenditures are often excluded from school district analyses because they are of this lumpy nature. Counting bond revenue as income and capital construction costs as expenditures would be peculiar for

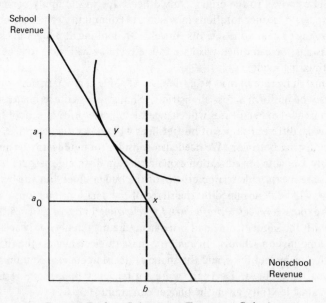

**Figure 6-2.** District Budget Selection: Tangency Solution

two reasons: the expenditure is unusual, and the revenue will be counted twice, since revenue to pay off the bonds will be counted in some other year. But factors of production may substitute for one another, and the decision to increase expenditures in the capital rather than the current account may signal a substitution rather than the lack of some resource. The solution is simple: We will analyze district revenues rather than expenditures. Thus revenue which pays off past bonds is counted, effectively smoothing out the capital expenditure pattern. Revenue from the sale of bonds is of course excluded, but income from cafeterias and admissions, fees, and so forth are included.[4]

### Budget Constraints

The budget constraint is usually referred to as a district's "ability to pay." Since most educational revenue is collected via the property tax, property valuation is a common measure of this ability.[5] But, no matter what the tax base, taxes falling on individuals are paid from current income. Average family income is therefore another common ability-to-pay variable. Family income and property valuation are not necessarily highly correlated: the two variables measure different aspects of fiscal ability and should both be included in any model.[6] Every study has found some measure of ability to pay to be significantly related to school expenditure. In fact, this is the only unequivocal result in the literature.

### Preference for Schooling

Variables measuring the preferences for education have included the median school years completed by the adult population, the occupational structure of a community or state (e.g., percentage employed in manufacturing, percentage employed as professionals), the distribution of income (e.g., the percentage of families with income over $10,000), the racial composition, percentage of children in private school, percentage unemployed, percentage of the population which is urban or rural, and other such socioeconomic characteristics. Family income may also reflect preferences for education. The presumption is that these variables capture the extent to which people view public education as important or unimportant because of the relationship (or lack of relationship) of formal education to their work, to perceived paths of social mobility, to their lifestyles, or merely because they have no children in public schools and do not care to support the education of others.

Most studies have generally found one or more socioeconomic variables reflecting demand for education to be significant, but there has been no agreement on which particular variables are crucial. Where identical models have been estimated for several states, the importance and even the signs of such variables are not always consistent.[7] Socioeconomic variables lack the precision in scale of monetary variables, adding another source of measurement error. It is difficult to choose a priori which of such variables to include in a model, and it is equally difficult to interpret these specific variables afterward. Often, they are highly collinear.[8] Hence it becomes necessary to rely on ad hoc methods of choosing the "best" variables, such as including those which maximize the explanatory power of the model. Since a large number of such socioeconomic variables are available from published data, we can have good hopes of capturing significant aspects of community preference for schooling.

### Relative Costs

Both the lack of data and conceptual problems hamper the process of translating theory into operational cost variables. An attempt to measure relative costs directly would necessitate cross-section price indices for school and nonschool services. This involves familiar problems: to derive such indices, it is necessary to specify both prices and weights for the goods and services which make up school service. Both lack of cross-section price indices,[9] and theoretical difficulties in specifying the weights[10] make this direct approach unmanageable.

Some studies have included variables designed to reflect the cost differences induced by "technology." Prominent among such efforts are the inclusion of population and population density as tests of whether economies of scale make large schools systems (or large schools) more or less expensive per pupil. However, any attempt to estimate economies of scale must control for school quality, since the economies of scale exist only if increased size decreases expenditure per pupil, with output per pupil held constant. Most studies which consider scale effects have made no attempt to control for school quality.[11] Their results must be interpreted as showing only whether district size or density has an effect on school funding. This might reflect urban preferences, political structure, or municipal overburden, but not technological differences. In sum, the evidence on economies of scale for districts is as yet inconclusive, and existing methods are not yet adequate to the task of relating expenditures to economies of scale.[12]

More generally, differences in relative prices among school districts will be related to the cost functions facing different districts, which are in turn determined by the production function and the prices in each district. Although there has been considerable attention devoted to the estimation of production functions, the results so far are too imprecise, inconsistent, and poorly specified to be used calculating relative price differences.[13] The principle result obtained so far is that the socioeconomic status of pupils has a more important effect on achievement tests scores than do school inputs. From this we might infer that schools and districts with large numbers of children from poor families may have high schooling costs relative to other districts. However, our discussions of municipal overburden would indicate that such districts might also have high costs of nonschool services. In addition, it becomes difficult to separate the different effects of socioeconomic variables: for example, would high adult education attainment in a district lead to greater preference for education and higher expenditures, or lower costs and hence lower expenditures?

### Nontangency Conditions

Several studies have included variables to measure the effects of the political structure on school resources. Most frequently a dummy variable reflecting whether a district is independent of other government units in its budget decisions is included, on the assumption that dependence on another governmental unit represents an additional constraint which may prevent voters' preferences from being fully realized.[14] Another variable frequently interpreted as reflecting political structure is the percentage of owner-occupied housing units. On the assumption that voters react to apparent rather than actual tax incidence, it has been hypothesized that this variable would be negatively related to educational expenditures.[15] However, this variable may be more complicated since it is also related to stability, longer-term residence, political power, greater wealth and income, and other socioeconomic variables.

The most thorough investigation of political structure is that of James, Kelly, and Garms (122). In their analysis of 107 large cities, they included seven variables designed to test whether governmental structure facilitates or hinders public access to wealth and the expression of demand for education. It is difficult to suggest a priori what the signs of these variables should be, and in fact none of them proved significant except when dummy variables for region were included in the regressions. The authors concluded that the effect of political structure is erratic: the sign and significance of any political variable may vary widely from district to district, with the result that the variable is insignificant unless the sample is quite homogeneous. Similar results were obtained by Dye (71).

Surprisingly, no one has specifically tested the possible impact of municipal overburden on school expenditures, except through the effects of population and population density. The variables generally associated with municipal overburden include nonschool public expenditures per person, high population and population density, predominance of low-income families, and heavy use of municipal facilities by nonresidents. As before, it is not always possible to separate the effects of some of these variables via municipal overburden from their effects as proxies for tastes, budget constraints, or price variables.

### Functional Forms of the Estimating Equations

In order to describe local district behavior, it is necessary to estimate the parameters of an equation which captures the four effects described in the previous section, using a set of observations on school districts. The first problem, then, is to specify a form for the equation to be estimated which is appropriate to the behavioral phenomena under investigation. The most rigorous way to proceed is to deduce from economic theory some a priori restrictions on the parameters to be estimated and to derive appropriate estimating forms from these restrictions. For this discussion we must ignore nontangencies, since economic theory proceeds from the assumption that observations represent equilibria and that the first derivatives of functions are continuous.[16] We thus assume that there is an objective function which is maximized subject to the budget constraint. Specifically,[17]

$$W = W(R,t) = W[(L(1 + m) + A, L/\text{PROP}] \tag{6.1}$$

where

$R$ = total revenue
$L$ = local revenue per pupil
$m$ = state matching rate
$A$ = state nonmatching aid
$PROP$ = equalized property valuation per pupil
$t$ = local property tax rate for schools ($t \cdot PROP = L$)

We specify the signs of the partials:

$$W_1 = \frac{\partial W}{\partial R} > 0 \qquad\qquad W_2 = \frac{\partial W}{\partial t} < 0$$

$$W_{11} = \frac{\partial^2 W}{\partial R^2} < 0 \qquad\qquad W_{22} = \frac{\partial^2 W}{\partial t^2} < 0$$

$$W_{12} = \frac{\partial^2 W}{\partial R \partial t} = 0$$

From this set of stipulations we can derive expressions for a change in a flat grant $(A)$, or a change in the matching rate $(m)$. The former case will involve only an "income effect," the response to a greater or lesser flow of total funds;

the second, an income effect (increasing the price of one good reduces the total income) and a price effect (rational behavior assumes a preference for less expensive goods). The object is to maximize the $W$ function with respect to the decision variable, local revenue, yielding the necessary condition:

$$\frac{\partial W}{\partial L} = W_1 (1 + m) + \frac{W_2}{PROP} = 0. \tag{6.2}$$

Since $L$ is a function of $A$ and $m$, we can set $dm = 0$ and solve for $dL/dA$:

$$\frac{\partial L}{\partial A} = \frac{-W_{11} \cdot (1 + m)}{W_{11}(1 + m) + \dfrac{W_{22}}{PROP^2}} \tag{6.3}$$

This expresses the pure income effect. From the signs of the partials we see this must be negative, and if $m \geqslant 0$, it must be between –1 and 0. This expression therefore indicates "substitution" of some increased nonmatching school aid for local school revenues, which are then free to be expended on non-school items. It is obvious from (6.3) that the extent of substitution of state for local funds depends on the matching rate $m$. When $m$ is high, the price of a dollar of school funds is low and more of a given increase in nonmatching aid will end up as an increment to local school expenditures rather than a tax decrease.

The expression for the effect on local expenditures from a change in $m$ contains a similar income effect weighted by local revenue $L$, and a price effect:

$$\frac{\partial L}{\partial m} = \frac{-W_1}{W_{11} \cdot (1 + m)^2 + \dfrac{W_{22}}{PROP^2}} - L \cdot \frac{W_{11} (1 + m)}{W_{11} (1 + m)^2 + \dfrac{W_{22}}{PROP^2}} \cdot \tag{6.4}$$

The sign of the entire expression is indeterminate, indicating that a price increase could result in either increased or decreased local funds, although we will assume that *total* school revenues would increase in either case.[18]

Matching grants will increase tax rates in some districts, lower them in others. If we accept the assumption that one objective function holds over all districts, then an increase in the matching rate induces greater tax increases in those districts in which local expenditure for schools is initially lower.

Following this utility function approach, we have already determined some restrictions on the parameters, and thus on the functions to be estimated:

1.  The substitution effect for nonmatching aid should be between zero and 1.
2.  The substitution effect should be a positive function of the matching rate.
3.  The effect of the matching rate on local revenue should not be restricted to be non-negative.

We can continue by formulating the price elasticity of local revenue explicitly. As above, the price of a school dollar is

$$P = \frac{1}{1 + m} .$$                                        (6.5)

We can express total revenue as

$$R = \frac{L}{P} + A.$$                                         (6.6)

The expression for the price elasticity of local revenue is

$$\eta_{L,P} = \frac{\partial L / \partial P}{L / P}$$            (6.7)

By differentiating $R$ with respect to price, we establish these relations:

$$\text{If } \quad \frac{dR}{dP} < 0, \quad \text{then } \eta_{L,P} < 1$$

$$\text{If } \quad \frac{dR}{dP} = 0, \quad \text{then } \eta_{L,P} = 1 \qquad (6.8)$$

$$\text{If } \quad \frac{dR}{dP} > 0, \quad \text{then } \eta_{L,P} > 1 .$$

We do not expect to observe $dR/dP > 0$, and hence should not observe a price elasticity of local revenue greater than 1 in equilibrium, though it could be greater than 1 in some districts due to nontangency conditions.

The important issue is to estimate a functional form which does not specify the price elasticity, but allows it to be calculated. We prefer it not to be restricted in sign, so we can freely determine the sign of $\partial L/\partial m$. One can posit a number of specific forms for the objective function $W$ and investigate the expressions for $\eta_{L,P}$ implied by them. Surprisingly few objective functions lead to both acceptable and readily estimable expressions for local revenue.[19] In addition, expressions for local revenue are not unique, so that estimating one does not yield definitive information on the objective function which lies beneath it.[20]

### Price Elasticity

A sensible procedure in this case is to estimate $\eta_{L,P}$ directly. This is conveniently and traditionally accomplished by specifying a multiplicative form which can be estimated by an equation which is linear in logarithms of the variables:[21]

$$L = P^{\eta_1} A^{\eta_2} \prod_i X_i^{\eta_i} \tag{6.9}$$

$$\log L = \eta_1 \log(P) + \eta_2 \log(A) + \sum_i \eta_i \log(X_i) \tag{6.10}$$

where $X$ represents other variables in the equation. Obviously $\eta_1$ is $\eta_{L,P}$. The well-known difficulty with this procedure is that the signs of cross-partial derivatives are determined by the signs of the parameter estimates, and may contradict the expectations specified above.

The linear additive form for $L$ is the most straightforward and prevalent in the literature. The usual approach is to estimate

$$L = \sum \alpha_i X_i - \beta S \tag{6.11}$$

where $S$ is state aid. This yields $\partial L/\partial S = -\beta$, which itself may be a function of other variables and thus may vary over districts.[22] Typically $0 < \beta < 1$, indicating that an increase in state aid of one dollar brings about a decrease in local expenditure of $\beta$, but an increase in total expenditure of $(1 - \beta)$. This specification

obviously fails to distinguish matching from nonmatching aid, or to make the
effect of nonmatching aid ($A$) dependent on the matching rate ($m$). Separat-
ing $S$ into its components

$$S = mL + A \tag{6.12}$$

we can replace (6.11) with

$$L = \sum_i \alpha_i X_i - \beta_1(mL) - \beta_2(A) \tag{6.13}$$

In equilibrium

$$L = \frac{\Sigma \, \alpha_i X_i - \beta_2 A}{1 + \beta_1 m} \tag{6.14}$$

Although $\partial L/\partial m$ is a relatively complex expression, the price elasticity is:

$$\eta_{L,P} = \frac{\beta_1 + m\beta_1}{1 + m\beta_1} \tag{6.15}$$

which is a function of an estimated parameter, and will be less than 1 when $\beta_1$
is less than 1. Thus the simple linear additive form, once state aid is separated
to allow for both price and income effects, yields an estimable equation with
the desired properties and flexibility.


### Other Approaches to Specifying Functional Forms

In the next chapter we will estimate one form derived from the maximization of a particular welfare function.[23]

$$W = \alpha R - 1/2 R^2 - 1/2 \beta t^2 \,. \tag{6.16}$$

This yields an expression for local revenue which is easily estimated using
an iterative technique. However, while it provides good estimates for most of
the variables under consideration, this form has the drawback of constraining
the price effect in undesirable ways.

Given the desirability of simplicity in the form to be estimated, another welfare function which leads to a particularly simple first-order condition, the so-called linear expenditure system, can be estimated. The objective function

$$W = \alpha_1 \log(R - \alpha_2) + \beta_1 \log(\beta_2 - t), \quad \alpha_1 + \beta_1 = 1 \tag{6.17}$$

yields the following expression for local revenue:

$$L = \alpha_2 \beta_2 \, \text{PROP} + \frac{\beta_1 \alpha_2 - \beta_2 A}{1 + m} \tag{6.18}$$

which can be readily estimated without resorting to nonlinear or iterative techniques. However, as shall be demonstrated in the next chapter,[24] this approach also constrains the price effect.

A final approach is to derive the marginal rate of substitution (MRS) between the tax rate and total revenue, and estimate it directly:

$$\text{MRS} = \frac{W_1}{W_2(1 + m)} = P \cdot \frac{W_1}{W_2} . \tag{6.19}$$

From our initial restrictions on the signs of the partials, we can determine that:

$$\frac{\partial \text{MRS}}{\partial L} = \frac{-W_{11} \cdot (1 + m)}{W_2} + \frac{W_1 W_{22}}{W_2^2 \, \text{PROP}} < 0$$

$$\frac{\partial \text{MRS}}{\partial t} = \frac{W_1 \cdot W_{22}}{W_2^2} < 0. \tag{6.20}$$

We can derive estimable equations from these restrictions.[25] However, failure to account for the identity $L = t \cdot \text{PROP}$ prevents meaningful estimation. The expression

$$\frac{\partial L}{\partial t} = P \cdot \frac{-W_1 W_{22}}{W_1 W_{11}} ,$$

derived from $\partial_{\text{MRS}}/\partial L$ and $\partial_{\text{MRS}}/\partial t$ above, is negative; but for any set of school districts $\partial L/\partial t$ will be positive because of the identity $L = t \cdot \text{PROP}$. Hence this approach cannot be useful at all.

Before leaving the objective function approach, we should consider a function which explicitly recognizes nonschool resources ($N$) as well as school revenues ($R$):

$$W = W(R, t, N),$$

$$
\begin{array}{lll}
W_1 > 0 & W_2 < 0 & W_3 > 0 \\[2mm]
W_{11} < 0 & W_{22} < 0 & W_{33} < 0 \\[2mm]
W_{12} = 0 & W_{23} = 0 & W_{13} \gtreqless 0
\end{array}
\qquad (6.21)
$$

If tax rates are fixed and local nonschool revenues increase, local school revenues must fall. This can be considered, for example, one concept of municipal overburden. More importantly, we can see that local noneducational revenues $L_N$ are a function of the matching rate for educational expenditures:

$$
\frac{\partial L_N}{\partial m} = \frac{-(W_{11} \cdot L \cdot (1 + m) + W_1)}{W_{13} \cdot (1 + m) + \dfrac{W_{22}}{\text{PROP}^2}}
$$

In the typical case, this expression will be negative, indicating that a decrease in the price of school revenue will tend to increase L at the expense of $L_N$.

At this point we can see a great weakness in considering the process of local public finance as abstractly as we have in this chapter. By specifying school and nonschool revenues, $R$ and $N$, we have disguised the fact that there is no determinate set of goods, services, or functions denoted by "school" or "nonschool" expenditures. Different districts purchase different things under the category "school," "recreation", "parks", "police", and so forth. In a world of rational price response with complete information, any price difference between school and nonschool funds should induce a shift of budget items into the cheaper (higher $m$) category.[26] Thus we might observe differences in the expenditures according to these expectations about rational responses to relative prices, but there might not be any differences in the services provided.

That large budget shifts in response to different matching rates are not usually recognized requires explanation. In most states, of course, there are no matching grant programs of any magnitude. In the states which are exceptions there are several reasons why this price effect has not been noted. State funds are usually restricted to some extent, and large transfers of functions to take advantage of matching rates might be noticed by the state and prohibited. It is likely that budgets represent power on the local level, so that transfer of funds and functions is politically difficult.[27]

Because we will be estimating a model of school district behavior for Massachusetts, where there are significant differences in the state's matching rate between the school and the nonschool sectors, it is appropriate to test the hypothesis summarized in equation (6.21): that local nonschool revenues are responsive to the matching rate for school revenue. Because of differences in accounting procedures among districts and because of constraints imposed by administrative and/or politically motivated behavior, it becomes much more difficult to specify an optimal form for the estimating equation. But as a simple test of this hypothesis, it should suffice to include the price of school resource revenues in an equation for local nonschool revenues. Conversely, we will include local nonschool revenues in the estimating equations for local school revenues $L$.

One implication of the preceding discussion is that several decisions are made simultaneously. Funds for schools and for nonschool public expenditures are determined together, each considering the other. In addition, the amount of state matching funds is endogenous to this system, depending as it does on the amount of local funds. Under equalizing plans, even the matching *rate* is endogenous, as it depends on some measure of the ability of the district to provide school funds (usually property valuation per pupil). Some state programs compensate districts according to characteristics of teachers (degree and experience), which may depend on characteristics of districts other than their demand for teachers of a certain type.[28] Property valuation may also be endogenous, being a function of the characteristics of the population and school quality.[29]

Hence a simultaneous equation system will be required, and we will utilize two-stage least squares for estimation. It will also be necessary to estimate nonlinear terms by iteration, the details of which are best left until Chapter 7.

### Sample Characteristics

Most previous authors have used samples of school districts within states, although these samples have usually been incomplete and often nonrandom. Some have used observation on cities from many states, and some have used state observations.[30] Nowhere is there any recognition that the sample itself might affect the specifications and results. Revenue variations among districts within a state may be due to different circumstances from interstate and intercity variations. Districts within a state interact with one another; they may compete for teachers and administrators, and communities may be conscious of the need to keep up the quality of their schools as a reflection of the kind of communities they are.[31] Neither states nor districts in different states share these conditions. Also, school districts are behavioral units with control over resources and the ability to formulate goals. Though they have legal responsibility for education, state decision-making powers are limited; states are aggregations of school districts and have little behavioral life of their own. Hence models based on state observations may describe multivariate associations but not behavioral patterns.

Two studies have estimated models for samples of districts from several states.[32] The effects of all variables vary widely among states. The political effects of dissimilar systems of state aid, and the fundamental differences in the structure of school districts among states (e.g., independent versus dependent, town versus county, deliberately segregated historically versus *de facto* segregated), are two explanations of these variations. In general, within-state and among-state variation in revenues for schools are separate aspects of the broader problem of inequalities, different in origin as they might be different in solution. This suggests that quantitative analysis should confine itself to one problem or the other, since studies which combine data from different states do not accurately reflect any integrated decision-making process. Because of our focus on intrastate disparities in educational resources, and on local funds which are the prime determinant of these disparities, our sample will consist of school districts within one state.

We would prefer to include all districts within a single state. Our search must be limited to seven states—Iowa, Massachusetts, New York, Pennsylvania, Rhode Island, Utah, and Wisconsin—because only these states have programs of general school aid which embody price effects.[33] Of these states, New York, Pennsylvania, and Wisconsin have school districts that are noncontiguous with towns and cities, so that district socioeconomic data has been impossible to obtain without using a complex and usually inaccurate mapping technique.[34] Rhode Island and Utah have small numbers of districts—39 and 17, respectively—making estimation rather problematic (especially in the case of the asymptotic estimators necessary in simultaneous equations models). It turns out, therefore, that one of the few cases where one can estimate the price and income effects of intergovernmental grants is that of Massachusetts school districts.

The sample used for estimation is comprised of 159 districts, including almost all of the large districts in the state and 85 percent of the public school pupils in 1968-69. Districts were omitted if they shared school facilities with neighboring towns or if socioeconomic data from the 1960 census was unpublished. Almost all of the omitted districts are therefore small and rural,[35] and the sample therefore overrepresents urban and suburban districts. There are two implications of this sample bias for the estimates presented below. The first is that, since the omitted districts include a large number of districts which are, for various reasons, peculiar,[36] their omission eliminates a certain amount of noise which would otherwise lower the explanatory power of the various regressions.[37] Secondly, sample bias may cause estimated coefficients to be biased upwards or downwards. However, it is not possible to predict, for any of the variables considered, the direction of the bias.[38] Because the sample covers such a large percentage of pupils, we will henceforth ignore possible bias due to the composition of the sample as relatively unimportant for the purposes of simulation.

### Summary

In this chapter we have provided a theoretical basis for the estimations and simulations to follow. We have discussed theoretical approaches to estimation and concluded that while economic theory can restrict the form which crucial parameters should take, it is not particularly helpful in delineating functional forms for estimation. Previous efforts to use economic theory to derive empirical models of public-sector financing, all of which can be reinterpreted within the framework of this chapter, have yielded similarly unspectacular results.[39] Our knowledge of the effects of economic variables, of production relations in education and other public services, and of political structures, is still too scanty to enable us to fill in the framework provided by theory. Many phenomena we suspect of being important in the provision of public services fit very poorly into economic models, such as political and economic power, historical factors, and market imperfections.[40] Largely, however, it is the current state of economic theory that is remiss: its highly abstract "maximization of objective functions" is not the powerful tool it pretends to be and usually leads to forms which are not better than the linear additive or log-linear forms most researchers start with.

In an attempt to categorize the variables of importance, we have sketched a political process using familiar economic tools, but have relaxed the maximization assumption. We have argued that the best way to observe this political behavior is within one state, a state which allows observation of both price and income effects. These preliminary steps led to the conclusion that we should estimate a simultaneous equations system to incorporate the endogeneity of several variables. Finally, we have tried to relate this necessary preliminary work to that of our predecessors, sparing the reader a straightforward review of the literature, but conveying, we hope, the notion of progress in the study of public school finance.

The next chapter will be concerned specifically with translating the concepts of this chapter into an empirical model. Although we do not claim complete victory over the problems of measurement and estimation, we will provide these advances over previous literature:

1.   A simultaneous equations model estimated by two-stage least squares.

2.  Nonlinear substitution of state funds for local.
3.  Estimation of the effect of municipal overburden.
4.  Estimation of separate district responses to the price and income effects in state aid programs.


## Notes

1.  The literature on the determinants of school expenditures or revenues, and on the provision of municipal services generally, is rather large and tedious to summarize. Reviews of this literature can be found in Miner (181), Oates (196), Davis (62), Bahn (8), Siegel (238), Hirsch (111), and Brazer (35).

2.  Tax rates vary greatly throughout the world, many total rates being far higher than rates considered unacceptable in the United States. Though the mix of services differs also, it seems safe to conclude that acceptability of a tax rate is largely a matter of history and custom.

3.  The model summarized here is common in the public finance literature. For a more detailed exposition, see Musgrave and Musgrave (191), pp. 614–20.

4.  Struyck (249) includes both revenues and expenditures and accounts for the relationship between them.

5.  Reliance on the property tax varies among states, but for the nation as a whole 84 percent of local revenue and 47 percent of total public school revenue came from property taxes in 1967. U.S. Department of Commerce, Bureau of the Census, 1967 *Census of Governments,* "Finance of School Districts," p. 9.

6.  Some property, of course, is business and manufacturing property, and the ability of these entities to pay is not reflected in personal income. The simple correlation coefficient between mean family income and property valuation per pupil is 0.22 in the 159 district Massachusetts sample employed in Chapter 7. See also James, Kelly, and Garms (122), James, Thomas, and Dyck (123), and Daniere (61) for similar evidence.

7.  James, Thomas, and Dyck (123) and Miner (181).

8.  Pidot (206) uses factor analysis to try to overcome this problem. Since results of such an analysis are expressed in linear combinations of variables. this technique still fails to provide an interpretation for individual variables.

9.  To our knowledge, only one set of cross-section price indices exist. These have been used by Owen (200), who concludes that accounting for price differences among cities does not eliminate the relationship between expenditure per pupil and median income.

10. As long as school districts are operating at their optimum, then actual purchases of the various goods and services making up school and nonschool

services can be used as weights. However, if a district is not operating at an optimum—either because of factors forcing it to operate at a nontangency point, as in Figure 6-2, or because of inefficiencies causing it to operate above its minimum cost function—then it will not be possible to separate price differences due to inefficiency from those due to market phenomena and differences in "technology."

11. See, for example, James, Kelly, and Garms (122); Pidot (206); Vieg et al. (268); Brazer (35); Scott and Feder (231). Others who claim to have found a significant contribution of size either have not published the statistics necessary to evaluate their claims (Sacks and Hellmuth [226], Hanson [100]), or have employed inadequate methodologies (Hettich [110], Schmandt and Stephens [229]). Henderson (108) did find population significant and negatively related to total governmental expenditures, but Dye (71) found size and expenditures positively related. Hirsch (111) did include a variable to control for school quality in a study of district expenditures and found the effect of size insignificant. However, his procedure yields biased coefficients. If the production relation for school output per pupil is assumed to be:

$$\text{Output} = f(\text{expenditures, size, } X) + M = a + b \cdot \text{expenditures} + c \cdot \text{size} + D \cdot X + M \tag{1}$$

where $D$ and $X$ are vectors, then the parameter $c$ indicates economies of scale. Hirsch estimates the inverse function:

$$\text{Expenditures} = \frac{-a}{b} + \frac{1}{b} \text{ output} - \frac{c}{b} \text{ size} - \frac{1}{b} DX - \frac{1}{b} \mu . \tag{2}$$

Since the covariance between output and the error term is nonzero,

$$E\left(-\frac{\mu}{b} \cdot \text{output}\right) = -\frac{1}{b} E(\mu \cdot \text{output}) \tag{3}$$

estimation of this equation yields biased coefficients.

There are other reasons why equations (1) and (2) are unacceptable. Not all expenditures are functionally related to outputs. If teachers prefer urban districts to rural areas and rural districts raise salaries accordingly, there will appear to be an economy of scale which has nothing to do with the technology of schooling and which could not be exploited by merging rural districts.

12. The conventional wisdom holds that very small districts may suffer diseconomies, but Bussard (42) concluded other reasons may have predominated in consolidation of rural districts. Levin (154, p. 129) concludes that "the evidence on the size-performance relationship suggests that high schools and school districts at the high end of the [size] spectrum probably

suffer from substantial diseconomies of scale." However, he fails to consider possible municipal overburden. See Michelson (171) for a discussion and investigation of economies of scale within one district. In general technological relationships must be studied using real variables rather than monetary variables, and adequate real variable data do not exist. See Levin (152) for a more detailed exposition of the difficulty of deriving technological relationships from public data.

13. See especially the criticism of this literature by Michelson (175).

14. There is some support from Miner (181) and James, Thomas, and Dyck (123) that independence increases expenditure, but the support is weak at best. See also James, Kelly, and Garms (122), p. 86 ff.

15. A negative relationship has been found by James, Thomas, and Dyck (123), James, Kelly, and Garms (122), and Davis (62). Although tax incidence studies usually assume that close to 100 percent of an increase in property tax is passed on to renters, it is apparently assumed that renters do not realize this and will vote to raise property taxes "on landlords." This seems highly unlikely.

16. If the budget line in Figure 6-2 were to move slightly in or out, we would observe no change in nonschool expenditures. However, with a great enough increase in the budget, more nonschool services would be provided when the minimum requirement of $b$ became nonbinding.

17. Other formulations of the objective function are possible and have been utilized by others, especially Barro (12). The one given here will prove more useful and can be defended on a priori grounds. See Grubb (90), Chapter 2.

18. Theoretically, however, even total revenues could increase in response to a price increase, but this is the case of a Giffen good and can be assumed an aberration.

19. The expressions for local revenue come from equation (6.2) with expressions for $W_1$ and $W_2$ from a specific objective function substituted in. For a thorough investigation of some possible forms for the objective function, see Grubb (90), Ch. 2.

20. That is, equation (6.2) is a partial differential equation in $L$ with no unique solution.

21. This approach was used by Feldstein (75).

22. A number of studies (Bishop [25], Renshaw [217], Struyck [249], and references cited in Osman [199]) have estimated equation (7) with total revenue or expenditure on the right left-hand side rather than local revenue or expenditure. In this case, the positive sign of $S$ is almost a truism. More seriously, this specification does not allow for the interrelationships among the components of revenue. When revenue sources are mutually dependent, as equations (6.3) and (6.4) indicate, then each revenue source must be considered a separate variable, and simultaneous estimation is

necessary to avoid least-squares bias. The failure of one-equation models to capture simultaneous interactions among sources of revenue has been discussed by Fisher (78), Morss (183), and Pogue and Sgnotz (210). Simultaneous models with state observations have been formulated by Horowitz (114) and O'Brien (197), although the latter denies the importance of simultaneity. Struyck (249) has estimated a simultaneous model with district observations.

23. This approach was that used by Stern (243). The estimation of this form is presented in equation i of Table 7-3.

24. See equation ii of Table 7-3. This presents a form in which the parameter $\beta_2$ is itself a function of other variables.

25. Barro (12), for example, suggests the forms

$$\text{MRS} = B_0\, e^{-\beta_1 R\, -\, \beta_2 t}\, \phi(X)$$

and

$$\text{MRS} = \beta_0 - \beta_1 R - \beta_2 t + \beta_3 X\ .$$

These lead to equations nonlinear in one parameter only, allowing solution by a search procedure which is not too expensive.

26. For more detailed comments, see Grubb and Michelson (96), p. 539, and reference therein.

27. For example, school buildings in many districts cannot be optimally used because of disputes over cost of maintenance when functions are shared. A major issue of debate in Boston for some time was whether the school committee of a city department would be responsible for evening adult classes initiated by the community but utilizing school facilities. With such overt and time-consuming debate, the state would surely act to prevent any fund switching the city might attempt.

28. See Johns (129) for a description of state aid programs, and Owen (200) for an argument that the supply of teacher characteristics depend on characteristics of the districts.

29. See Kain and Quigley (134), Oates (196), and the discussion in Chapter 7.

30. O'Brien (197), Horowitz (114), Fisher (79), Sacks and Harris (225), Deitch (64), Renshaw (217), and Shapiro (235) used state samples; James, Kelly, and Garms (122) and Dye (71) used samples of large cities.

31. See Benson (15).

32. James, Thomas, and Dyck (123); Miner (181).

33. See Johns (129). All of these use some variant of percentage equalizing, usually with a floor in the matching rate (or "reimbursement percentage"). Other states rely on flat grants and foundation programs, which have income effects but no price effect. A larger number of states distribute revenue,

for both school and nonschool purposes, through matching grant programs. However, the expenditures of such funds tend to be restricted, the amounts of aid are relatively insignificant, and there is usually little variation in the effective price among districts, which leads to identification problems in estimation.

During the 1972–73 legislative year, seven additional states passed legislation incorporating rates in percentage equalizing formulas. However, because of save-harmless and transitional clauses, it will be some time before it will be possible to isolate price effects in these states.

34. With the appearance of the school district fourth count tapes, based on mapping procedures and the 1970 census data, availability of at least some socioeconomic data will not longer be so time-consuming. The accuracy of such data is still open to question, however. In addition, there are serious conceptual problems involved in analyzing noncontiguous districts, principally the nature of the relationship between school revenues and nonschool revenues and the interaction between elementary and secondary districts.

35. A few medium-sized, suburban districts were omitted because of sharing facilities.

36. For example, towns which have abnormally high property valuation per pupil, like Rowe with its nuclear power plant, tend to be small and therefore excluded. Many towns with considerable amounts of vacation property, on Cape Cod and in the Berkshires, are likewise omitted. Residuals for Nantucket and Provincetown, which are in the sample, indicate that such resort towns are always outliers, generally having negative residuals in regressions for local revenue per pupil

37. This was confirmed by some earlier regression weighted by a number of pupils in each district. These results, relatively dominated by larger districts, displayed greater explanatory power (in terms of the standard error of the equation) than did unweighted regression of the same specification.

38. For example, many of the omitted districts are predominantly farming communities, which are property-rich and income-poor but with low school spending; their omission implies that the impact of property valuation on local revenue is likely to be overestimated. On the other hand, such high-spending towns as Rowe and resort towns are also property-rich and income-poor, causing a bias in the opposite direction.

39. Siegel (238) posits demand and supply functions for municipal services, another expression of the utility functions and production relations implicit in the utility-maximizing model; his reduced form is simply a linear form of equation (6.3). Similarly, the utility-maximizing models of Henderson (108) and Stern (243) are methods of deriving estimable forms of equation (6.1), linear in the case of Henderson and nonlinear in Stern's case (discussed in the next chapter). Inman (119) has developed

a comprehensive model of the provision of public services and used it to analyze the *Serrano* decision. However, his results depend crucially on perfect knowledge of the cost function in each school district, including the economies of scale involved. Brown (38) has criticized the literature for failing to use models properly and estimating confused combinations of demand functions and production relations; but his model, a straight-forward exposition of utility maximized subject to production constraints, yields no additional insights and, given our current state of knowledge, no helpful ways of untangling demand and production relations.

40. One of the clearest statements of this problem is Margolis' (165) criticism of Samuelson's (227) classic article in the theory of public goods.

# 7 Estimates of School District Behavior

In this chapter we set out the variables and then the equations which describe the behavior of Massachusetts school districts in 1968-69. A highly modified percentage equalizing formula was then in its third year of operation. Because of the particular way in which the aid formula operated (described in Appendix 7A of this chapter), the data will permit estimating local responses to both the income effect of nonmatching aid and the price effect induced by matching aid. The equations are interesting in themselves as descriptions of district behavior, but they also provide the basis for simulating the results of different state aid formulas in Chapter 8.

After presenting the relevant variables and the expected relationships among endogenous variables, we will discuss five equations for local school revenue. Three of these will be retained for simulation in the next chapter. We will present only one equation for each other endogenous variable. Finally, the observed interrelationships will be discussed along with some implications for school finance reform.

It should be kept in mind that we are looking for the differences in school revenue distributions under alternative state aid programs, all of which allow district choice. The retention of three equations for local revenue, with three different estimates of crucial parameters, may appear inconclusive. But, to anticipate the results of the following chapter, the results of simulations depend on a complex interaction among behavioral estimates and the parameters of hypothetical state aid programs. The simulations prove to be relatively robust, in the sense that the observed variations in parameter estimates make relatively little difference to the substantive conclusions of the next chapter.

Because the nature of local school finance requires the estimation of a system of simultaneous equations, the dominant estimation technique is that of two-stage least squares. In addition, nonlinearities suggested by the theoretical considerations of Chapter 6 sometimes require estimation by iteration. The complexity of estimating the price effect compounds the statistical problems. Most econometric details have been relegated to Appendix 7A so as not to hinder the presentation of the substantive information yielded by the equation estimates.

## Variables

It will be convenient to refer to variables by mnemonic labels. Table 7-1

115

**Table 7-1**
**Variables Used in Model Estimation, Massachusetts Sample**

*Endogenous*

| | |
|---|---|
| LEDR | Local school revenue per pupil, 1968–69 |
| CH70 | Noncategorical (Chapter 70) state aid for education, per pupil, 1968–69 |
| CSA | Categorical state aid per pupil, 1968–69 |
| LNER | Local noneducation revenues, per pupil, 1968–69 |
| NESA | State aid for noneducational purposes, per pupil, 1968–69 |
| SCHRATE | School tax rate, equalized, 1968 |
| NERATE | Tax rate for nonschool local revenues, equalized, 1968 |
| PROP | Property valuation per pupil, equalized, 1968–69 |

*Exogenous*

| | |
|---|---|
| A | Nonmatching aid under the Chapter 70 formula, 1968–69 |
| M | Matching rate under the Chapter 70 formula, 1968–69 |
| PRICE | $1/(1 + M)$ |
| TIT1 | Aid from Title I of the Elementary and Secondary Education Act of 1965, per pupil, 1968–69 |
| OTHFED | Federal aid other than Title I aid, per pupil, 1968–69 |
| Y | Mean family income, 1960 |
| POOR | Percentage of families with income less than $3,000, 1960 |
| AFDC | Percentage of children in families receiving Aid to Families with Dependent Children, 1968–69 (based on net average membership) |
| PROF | Percentage of employed males working as professional, technical, and kindred workers, 1960 |
| ED | Median years of school completed for the male population age twenty-five and over, 1960 |
| CHILD | School membership (NAM) as a percentage of the population, 1968–69 |
| OWNED | Percentage of occupied housing units which are owner-occupied, 1960 |
| POPGROWTH | Increase in population from 1960 to 1970, as a percentage of 1960 population |
| MAN | Percentage of those employed in a district employed in manufacturing, 1968 |
| POP | Population, 1970 |
| POPDEN | Population density, 1970 |
| SOUND | Percentage of the 1960 housing stock which is neither delapidated nor deteriorating |
| RES | Percentage of property which is residential. |

**Table 7-1 (Continued)**

Sources: Components of school revenue, school membership (net average membership or NAM) and PROP were obtained for 1968–69 from unpublished data of the Massachusetts Department of Education, corresponding to the data for 1966–67 published in the *Annual Report of the Department of Education for the Year Ending June 30, 1967,* part II, section B. The tax rates, SCHRATE and NERATE, are taken from "School Tax Rates and Total Tax Rates for 1968," Massachusetts Teachers Association Research Bulletin 689-8, (October 23, 1968), and from "1968 Tax Rates-Actual and Full Value," Massachusetts Taxpayers Foundation (November 1968), which also lists assessment ratios for all towns in Massachusetts. LNER is derived from the application of the *unequalized* NERATE to the unequalized property valuation in each town; it therefore measures the local revenue for noneducational purposes from the property tax. State aid (noneducational) to towns and cities (NESA) was taken from unpublished worksheets of the Massachusetts Department of Corporations and Taxation; federal aid for noneducational purposes, in the town reports in the Massachusetts Bureau of Accounts, was unavailable for most districts in the sample.

Y was calculated from a special tabulation of 1960 census data for Massachusetts Department of Education, published (somewhat transformed) in Appendix Table IA of Daniere (61).

MAN is calculated by the Massachusetts Division of Employment Security, and published in the various "Town and City Monographs" of the Massachusetts Department of Commerce. All other variables were taken from the *U.S. Census of Population,* 1960 and 1970, state reports for Massachusetts. For a few towns, the "Town and City Monographs" provided data not published in the census volumes.

RES was generously provided by Helen Ladd, based on unpublished data from the Massachusetts Department of Taxation.

contains the variable names, their status (endogenous or exogenous), definitions, and sources. In Appendix Table 7C-1 we provide the means and standard deviations of these variables, and Table 7C-2 contains the correlation matrix.

### Revenue Sources and Property Value

The variable of greatest interest is local educational revenue, LEDR. The equations for this variable will summarize the response of school districts to their populations and to fiscal circumstances in raising school revenues. We are also interested in local noneducational revenues, LNER, both to describe the raising of nonschool funds and to investigate possible interactions between school and nonschool funds. All other revenues are of less interest, but they affect the behavior of districts as estimated by equations for LEDR and LNER.

Chapter 70 aid (CH70)[1] is the basic source of school funds flowing from the state to school districts. In 1968-69 CH70 comprised 67 percent of total state aid. The basic act was based on the percentage equalizing formulation:[2]

$$S_i = r_i R_i$$

$$r_i = 1 - k \cdot \frac{PROP_i}{\overline{PROP}}$$

where $R_i$ is total revenue $(R_i = S_i + L_i)$, and $S_i$ and $L_i$ are state and local revenue. In such a formulation $r_i$ and consequently the matching rate

$$M_i = \frac{r_i}{1 - r_i}$$

varies among districts. Without such variation we could not estimate district
response to price differences.

The actual matching rate $M_i$ for each district is derived from a more complex formula, including floors, ceilings, and exceptions. The complete formula
is described in Appendix 7A. In practice CH70 aid is based on the *previous*
calendar year's expenditure, or on expenditure during the two preceding fiscal
years. A correct model of school expenditures would require a dynamic formulation in which one year's activities would depend on variables generated
the previous year, and district behavior would consider the effect that this
year's decisions will have on next year's finances. For a number of reasons,
we have not employed a dynamic model here, including lack of annual data for
exogenous variables, and the belief that although the law may have been old
enough to allow the assumption of an equilibrium, it was not old enough to
show us the continuing equilibrium adjustment process.

To summarize: we generated the matching rate facing each school district in 1968-69 by application of the CH70 formula. This variable M is
then treated as exogenous; but since state aid in the percentage equalizing
formula also depends on local revenue (LEDR), the *amount* of aid under
the matching provision is endogenous. Because of the numerous changes
in the Chapter 70 Act from the textbook percentage equalizing formula,
some districts receive nonmatching aid rather than matching aid from the
state. This aid, denoted A, is exogenous, since it is not a function of local
revenue.

Categorical state aid (CSA), which comprised 33 percent of total state
aid in 1968-69, is composed of several restricted grants: about 45 percent
aids school construction, 25 percent aids pupil transportation, 21 percent
is earmarked for special education, and the remainder supports school lunches
and wards of the state. Because construction aid is disbursed through a matching grant formula, CSA and local revenue are interdependent; therefore CSA is
an endogenous variable in the equations to be estimated.[3]

Title I aid is allocated to districts through a formula depending largely on the presence of children in families receiving Aid to Families with Dependent Children (AFDC), with the preponderance of poverty in 1960 (POOR) also having some effect. If Title I aid were *disbursed* by this formula, a nonstochastic process, there would be no reason to estimate an equation for it. However, about 7 percent of Title I aid in 1968-69 was never applied for and was available to other districts upon application.[4] This raises the possibility that a behavioral relation reflecting both the failure to apply for allocated funds and success in obtaining leftover funds can be estimated. We have therefore estimated an equation for Title I aid, that will reflect both the Title I distribution formula and behavioral elements.

The bulk of non-Title I aid (OTHFED) comes from PL81-874 aid, distributed to districts where federal land and buildings deprive a school district of property tax revenue, but where the children of federal employees attend public schools. In Massachusetts this describes districts which include military installations almost exclusively. OTHFED is exogenous, unaffected by the variables in this system.

Finally, noneducational state aid (NESA) is endogenous like CSA. Although part of this aid (for construction purposes) is disbursed through matching grants, determining a price variable would have entailed detailed study of the various noneducational aid provisions, stating them in terms of variables as was done with CH70, and calculating a price for each district. As in the case of CSA, the data to do this is unavailable. Hence, we have treated NESA simply as an endogenous variable, in lieu of an explicit treatment of price. Such an approximation is justified by the fact that the matching rate which determines part of NESA is constant among districts, and hence the effective price of nonschool revenues therefore does not vary as it does for school revenues. No information on a district basis is available for federal aid to nonschool services, and such a variable has been omitted by necessity. However, much of such aid supports specific projects and should not affect general local behavior.

In summary, we are treating sources of funds as follows:

|  | *Endogenous* | *Exogenous* |
|---|---|---|
| Local | LEDR | |
| | LNER | |
| State | CH70 | M |
| | CSA | A |
| | NESA | |
| Federal | TIT1 | OTHFED |
| | (predetermined) | |

One nonrevenue variable will be considered endogenous—property valuation per pupil (PROP). The discussion of Chapter 6 focused on the local decision process for generating school and nonschool services. However, there is another mechanism available to individuals (though not to communities) for choosing among alternative levels of public goods and services—mobility among jurisdictions. If there are relatively few communities among which potential residents in an area may choose, then there will be a relatively greater demand for residential property in those jurisdictions where the patterns of public services and taxes are in greatest demand, and property values will be relatively higher.[5] More specifically, property values should reflect local tax rates and expenditure patterns as long as expenditures are a rough indication of real services received. Thus property valuation may depend on local decisions about school and non-school expenditures and should be treated as an endogenous variable.[6]

While we will treat PROP as endogenous and estimate an equation for it, there are several reasons for caution in the interpretation and use of the results. First of all, the process of capitalization may work with a lag, whereas we have confined ourselves to a one-period model. Secondly, school and nonschool *services* should be reflected in property values, and the use of revenues ignores the extent to which expenditures are ineffective, the differences among districts in the relative costs of providing services, and the extent to which local expenditures reflect perceived differences in services rather than some other factor.[7] Third, the measure of the PROP variable may be biased[8] and may be subject to some political manipulation which affects both taxes and state aid.[9] Fourth, by using district summary data rather than values of individual property or classes of property, the precise relationships between property value and its type (commercial, industrial, residential) or its ownership (landlord versus resident) cannot accurately be estimated. These caveats should be served to stress the tentative nature of our conclusions based on the PROP estimation.

The set of *hypothesized* interrelationships among endogenous variables is presented in Figure 7-1. Procedurally, this figure indicates that we will

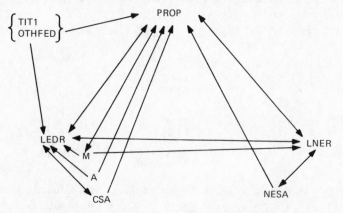

**Figure 7-1.**   Endogenous Variables: Hypothesized Interrelationships.

estimate the equations for all the endogenous variables except TIT1 by two-stage least squares, and TIT1 by ordinary least squares.[10]

### Socioeconomic Characteristics

Population characteristics of individual district were taken from the 1960 census of population. Census data for 1970, closer to the school year 1968-69, provided similar equation specifications, but poorer fit. It should not be surprising, however, that current expenditures are related to *past* population characteristics. In the first place, it may take the political process several years to respond to changes in the composition of a district's population, so that expenditures respond to socioeconomic characteristics with a lag.[11] Secondly, the budgetary process itself may exacerbate this lag effect. Sharkansky describes budget determination as an incremental process, where the most important consideration in determining a budget item appears to be what has been spent on that item in the past.[12] Thus past population characteristics, which have affected previous budget decisions, may continue to have an effect over time.

Finally, socioeconomic characteristics of political jurisdictions are remarkably stable over time, as the correlations between 1960 and 1970 variables in Table 7-2 indicate.[13] Between a decision process with considerable inertia built in and stable population characteristics, it is hardly surprising to find school revenues more responsive to past than to present characteristics. But this finding does indicate that the most accurate description of local behavior would be an explicitly dynamic specification, incorporating population characteristics for several previous years. With a decennial census, this approach is clearly impossible.

However, the use of 1970 values for the variable POP was found to result in marginally better fit than the use of 1960 values. To a greater extent than the socioeconomic variables, population size reflects necessity rather than taste,[14] so that the effects of population changes will be more quickly felt. In addition, local governments must consider per capita service levels in their

**Table 7-2**
**Correlations between 1960 and 1970 Values of Socio-economic Variables**

| Variable | Correlation |
| --- | --- |
| Y | 0.915 |
| ED | 0.869 |
| PROF | 0.915 |
| OWNED | 0.849 |
| POOR | 0.759 |

allocation decisions, an additional reason why current rather than lagged population levels affect resource allocations.

### Equations for Local Revenue

The equations estimated for LEDR appear in Table 7-3. Several equations have been presented, for two reasons.[15] The first is the comparison of different estimating forms outlined in Chapter 6. The second is that different estimating techniques give different results, and it seems more appropriate to indicate the range of results than to choose one for presentation. As mentioned earlier, the results of the simulations in the next chapter are not sensitive to the differences in the estimates reported here.

The usual criterion for elimination of variables is statistical significance at the 5 percent level, usually with a one-tailed test. This standard is not always maintained if the variable improves the fit of the regression since for purposes of simulation, no matter what the standard error, the resulting regression gives the best parameter estimate available. Differences in specifications come not so much from experimenting with variables, but from looking at different forms.[16] In a number of instances, a nonlinear parameter was estimated by an iterative routine, specifying an initial value and varying it to maximize $R^2$. These parameters are indicated by an asterisk in Table 7-3. The equations are also labeled according to their theoretical source as discussed in Chapter 6.

Each equation generates a number of parameters which were discussed in Chapter 6, particularly the response to the matching rate for state funds and to nonmatching state aid. The price elasticity $\eta_{LEDR,PRICE}$ and the response to a marginal dollar of nonmatching aid (for districts with no matching aid) $\partial LEDR/\partial A$ are presented in Table 7-4. Clearly, the values of these parameters are sensitive to equation specification. Since we are most interested in the response of the district to state aid, we will have to discuss the relative merits of the specifications here in order to proceed.

The utility function approach yields perverse estimates of the price elasticity and the response to A. They imply that the state is unable to increase total school expenditures by increasing the matching rate on local school funds or by increasing funds directly. If this were a finding from time-series data which might be dominated by inertia rather than response to incentives, or a robust finding holding over different equations forms, we would be more inclined to investigate the possibility that the state actually can do nothing to affect total revenue (hypothesis I of Chapter 3). Although many investigators have estimated that a dollar increase in state aid does not necessarily increase total revenue by a dollar, none has ever claimed the resulting increase to be zero or negative. Since we had theoretical objections to the utility function approach, and since the empirical results are at odds with other estimates, we shall say no more about it.[17]

**Table 7-3**
**Equations for Local Revenue, 159 Massachusetts Districts, 1968-69**

*Utility Function Specification*

i. 
$$LOCR = \underset{(0.728)}{(2.882} PROP + \underset{(0.0140)}{0.0823Y} + \underset{(7.73)}{28.05ED} - \underset{(72.1)}{107.9OWN} - \underset{(57.79)}{110.24RES} - \underset{(0.131)}{1.134A} + \underset{(0.735)}{1.836} CSA + \underset{(1.24)}{3.97TIT1} - \underset{(0.187)}{0.759OTHFED}$$

$$\underset{(82)}{- 110)/(1 + m} - \underset{(*)}{0.017Y/(1 + m)} PROP^2)$$

$SEE = 73.41$

$R^2 = 0.7706$

*Linear Expenditure Function*

ii. 
$$LOCR = \underset{(2.130)}{(-4.299} + \underset{(0.00032)}{0.00173Y} - \underset{(1.544)}{3.148} RES) PROP + \underset{(171.2)}{(701.23} PROF - \underset{(0.140)}{1.016A} + \underset{(0.660)}{1.424} CSA + \underset{(1.102)}{3.362} TIT1 - \underset{(0.179)}{0.759} OTHFED + \underset{(52.49)}{432)/(1 + m)}$$

$SEE = 74.29$

$R^2 = 0.7634$

*Linear Additive Specifications*

iii. 
$$LOCR = \underset{(1.67)}{(4.102} PROP + \underset{(0.015)}{0.092Y} + \underset{(7.55)}{21.17ED} - \underset{(57.3)}{106.45} RES - \underset{(0.623)}{0.740A} + \underset{(0.67)}{1.21CSA} + \underset{(1.22)}{4.379} TIT1 - \underset{(0.225)}{0.498OTHFED} - \underset{(0.57)}{225.5)/(1 + m} - .608)/(1 + m \cdot .608)$$

$SEE = 83.85$

$R^2 = 0.6771$

## Table 7-3 (Continued)

iv. $\text{LOCR} = (5.414 \text{ PROP} + 0.0844Y + 634.9 \text{ PROF} - 117.10 \text{ RES} - 0.321 A + 0.812 \text{CSA} + 4.178 \text{ TIT1} - 0.375 \text{ OTHFED}$

    (0.774)    (0.0146)    (175)    (50.9)    (0.120)    (0.615)    (1.136)    (0.163)

$- 0.000000124 \cdot \text{POP} \cdot \text{LNER} - 75.7)/(1 + m \cdot (1.51 - 0.0667 \cdot \text{SCHRATE}))$

    (0.000000086)    (84.6)    (*)    (*)

$SEE = 75.75$

$R^2 = 0.7208$

*Log-Linear Specification*

v. $\text{LOCR} = \text{PROP}^{0.400} Y^{0.823} \text{PROF}^{0.089} \text{RES}^{-0.069} \text{PRICE}^{1.352 - 0.0643 \text{ SCHRATE}} A^{-0.012} \text{CSA}^{0.092} \text{TIT1}^{0.6521} \text{OTHFED}^{-0.010} e^{-2.27}$

    (0.074)(0.174)    (0.042)    (0.063)    (0.778)    (0.029)    (0.018)    (0.043)    (0.017)    (0.015)    (1.57)

$SEE = 0.137$

$R^2 = 0.7103$

$SEE_c = 80.84$

*Estimates for Seventy Districts with Nonmatching Aid Only*

vi. $\text{LOCR} = 4.011 \text{ PROP} + 0.0683 Y + 44.67 \text{ED} - 200.65 \text{ RES} - 0.743A + 1.476 \text{ CSA} + 4.173 \text{ TIT1} - 0.904 \text{ OTHFED} - 273$

    (1.572)    (0.0176)    (11.53)    (77.07)    (0.578)    (0.665)    (1.713)    (0.264)    (164)

$SEE = 76.96$

$R^2 = 0.8416$

Note: Standard errors in parentheses; asterisks denote parameters estimated by iteration. $SEE_c$ denotes the standard error of the estimate corrected for the log=linear form. Instrumental variables includes A, TIT1, OTHFED, Y, PROF, ED, RES, OWNED, MAN, SOUND, POP, POPDEN, POP-GROWTH, AFDC, and POOR; M is an instrumental variable in i–iv, and PRICE is an instrument in v.

**Table 7-4**
**Parameters Describing the Substitution of State for Local Funds**

| Equation | Price Effect $\eta_{LEDR, PRICE}$ | Income Effect $\partial LEDR/\partial A$ |
|----------|------------|-------------|
| i | 1.20 | –1.08 |
| ii | 0.833 | –0.85 |
| iii | 0.499 | –0.740 |
| iv | 0.218 | –0.321 |
| v | 0.142 | –0.19 |
| vi | – | –0.743 |

NOTE: All values are calculated at the sample mean.

The estimates based on the linear expenditure system (equation [ii]) are plausible, though peculiar in one critical sense. Although the price elasticity is theoretically free to vary, two alternative specifications[18] yielded the same price elasticity (0.85), essentially the same as in equation ii (0.83). These estimates seem perilously close to one; that is, they indicate a relatively low price response. We clearly cannot reject the estimates on such grounds. However, the fact that the price elasticities are so similar signals an important weakness: the linear expenditure system implies a price elasticity which is not responsive to parameter differences and, like the utility function specification, which depends critically on coefficients not intended to measure price effects. (Here, the coefficients of $\partial LEDR/\partial PROP$ are crucial to the price elasticity.) Finally, we should note that equation ii (as well as the other unreported equations of this form) imply that a marginal dollar of nonmatching aid A decreases LEDR by $0.85, which appears rather high but is at least plausible.

Equations iii and iv are two regressions derived from the linear additive approach described in the previous chapter. In equation iii, the effect of an additional dollar of matching aid is to reduce local revenue by $0.608, implying a price elasticity of 0.499. The standard error of the parameter estimate is high, so that this coefficient is insignificantly different from zero; but for purposes of simulating the results of changing state aid programs for the majority of pupils in Massachusetts, this estimate is the best available.

However, the insignificance of this coefficient raises the possibility that the "substitution effect" of nonmatching aid—that is, the price elasticity—is not constant over all districts, but rather varies systematically as some other district characteristic varies. We did find this to be the case, as equation iv indicates: the marginal effect of an additional dollar of matching aid under the CH70 formula is –1.51 + 0.0667 SCHRTE, so that the price elasticity is a function of the local school tax rate.[19]  There are two explanations for this result. In the first place, districts with low school tax rates are relatively unburdened providing resources to schools. Either they have an extraordinarily large property base, or their preferences for schooling are relatively low. One implication is that such districts are in equilibrium with respect to their preferences for schooling services relative to other goods and services, since they could so easily increase school revenues. Whether the low tax rate is due to high property valuation or preferences, additional revenues from the state from a higher matching rate are more likely to be used to reduce school taxes than to increase expenditures. Conversely, districts with high tax rates are more likely to be constrained by low property valuation to spend less for schooling than they otherwise would, or are districts with preferences for high levels of school services. Both groups will be more likely to increase total spending if matching rates (and matching state funds) increase. Hence the price effect is a function of the school tax rate. A second explanation, less intuitive, refers to the utility analysis of the previous chapter. From equation 6.4, $\partial$LEDR$/\partial(m \cdot$ LEDR) increases with LEDR and decreases with PROP$^2$. Both of these conditions are met when this partial derivative increases as the school tax rate, which equals LEDR/PROP, increases.[20] The point is, then, that price effects are not constant across districts, but vary according to the relative burden of raising the revenues for public education.

The final estimate of LEDR, equation v, is a log-linear specification. The parameter estimates are elasticities, and thus $\eta_{\text{LEDR,PRICE}}$ = 1.352 –0.0643 · SCHRTE. At the sample mean this takes a value of 0.142, quite close to the estimate from equation iv. As before, the price effect is a function of the school tax rate; the coefficient of SCHRTE is significantly different from zero at better than the 0.1 percent level. However, contrary to the previous results, equation v indicates that nonmatching state aid has no significant effect on local revenue.

The discussion of Equations iii-v indicate that their price elasticities differ, but no equation is clearly superior to the others. We can utilize all three equations in preliminary simulations and choose one which best reproduces the current funds distribution. However, the wide range of estimates for the income effect, $\partial$LEDR$/\partial$A, remains troubling. The simple substitution effect of nonmatching state aid should be clear without going through the tedious process of simulation. One approach is to estimate an equation for local revenue for those districts with nonmatching state aid only. This result is presented in equation vi and indicates that the best estimate of the substitution effect is -0.743, very close to the estimate from equation iii. The estimate is significantly different from zero at only the 10 percent level, but it remains the best available estimate.

### General Properties of Local Revenue Equations

The equations in Table 7-3 support a number of traditional conclusions.

Local revenue is higher when the value of property is high, when the family income of residents is high, and when the educational level or occupational status of the population is high. Local revenue is lower when state general purpose aid is higher and when non-Title I aid is higher. Categorical aid tends to increase local revenue, a reflection of the stimulating effect of the matching provision. Finally, and inexplicably, the coefficient of Title I revenue is high and positive rather than negative as expected. This peculiar result is robust over all specifications. It has been suggested that Title I regulations requiring all schools within a district to be comparable *before* the addition of federal aid have induced districts with Title I funds to upgrade previously neglected schools, thereby increasing average local revenues. Alternatively, Title I may serve as a proxy for cost variations. These explanations are not satisfactory, and we remain puzzled about this coefficient.

The property base composition, RES, has a consistently negative effect. That is, districts with a higher proportion of commercial and industrial property relative to residential property raise more school revenue, *ceteris paribus.*[21] This can be interpreted as a price effect. Only that portion of the property tax which falls on residential housing is directly paid by residents. That falling on industrial and commercial property might be paid by residents as customers, employees, or owners of businesses, but this portion of the tax is potentially invisible and—perhaps more to the point—a large fraction may be exported to nonresidents. Hence local revenue costs less in terms of direct payments by residents when there is relatively less residential property, and a "rational" price response would require that residents raise more local revenue, *ceteris paribus.* The negative coefficient of RES confirms this hypothesis. It should be clear, however, that this is a very different price effect, both conceptually, and empirically, from the price effect induced by the state's matching rate. The price elasticity from equation iv due to the matching rate is 0.218, while the elasticity of LEDR with respect to RES is –0.134. Hence it is inappropriate to use one measure of price response as a substitute for the other.[22]

In the previous chapter we hypothesized that local nonschool revenue might affect the generation of local school revenues. This hypothesis was not confirmed by any of the nonlinear forms, but it was consistently confirmed at about the 7 percent confidence level for the linear additive forms estimated.[23] As can be seen from equation iv, the effect of LNER increases as population increases. This is consistent with a popular notion of municipal overburden, which claims that cities may be so burdened by large and irreducible requirements for noneducational services that school expenditures suffer as a consequence.[24] For most of the districts in Massachusetts, the effect of LNER on LEDR is negligible. But for Boston, with a 1970 population of 641,071, a marginal dollar raised for nonschool purposes decreases LEDR by $0.083. For a smaller city such as Springfield, with a population of 163,905, the corresponding reduction in LEDR is $0.021. Further evidence as to the validity of the municipal-overburden argument will be discussed below in conjunction with the equations for LNER.

Finally, two comparisons should be noted. The first is between two measures of community socio-economic status, ED and PROF. Either of them enters significantly in every equation, but—because of high collinearity[25]— they never appear together. They function as fairly close substitutes for one another, with essentially the same impact on school finance decisions. The second interesting comparison is that between the effects of income and property valuation. From equation v, the income variable is twice as important in explaining LEDR as property valuation, in terms of elasticities. The same pattern can be shown to hold for the impact of PROP and Y on total revenues.[26] This suggests that emphasis of school reformers on the effects of property variations would be misplaced in Massachusetts, where income variations are considerably more important in explaining resource inequities.[27]

### Equations for Other Variables

To complete the description of endogenous interrelationships, we include here a discussion of the other equations we have estimated. These are presented in Table 7-5.

### *Local Nonschool Revenues*

As with school revenues, property valuation is an important determinant of nonschool revenue. Indeed, the marginal propensity to raise revenue for nonschool services is larger than the marginal propensity to raise revenue for school items, as summarized in Table 7-6. One possible explanation of this difference is that different prices from state matching rates induce the greater response of nonschool revenue; but because the price of school revenue is on the average slightly lower than the price of nonschool revenue,[28] we would expect the marginal propensity to raise school revenue to be higher. Hence this explanation is invalid. A more plausible reason relies on the disequilibrium analysis of the previous chapter: If state laws, national norms, and other exogenous factors constrain school spending so that many districts are spending more on schools than they would in equilibrium, any increase in income (property value) would induce a larger increase in nonschool revenues than in school revenues. Although the concept of disequilibrium is often applied to cities, where the requirements of nonschool services are claimed to be inordinately large, the majority of districts in the Massachusetts sample are not central cities. They are small enough so that some vague set of minimum standards or costs may

**Table 7-5**
**Equations for Other Endogenous Variables, 159 Massachusetts Districts, 1968-69**

vii. LNER = 7.74 PROP + 0.00048 POP + 0.0178 POPDEN - 30.38 POPGROWTH + 1519 AFDC - 289.39 OWNED + 32.08 ED
   (1.07)     (0.00025)      (0.0032)           (5.24)              (319)            (84.23)            (11.85)

   - 792.8 CHILD + 1282·PROF²·PRICE + 160.4
     (294)              (710)            (116)

SEE = 104.6
$R^2$ = 0.8529

viii. PROP = 0.014 TER + 0.031 TNER - 0.81 TAXRATE - 6.67 MAN + 18.216 SOUND - 0.00028 POPDEN + 0.443 POPGROWTH + 0.8
      (0.003)        *          (0.04)          (1.50)        (5.42)           (0.0001)           (0.172)           (5.6)

SEE = 3.826
$R^2$ = 0.8838

ix. CSA = 1.078 LOCR - 0.54 PROP + 2.00 POPGROWTH - 0.0017 POPDEN + 108 CHILD - 4.07
     (0.021)       (0.25)        (0.87)             (0.0005)          (43)        (12)

SEE = 2.72
$R^2$ = 0.3342

x. NESTA= 0.14 LNER + 240.6 POOR + 0.000086 POP - 276.6 CHILD + 102.6
    (0.019)       (68.7)         (0.00007)           (74)         (24)

SEE = 37.25
$R^2$ = 0.6848

xi. TIT1 = 122.69 AFDC + 23.56 POOR + 9.68 PROF - 1.76
      (4.92)         (6.71)        (4.88)        (1.18)

SEE = 2.945
$R^2$ = 0.8683

**Table 7-6**
**Effects on Property Value of School Revenues and Nonschool Revenues**

|          | Equation | $\frac{\partial REV}{\partial PROP}$ | $\eta REV, PROP$ |
|----------|----------|--------------------------------------|------------------|
| LEDR     | iii      | 3.722                                | (0.167)          |
|          | iv       | 4.515                                | (0.203)          |
|          | v        | –                                    | 0.400            |
| LNER     | vi       | 7.74                                 | $0.752^a$        |

[a]This represents the coefficient of PROP in a log-linear specification, reported in Grubb (90), Ch. 3.

apply to school revenues. A final possibility is that a relatively higher income or wealth elasticity for nonschool revenues is simply a basic attribute of tastes and preferences for public goods and services.[29]

The coefficient of LNER in equation iv suggests that LNER influences the amount of spending on schools, but we find no evidence that the opposite occurs. LEDR is not a significant variable in any specification of LNER. The implication is that schooling is less "necessary," so that school expenditures decline when nonschool expenses rise. That finding, however, is a function of population, so that only in large districts do nonschool expenditures seriously reduce school expenditures. This might lead us to accept the municipal-over-burden argument. In large school districts, then, school expenditures may *not* be in equilibrium, but appear restricted by nonschool expenses which are necessary for the maintenance of the district's integrity rather than expressive of local preferences.[30]

The exogenous variables entering into the equation for LNER lend support to the contention that nonschool expenditures are less a function of prefer-ences than of necessity. Nonschool revenues increase with population, popula-tion density, and with the preponderance of families receiving welfare. In addition, communities with faster population growth tend to spend relatively less on nonschool goods and services. While this may reflect a lag in adjusting service levels to population,[31] it may also represent another dimension of those towns and cities which are stagnant in terms of population growth—generally, central cities and their inner suburbs[32]—and which require larger per capita expenditures for highways, police, and fire protection. The negative coefficient of OWNED supports the "political" nature of this variable. As for school reve-nues, socioeconomic status as measured by ED is positively related to nonschool revenues. The variable CHILD corrects for the fact that LNER is in per pupil, rather than per capita, terms.

Finally, as hypothesized in Chapter 6, the price of school funds affects the amount of nonschool funds, the response to price being higher as the occupational structure is more professional.[33]  This may indicate either of two very different kinds of behavior:  a typical price response, with larger purchases of cheaper goods; or budget maneuvering, placing some items (e.g., recreation, health services, and libraries) in the school budget where a dollar of expenditure costs less in terms of local revenue than it does in the nonschool budget.  If the latter is the case, then school finance laws subsidize nonschool activities, and do so to a greater extent in communities of higher socioeconomic status.  If the former, then there are distortions in the "proper" amount of various public services due to the price differentials created by the state.

The coefficient of the price variable in equation vii indicates that, at the sample mean, a change from a matching rate of zero to a matching rate of one-third—implying a price of school revenue of 0.75—would induce LNER to fall by $6, compared to a mean of $530 per pupil.[34]  Thus while the hypothesis that the price of school expenditures affects local nonschool revenues has been sustained, the magnitude of this effect is rather small.  But the interaction of the price effect with socioeconomic status (PROF) may give a clue as to why this is true.  There are undoubtedly many ways in which cities could move expenditure items from one category into another, especially from nonschool into school expenditures.  Local bureaucracies may not be anxious to give up control of their own budgets to increase the city's total resources, and they may not be aware of the implications of price differentials.  But they seem more willing and able to make such substitutions when the citizens are wealthier or of higher socioeconomic status.[35]  Hence price manipulation—attempting to induce local funds for a particular service through a matching grant from the state—has several dangers.  It may induce only budget manipulation, and it may be differentially effective, subsidizing the public expenditures of wealthy communities more than those of the poor communities.

### Property Valuation

The estimation of the equation for PROP is explained in Appendix 7A. Our reservations about this equation were pointed out above, and because of them we do not want to make more of our findings than they can bear; but the results are neither irrelevant nor unexpected.

First, expenditures for school and nonschool services do increase property value, and taxes to pay for them decrease that value. However, nonschool services increase the value of property more than school services.[36]  One possible explanation is that nonresidential property valuation is heavily affected by nonschool expenditures but not by school expenditures. Once again, the magnitude of these effects is not large, but they are biased in favor of wealthy districts. At the sample mean, a 1 mill increase in the tax rate produces the following:

|                    | Changes in Revenues | Change in PROP |
|--------------------|:-------------------:|:-------------:|
| School revenue     | $15.77              | $126          |
| Nonschool revenue  | 20.05               | 661           |
| Total revenue      | 35.82               | 787           |
| Taxes              | 27.83               | –810          |
| Total effect       | +$ 7.99             | –$ 23         |

In the rational world, a large positive change in property value would induce owners to vote for increased services because the services increase their property value. On the other hand, renters would vote for increased services when the balance is negative, because even if the taxes are passed to them, they should pay lower rents from decreased property value. The figure shown is a virtual stalemate, amounting to about 0.1 percent of mean property valuation per pupil.

But wealthy communities, those with high property value, will raise more revenue from a given tax rate than poor communities, and demand for property in these communities should be relatively higher. Hence equation viii describes a disequilibrium situation, where increased tax rates in districts of above average property value tend to increase property value and thus encourage greater spending on public goods. Similar tax increases in districts of low wealth will only decrease property valuation.

There are, of course, a number of forces which interfere with this process. On one hand, some high-wealth districts are undesirable for residences because of a high concentration of commercial property value,[37] and thus property values will be bid up by businesses more than families. On the other hand, minimum lot and other "snob" zoning laws, unavailability of rental units, disequilibrium in the mortgage market, and lack of transportation to employment artificially restrict demand for housing in high income districts. Nonetheless, to the extent that the disequilibrium process operates, there is another inequitable effect of relying on local taxation: richer communities recapture some of their increased spending in property values, but poorer communities suffer twice, once through the level of taxes required to support schools and again through the reduction in property values induced by high tax rates which produce relatively lower revenues.

The incidence of these effects on individuals is less clear than their effects on property. The question remains: who bears the cost of property taxes? If owners of property do, then absentee landlords pay the cost of educating tenant children, but they also capture the benefits (or costs) of capitalization of taxes and expenditures, including the capitalization which would result from a change in state aid programs. It seems more likely that owners and tenants (including businesses) share these benefits and costs to varying extent. We cannot pursue the question of incidence here. Indeed, the equation for PROP is not designed to carry the discussion very far. But it does emphasize another peculiarity of financing schools by manipulation—through the state's price and income effects—of local activities. This will be one of several arguments leading us to advocate a less manipulative state aid system.[38]

### Categorical State Aid

Equations ix and x describe the allocation of categorical state aid for school and nonschool purposes. Because of matching provisions, both CSA and NESA depend on local revenue. School aid is "progressive," in that less of it flows to wealthy communities, but more flows to growing communities because of increased construction aid. The sign of population density in the equation for school aid reflects transportation aid to rural districts, and the positive coefficient for CHILD reflects services such as school lunches and money flowing to state wards. Nonschool categorical aid flows to urban districts, those with large populations and with high concentrations of poor families. The negative coefficient for CHILD is a correction for stating aid in per-pupil terms. Finally, the explanatory power of the equation for nonschool aid is much better than that for school aid.

### Title I

The ordinary least-squares equation for Title I funds reflects primarily an additive linear estimate of the distribution formula, which dictates that funds flow to districts where the variables AFDC and POOR are high. Secondarily, funds go to districts of higher socioeconomic status. We assume that this surprising result indicates the ability of such districts to obtain unallocated funds, through a greater ability to get information about available funds and to act accordingly. If this result reflects the truism that aid systems which permit any local manipulation will benefit most those districts which are adept at manipulation, then it also indicates that such abilities are not random but are related to class status.

### The System of Simultaneous Equations

Much of the substance of this chapter is contained in the detail of individual regressions, particularly in the regressions for LEDR and LNER. What distinguishes this model from previous attempts to ascertain the determinants

of municipal expenditures, however, is the effort to estimate a system of
simultaneous equations.

Any one of the equations for local revenue in Table 7-3, together with the
equations of Table 7-4, constitutes a system of simultaneous equations. If we
choose equation iv from the alternatives for LEDR, the pattern of interactions
among the endogenous variables of the system is as shown in Figure 7-2. This
figure contains a number of interactions which are different from those hypothesized earlier in this chapter. In particular, an influence of school revenue on
nonschool revenue was not found. In fact, the connections between the school
and the nonschool sector appear rather weak. The only connections are that
via the coefficient of LNER in equation iv—which is statistically significant at
only the 7 percent level—and that via the effect of the price of school revenue
on LNER, in equation vii. This disturbing lack of connection is obvious struc-
turally in separate school and municipal administrations. But our expectation
that the two sectors are interdependent because of their economic interaction
has been only weakly supported.

A second striking feature of the system of equations is the consistent
appearance of socioeconomic status as measured by PROF. The typical
explanation, that social class variables reflect "taste" for public services, is
insufficient. PROF enters that way, perhaps, in explaining local school revenue,
but certainly not in explaining Title I allocations or in the price response of nonschool funds.[39]    As we suspected in Chapter 6, we cannot always discern what
role a variable is playing. A plausible explanation is that PROF reflects the
ability of districts to perceive and respond "rationally" to intergovernmental

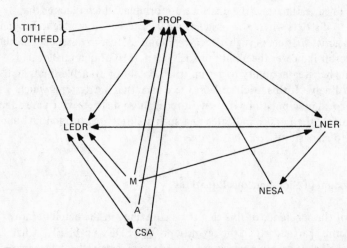

Figure 7-2.  Endogenous Variables:  Empirical Interrelationships

aid programs, rather than (or in addition to) a measure of preferences. One crucial question for rational school budgeting—what the matching rate for a district is—is not obvious and may not always be known.[40] Information about federal programs and the ability to follow federal procedures may similarly be imperfect.[41] To the extent that information and relevant expertise is in short supply, complexity in intergovernmental allocation programs is itself a source of bias in the process of local financing.

The possibility that information costs affect behavior raises disturbing questions about what simulations mean, especially simulations of other distribution systems. On one hand, a new system (such as district power equalizing) would require new information to be disseminated, which might again advantage higher status districts. On the other, the new system might be simpler, or might be accompanied by better information and better training of responsible local officials. This should especially be true of systems like DPE which are predicated on price effects and rational responses to price. Thus even if district behavior is itself predictable, observed behavior under a different state program may differ from predicted behavior because of changes in information patterns.

This point is intended to stress the fragility of simulations, but not to undermine their importance. The next chapter will be concerned with the school resource distributions which these equations would predict. We have described the income and price effects of the equations, and the interactions among the various equations of the model. But the question still remains what effect on measures of the distribution of funds these parameters have. The simulations presented in the next chapter are simply the logical extensions of the regressions in Tables 7-3 and 7-5.

## Appendix 7 A : Estimation Procedures

This appendix will describe some of the estimation procedures which were followed for the model of school district behavior. Specifically, the particular form which matching aid under the CH70 formula takes necessitates some choices of estimation technique. After describing the CH70 formula, the estimation problems for local revenue will be presented. Finally, the iterative estimation procedure for property valuation will be discussed.

### The Chapter 70 Formula

In the "pure" form of percentage equalizing which formed the original basis of the CH70 formula, every district faces a matching rate, which can be positive or negative. The general form for percentage equalizing is:

$$S_i = 1 - k \frac{PROP_i}{\overline{PROP}} \cdot (S_i + L_i) \qquad (7.1)$$

However, the final version of the CH70 formula incorporated a number of changes.[42] First, the "reimbursement ratio" $(1 - k \cdot PROP_i/\overline{PROP})$ was applied (in 1968-69) to reimbursable expenditures from local revenue, rather than to state plus local revenue as equation (7.1) indicates. Second, with the introduction of a floor and a ceiling in the amount of local expenditures which can be matched, the CH70 formula divides districts into two groups. One faces a matching rate given by the expression[43]

$$m_i = 1 - 0.65 \, PROP_i/\overline{PROP}.$$

The other group, those with local reimbursable expenditures below $370 or above $509, receive what is effectively nonmatching aid, since increases or decreases in local revenue will not affect the amount of state aid they receive. The amount of aid is calculated by applying the matching rate from equation (7.2) to the floor of $370 for low-spending districts, and to the ceiling ($509) for high-spending districts.[44] For these districts the matching rate is zero.

In addition, for both groups of districts, there is a ceiling in the matching rate of 0.75, and a floor of 0.15. A reduction in aid if federal aid is large

137

affected a small group of districts. Finally, total entitlements were prorated according to the allocation by the legislature, which amounted to 70 percent of entitlements in 1968-69.[45]

In one sense the complexity of the CH70 formula is critical to the success of estimation. If all aid were distributed according to a matching rate like that of equation (7.2), then it would be impossible to distinguish between the effect of PROP and the effect of the matching rate (which would be a linear function of PROP) on local revenue. However, the presence of the various floors and ceilings means that the matching rate and property valuation per pupil are not particularly collinear. The simple correlation coefficient between the two is only $-0.441$.

Strictly speaking, the matching rate itself is endogenous, in that it is a function of two endogenous variables: the local property valuation value per pupil, as indicated in equation (7.2), and local revenue, which determines whether a district is to receive matching or nonmatching aid. But because of the nonlinearities in the matching rate, it proved impossible to treat it as endogenous for purposes of estimation.[46]    Hence the solution was to treat the matching rate as an exogenous variable.

### Estimation of Local Revenue Equations

If we assume, as in equation (6.3), that school districts respond to the dollar amounts of state aid—both matching aid and nonmatched aid—then the corresponding regression equation is:

$$\text{LEDR} = \sum_i \alpha_i X_i - \beta_1 \cdot (m \cdot \text{LEDR}) - \beta_2 \cdot A + e \qquad (7.3)$$

where $X_i$ denotes other variables and $e$ is an error term. The solution of this equation for LEDR results in an error term which is divided by $(1 + B \cdot m)$, so that direct estimation of equation (6.14) would suffer from heteroskedasticity. Therefore estimation of equation (7.3) provides the most efficient estimates of equation (6.4).

These are two possible methods of estimating equation (7.3). The first is to use two-stage least squares, with the term $m \cdot \text{LEDR}$ endogenous; this procedure was the one used for equation iii of Table 7-3.[47] Alternatively, it is possible to estimate the parameter $B_1$ by adding $B_1 m \cdot \text{LEDR}$ to both sides of the equation, and iterating over $B_1$ to minimize the standard error of the equation. This was the method used for equation iv of Table 7-3. The result is equivalent to that obtained by treating the term $m \cdot \text{LEDR}$ as exogenous, in the sense that it is not instrumented in equation (7.3), but the term does not enter the list of exogenous variables. One justification is essentially the same as that for keeping *m* exogenous: Because of the nonlinearities in the Chapter 70 formula, endogenous treatment of this term will not capture the critical variation. But more to the point, matching aid is strictly predetermined, since it depends on local expenditures in previous years. In the absence of severe serial correlation of the error terms, this justifies the exogenous treatment. The choice of estimation techniques is somewhat arbitrary, since both can be shown to yield parameters which are biased upward, but the estimation of $\beta_1$ by iteration is supported by the fact that the price elasticity of equation iv is close to that obtained by the log-linear specification of equation v, where the estimation problem is simpler. In this specification, PRICE is treated as an exogenous variable, and estimation via two-stage least squares is otherwise straightforward. Finally, it should be noted that, wherever the school tax rate appears as an argument of the price coefficient $B_1$, it is considered endogenous and therefore instrumented.

### Estimation of the Equation for PROP

The hypothesis that local expenditures and taxes are partially capitalized in property values can be tested by specifying the following regression:

$$\text{PROP} = \alpha \text{TEDR} + \beta \text{TNER} - \gamma \text{TOTRATE} + \sum_i a_i X_i + e \qquad (7.4)$$

where the $X_i$ refer to exogenous variables, and TOTRATE is the total tax rate. However, since it is true by definition that

$$\text{TEDR} + \text{TNER} = \text{TOTRATE} \cdot \text{PROP} + \text{CH70} + \text{CSA}$$
$$+ \text{TIT1} + \text{OTHFED} + \text{NESA} \qquad (7.5)$$

equation (7.4) amounts to a linearized version of the identity

$$\text{PROP} = \frac{\text{TEDR} + \text{TNER} - \text{CH70} - \text{CSA} - \text{TIT1} - \text{OTHFED}}{\text{TOTRATE}} \qquad (7.6)$$

To eliminate this identity, it is possible to solve (7.6) for TNER, substitute this expression into (7.5), and estimate the following regression:

$$\text{PROP} \cdot (1 - \beta \text{TOTRATE}) + \beta (\text{LEDR} - \text{NESA}) = \alpha \text{TEDR} -$$
$$- \gamma \text{TOTRATE} + \sum_i a_i X_i + e . \qquad (7.7)$$

Iterating over $\beta$ and minimizing the standard error of the equation yields a maximum likelihood estimate of $\beta$. The result is presented as equation viii of Table 7-5. Alternatively, one can solve (7.6) for LEDR and substitute this expression into equation (7.5) to derive an estimable form similar to (7.7). This result is slightly inferior in terms of goodness of fit, and hence equation viii has been chosen from the two alternatives.

## Appendix 7 B: The Price Effects of District Power Equalizing

We have couched the analysis of Chapters 6 and 7 in terms of the price and income effects of intergovernmental aid, an approach which is standard in the public finance literature.[48] However, this is quite different from the view taken in most legal and economic analyses of district power equalizing formulas, which most often assume that the "effective property value" which each school district faces is made equal. These two approaches amount to different models of how school districts behave with respect to state aid programs, and not surprisingly they have quite different implications for policy. The purpose of this appendix, therefore, is to clarify the difference between these two views, and to test which one is a more appropriate description of school district behavior.

We can start with a simple representation of the process which generates total school revenues:

$$R = f(P, Y, SES, \ldots; S. F., \ldots) \tag{7.8}$$

That is, total revenues per pupil $R$ are a function of local property valuation $P$, income $Y$, other socioeconomic variables $SES$, other variables unspecified by this general function, and federal aid $F$. If the state distributions non-matching aid $A$ and matching aid through a matching rate $m$, total revenue can be expressed as

$$R = (1 + m) \cdot L + A = (1 + m) \cdot t \cdot P + A \tag{7.9}$$

where $t$ is the local tax rate.

In the behavioral model which has been served as the basis for policy recommendations of most school finance reformers since 1970, districts are assumed to choose a level of revenues according to the schedule of tax rates required for each particular expenditure level, or (equivalently) according to the yield per mill of tax. Since an additional mill of tax yields $(1 + m) \cdot P$, equation (7.8) becomes:

$$R = f[(1 + m)P, Y, SES, \ldots; A] \tag{7.10}$$

In the case where the matching rate is zero and the state distributes aid through flat grants or foundation programs, then equation (7.10) indicates that revenues are influenced by property valuation per pupil. However, if state aid is distributed through a district power equalizing formula where $m = k/P - 1$

141

and the yield per mill is a constant, $k$, for all school districts, then property valuation $P$ disappears from equation (7.10). The *Serrano* mandate—that school district resources not be a function of local wealth—is upheld. That is, this view of school district behavior assumes that districts will react to their "effective" property base $(1 + m)P$, so that all DPE formulas will free district revenues from local wealth because they equalize the "effective" base across districts.

The second view of school district behavior applies utility theory, treating a district like a utility-maximizing consumer who has utility increasing with additional resources per pupil but decreasing as the local tax rate increases. In particular, districts behave like consumers in reacting positively to increases in property valuation (analogous to income effects in the usual consumer model) and negatively to increases in the "price" of revenue per pupil, $1/(1 + m)$. In the usual case, an increase in this price will cause a decrease in total revenues per pupil, and vice versa. Hence the state's matching rate is important not because it establishes an effective property base, but because it determines a price to which districts react.

The difference between these models can be stated quite succinctly: the first of them assumes that the district reacts to the effective property base $(1 + m)P$, so that a change in $(1 + m)$ and a change in $P$ have similar effects. That is, if $E = (1 + m) \cdot P$,

$$\frac{\partial R}{\partial m} = \frac{\partial R}{\partial E} \cdot \frac{\partial E}{\partial m} = \frac{\partial R}{\partial E} \cdot P \text{ and } \frac{\partial R}{\partial P} = \frac{\partial R}{\partial E} \cdot \frac{\partial E}{\partial P} = \frac{\partial R}{\partial E} \cdot (1 + m) \quad (7.11)$$

$$\frac{\partial R}{\partial m} \bigg/ P => \frac{\partial R}{\partial P} \bigg/ (1 + m) \ . \quad (7.12)$$

The second model, on the other hand, indicates that reactions to changes in $(1 + m)$ (price effects) and to changes in $P$ (analogous to income effects) are different.[49] This difference provides us with a basis for distinguishing between these two hypotheses empirically.

Three tests of the alternative models are possible. First, from equations (7.9) and (7.12), it follows that

$$\frac{\partial R}{\partial m} = L + (1 + m) \cdot \frac{\partial L}{\partial m} \quad (7.13)$$

$$\frac{\partial R}{\partial P} = (1 + m) \frac{\partial L}{\partial P} + L \frac{\partial m}{\partial P} \ . \quad (7.14)$$

Therefore, if the first model is to hold and equation (7.12) is to be true, then it must be true that

$$\frac{L + (1 + m) \dfrac{\partial L}{\partial m}}{P} = \frac{(1 + m) \dfrac{\partial L}{\partial P} + L \, \dfrac{\partial m}{\partial P}}{1 + m} \tag{7.15}$$

$$=> \eta_{L,(1 + m)} + 1 = \eta_{L,P} + \eta_{(1 + m),P} \tag{7.16}$$

where $\eta$ denotes elasticities. The validity of equation (7.15) is easily tested
with the information from equation i of Table 7B-1.[50] Evaluating the left-hand
side of equation (7.15) yields a value of 4.71 while the right-hand side takes a
value of -5.413 at the sample mean. The difference between these two is statistically different at better than the 5 percent level (t = 2.03). Hence we can
reject the first of the two models presented here at least in the vicinity of the
sample mean. Furthermore, equation (7.15) holds true only when the school
tax rate (which is one of the arguments of $\partial L/\partial m$) takes on a value of 2.03 mills,
which is far below the range of observed values. This again supports the rejection of the first model.

The test summarized by equation (7.15) is, however, somewhat awkward
because it requires the use of specific values for $L$, $m$, $\partial m/\partial P$[51] and the school
tax rate. A more direct test is possible, utilizing regressions for total revenue
rather than local revenue and testing equation (7.12) directly. Equation iii
of Table 7B-1 presents such a regression. From this it is clear that

$$\frac{\dfrac{\partial R}{\partial m}}{P} = \frac{-483.6 + 15.6 \cdot t}{P} = 6.64 \text{ at the sample mean,}$$

$$\frac{\dfrac{\partial R}{\partial P}}{(1 + m)} = \frac{6.583}{(1 + m)} = 5.64 \text{ at the sample mean,}$$

and $\partial R/\partial P \big/ (1 + m)$ and $\partial R/\partial m \big/ P$ are significantly different at about the
2.5 percent level (the associated $t$-statistic is 2.21). Only where the school
tax rate is in the vicinity of 41.11 mills—which is outside the range of observed
tax rates—is the marginal impact of a change in the matching rate approximately
equal to the marginal impact of a change in property valuation. Again, the
second model of school district behavior is compatible with these results,
while the first one is not.

**Table 7-B1**
**Equations for Local Revenue, 159 Massachusetts Districts, 1968-69**

i.   $LEDR=$ 6.953 P-(689 + 14.38 SCHRATE) (1 + m) + 0.0735 Y + 429 PROF - 133.2 RES - 1.10 A - 0.213 CSA + 4.323 $\frac{TIT2}{TIT1}$
       (1.45) (201)   (4.40)          (0.0146)   (175)     (50.3)   (0.359) (0.709)

      -0.363 OTHFED - 0.000000176 POP·LNER + +542.9
      (0.167)       (0.000000091)     (129.39)

    $SEE$ = 73.45

    $R^2$ = 0.7555

iii.   $LEDR=$ $P^{0.400}$ $(1+m)^{(-1.351\ +\ 0.064\ SCHRATE)}$ $Y^{0.823}$ $PROF^{0.894}$ $RES^{-0.069}$ $A^{-0.012}$ $CSA^{0.092}$ $TIT1^{0.052}$ $OTHFED^{-0.010}$ $e^{-2.27}$
       (0.074)    (0.778) (0.643)      (0.174)   (0.042)   (0.063) (0.018)   (0.043)   (0.017)    (0.015)   (1.57)

    $SEE$ = 73.45

    $R^2$ = 0.7103

iii.   $TREV=$ 6.583 P - (483.6 - 15.6 SCHRATE) (1 + m) + 0.068 Y + 428 PROF - 123 RES - 0.533 A + 0.733 CSA + 5.934 TIT1
       (1.529) (211.8) (4.64)          (0.154)   (185)    (53)    (0.378)   (748)     (1.183)

      + 0.526 OTHFED - 0.000000175 POP·LNER + 395
      (0.176)       (0.000000096)     (252)

    $SEE$ = 77.40

    $R^2$ = 0.6971

A third test is possible, based on the elasticities of equation (7.16) rather than on partial derivatives. Equation (ii) is a log-linear specification for local revenue, and the parameters are estimates of elasticities. From these estimates the left-hand side of equation (7.16) is 0.8534 at the sample mean; the right-hand side becomes 0.1315. The difference is significant at better than the .1 percent level, as the corresponding $t$-statistic is 3.43. As in the previous two tests, the two sides of equation (7.16) can be equal only with variable values which are far outside the range of observed values. Hence the validity of the three tests of equation (7.12) is rather conclusive, since the results do not depend on any particular formulation. We can therefore reject the hypothesis that districts respond to their "effective property base" $(1 + m) \cdot P$ and accept the hypothesis that they react "rationally" to the price effect embodied in the matching rate.

If this result had no policy implications, then it would be rather irrelevant in view of the fact that courts and legislatures are now in the midst of forming new state aid programs. However, the first model implies, as mentioned earlier, that *any* district power equalizing formula will satisfy the *Serrano* mandate. That is, it does not matter what value $k$ takes on, since "effective" property valuation will be $(1 + k/P - 1) \cdot P = k$ for each district, and therefore constant among districts. However, the second model implies that $k$ must take on a precise value if the present correlation between revenues and property valuation is to be eliminated. If $R$ is a function of $P$ (the "income" effect) and $\tau$ (the price $1/(1 + m)$) then the following must hold:[52]

$$\frac{dR}{dP} = \frac{\partial R}{\partial P} + \frac{\partial R}{\partial \tau} \cdot \frac{\partial \tau}{\partial P} \tag{7.17}$$

For the correlation between $P$ and $R$ to be zero, $dR/dP$ must be zero, implying that

$$\frac{\partial \tau}{\partial P} = \left. \frac{-\partial R}{\partial P} \middle/ \frac{\partial R}{\partial \tau} \right. \tag{7.18}$$

and implying in turn that matching rate $m$ in a DPE formula satisfying this requirement must be

$$m = \frac{1}{C - \left( \frac{\partial R}{\partial P} \middle/ \frac{R}{\partial \tau} \right) \cdot P} - 1 \tag{7.19}$$

yielding, in the case where $C$ (a constant) is zero, a district power equalizing formula with

$$k = \frac{-\partial R}{\partial P} \Big/ \frac{\partial R}{\partial \tau} \ . \tag{7.20}$$

Thus, contrary to the implications of the first model, the value which $k$ assumes is critical to the outcome. If $k$ is lower than the value indicated in equation (7.20), some positive correlation between property valuation and revenue might remain; if higher than this value, a *negative* correlation would result.

The simulations in Chapter 8 indicate that the usual DPE formulas, where $k$ is usually at or above the state's mean property valuation per pupil, would result in a negative correlation. This result indicates that the price effect is much stronger than is usually thought—at least in Massachusetts—and that a state aid formula with greater variation in matching rates than those which have existed in the past would induce radical shifts in behavior, including attempts to circumvent the state aid formula, partial abandonment of public schools, and thorough changes in the behavioral patterns which underlie models such as that given in equation (7.8).

In Massachusetts, the magnitude of the price effect is presumably known, so that school finance policies can consider the strength of this effect. However, there is little reason to believe that behavioral parameters estimated for one state can be assumed to hold for other states. Because of the problems which make the estimation of price effects difficult, few states can obtain information on the likely reaction to the price effects implicit in district power equalizing formula.

In sum, it is empirically inappropriate to view districts as responding to the "effective property base" of a matching grant program. Instead, as we have done in the text, district behavior conforms to that expected from the application of a utility model, in the sense that districts react appropriately— and in quite different ways—to price and income effects.

### Notes

1. "School Funds and State Aid for Public Schools," Chapter 70 of the General Laws of the Commonwealth of Massachusetts, enacted 1966 with subsequent amendments.
2. See Chapter 5 or Benson (17). The passage of a percentage equalizing plan in Massachusetts is generally attributed to Benson's influence.
3. The price effect resulting from the matching provisions of construction aid were not specifically considered, in the way price effects from the CH70 formula were, largely because of data unavailability: data on both state construction aid and local construction expenditures are not published.

Failure to consider this price effect appears to be of little import, since there is relatively little variation among districts in the matching rate for construction: the matching rate has a floor of 0.40 and a ceiling of 0.50, varying inversely with property valuation. See Johns (129), p. 135.

4. Oral communication, Mr. Robert Jeffrey, Massachusetts Department of Education.

5. If there are infinitely many communities among which individuals and firms may choose, then one can always find a community where taxes accurately reflect the value of local public services to that family (or firm). In this case there will be no reason for taxes and expenditures to be reflected in property values. The capitalization of taxes and expenditures is thus due in part to the fact there are relatively few communities among which one might choose.

6. For the development of this the theory, see Tiebout (254). An application of Tiebout's model to property value in northern New Jersey, with estimated equations similar to those we will present here, is that of Oates (196).

7. Expenditures on schools, for example, could be perceived as a measure of the social class of children, or of the attitudes of adults, or of the political power of parents, and mobility patterns may be affected by these factors. For further discussion, see Chapter 8 and Appendix 8A.

8. The ratio of assessed valuation to market valuation is referred to as the *assessment ratio*. Even within a community, different kinds of property are assessed at different ratios: commercial property and low-valued property appear to be assessed at higher ratios, making the property tax more regressive than it otherwise would be (Oldman and Aaron [198]). Important as this may be to the incidence of the property tax and to taxpayer response to local expenditure decisions (see Barlow [11]), it is extremely difficult to quantify.

9. Property is evaluated locally and converted to an "equalized value" through assessment ratios calculated by the Massachusetts State Tax Commission. This process is somewhat mysterious: it is as difficult as assessing itself, especially since districts vary in the amounts of property which are sold in any period of time. But it is less overt and, although we have no evidence to this effect, it is obviously subject to political pressures. One has to hold as a hypothesis, though the hypothesis may be false, that $PROP_i$ for state school aid is somewhat manipulable.

   Rothenberg (223) has recalculated assessment ratios for a sample of twenty-one communities in the Boston area, with considerable divergence from the state's assessment ratios in some cases. When we estimate our model for the twenty-one districts using state assessment ratios and using Rothenberg's values, the estimates are almost precisely the same.

10. More detail on these procedures and the rationale for them can be found

in any but the most elementary econometrics text. See, for example, Johnston (130).

11. Corroborating evidence supporting the existence of lag in expenditures comes from expenditure functions for California unified school districts, estimated by Grubb with Jack Osman. When 1969-70 school revenues or expenditures are regressed on 1969 district income from the 1970 census, the coefficient of income is insignificantly different from zero. However, when 1971-72 revenue and expenditure data are regressed on 1969 income, the coefficient is significant and positive as expected.

12. For example, Sharkansky calculates the correlation between the level of state government expenditure in 1965 and in 1952 to be 0.85. See Sharkansky (234), Table III-1.

13. The relatively lower correlation for POOR is due to the fact that, with increasing incomes, a family income of $3,000 in 1960 represents a different level of poverty than $3,000 in 1970.

14. See the discussion of local noneducational revenue below.

15. Readers who are interested in even more detail on equation specification and estimation than provided here and in Appendix 7A should consult Grubb (90).

16. There are two exceptions to this statement: The variable ED and PROF are substituted for each other to see which better captures the "preference for education" effect. Variables describing nonlinear price effects were also found by experimentation.

17. In fact, the peculiar estimate of the price elasticity from equation i comes from that aspect of the utility function specification to which we objected. The price elasticity of equation i depends critically on the parameter of Y in the denominator, $-0.017$. However, there is little reason to suspect that this parameter will pick up the price effect rather than a nonlinear effect of income on LEDR. Similarly, in Stern's (243) formulation, OWNED appears in the denominator and its coefficient is a crucial element of the price elasticity. In our estimation OWNED appeared in the numerator rather than the denominator; and it seems reasonable that Stern's parameter estimate reflects the influence of homeownership on local revenue rather than the price effect.

18. These are presented in Grubb (90), Ch. 3. They differ from equation ii in having different variables as arguments of $\partial LEDR/\partial PROP$.

19. The introduction of the school tax rate increases the explanatory power of the equation greatly, as comparison of the $R^2$'s and standard errors from equations iii and iv indicate. The coefficient of the school tax rate in equation iv is estimated by an iterative technique, and therefore has no standard error calculated for it. However, from other specifications in which a standard error was calculated, the $t$-statistic associated with the school tax rate varies from about 1.5 to over 2. See Grubb (90), Ch. 3.

20. The fact that SCHRATE appears on the right-hand side of equation iv (and, in the log-linear specification, on the right side of equation [v]) might seem to reflect a tautology. Since LEDR = PROP $\cdot$ SCHRATE, $\partial$LEDR/$\partial$SCHRATE = PROP, which is always positive; and similarly, $\partial$LEDR/$\partial$SCHRATE from equations iv and v is positive. However, in the linear form this partial derivative is precisely $\partial$LEDR/$\partial$SCHRATE = $\beta_1 \cdot m \cdot$ LEDR where $\beta_1$ is the estimated coefficient and is positive. If $m \cdot$ LEDR were highly collinear with PROP, then we might have reason to fear a spurious association causing the appearance of SCHRATE as a variable in $\partial$LEDR/$\partial(m \cdot$ LEDR). However, the correlation coefficient between m $\cdot$ LEDR and PROP is *negative* (–0.411). Similarly, from the log-linear specification in equation iv, $\partial$LEDR/$\partial$SCHRATE = $-B$ log (PRICE) $\cdot$ LEDR, and the correlation coefficient between this and PROP is – 0.420. Hence there is no danger that the appearance of SCHRATE as an argument of the price effect is due to spurious association.

21. Note, however, that the simple correlation coefficient between LEDR and RES is slightly positive, 0.093.

22. For example, Barlow (11) used a measure of the response of districts to property composition to reflect price response to a state aid program.

23. See Grubb (90), Ch. 3. Equation iii of Table 7-3 was in fact the only linear additive specification in which LNER added nothing to the explanatory power of the regression.

24. See, for example, Callahan, Wilken, and Sillerman (43).

25. The correlation between ED and PROF is 0.792.

26. This is explained in W. Norton Grubb, "Wealth, Price and Income Effects in Local School Finance," paper delivered at meetings of the American Educational Research Association in April 1974. This paper is being revised for publication.

27. The example of Massachusetts, with income more important than property value, is far from universal. At the opposite extreme, income makes no significant difference at all to revenue variations in South Carolina. California is an example of a state where both are important, but property is more important than income. One can hypothesize that these differences among states are due to the number of relative size of districts within a state, but it would be impossible to test this hypothesis without well-specified revenue equations for a large number of states.

28. The average school matching rate is 0.1676, so the price of school services is 1/1.1676 or 0.856. From equation ix the average matching rate for nonschool revenue is 0.14, with a price of 1/1.14 = 0.877.

29. Another finding related to the effect of property should be noted. Unlike the case of LEDR, property composition (RES) does not significantly affect LNER. This indicates that any tendency for towns with high proportions of nonresidential property to raise higher tax revenues because of a lower "price" to residents is offset by a tendency for towns with

high percentages of residential property to raise more revenue for non-school purposes, *ceteris paribus*. It seems reasonable that this is due to differences in the composition of nonschool services among communities: those with concentrations of nonresidential property may have to spend more for utilities, road maintenance, and services to poorer residents, while those with high proportions of residential property spend relatively more for parks, recreation facilities, and libraries. Such consumption patterns hold within towns; see Benson and Lund (19). But without more detailed data on the composition of LNER, it is impossible to test this hypothesis.

30. Devout economists would insist that this constitutes an equilibrium, but that prices are different for big cities—for example, the price of failing to provide police protection is larger—and the community responds rationally to these prices. We will not pursue this semantic debate, but prefer the disequilibrium terminology to emphasize that some conditions are *imposed* on large cities—partly by suburban zoning laws, restrictive covenants, prices of land and labor-market structures—and that the consequent limitation of choices distorts the operation of preferences.

31. Brazer (35) also found nonschool revenues negatively related to population growth and suggested the interpretation of a lag in service levels.

32. See ACIR (4).

33. In a log-linear specification for LNER, the price entered significantly, but as a function of Y rather than PROF. The interpretation is essentially the same: that sensitivity to price increases with socioeconomic status.

34. At the mean plus one standard deviation of PROF, the comparable fall in LNER would be $12.

35. While it is plausible that this is due to either better information or political pressure for more effective local government in such jurisdictions, the statistical results can only indicate the presence of such effects and cannot distinguish between these explanations.

36. In the most rational of worlds this would help explain why the price effect on LNER was not stronger: shifting from nonschool to school services may provide a dollar of services for less cost, but may return less in increased property value. Whether this actually happens seems doubtful.

37. Industrial enclaves are usually cited as examples. However, in the Massachusetts sample the correlation between PROP and RES is an insignificant −0.042.

38. See Chapter 9 and Michelson (175).

39. In addition, in one specification for LOCR, PROF entered as an argument of the price effect on local school revenue, with high socioeconomic status districts exhibiting greater responsiveness to price variations. See Grubb (90), Ch. 3.

40. While this may seem implausible, conversation with officials of the Massachusetts Department of Education, in the course of collecting data and clarifying its meaning, indicated that most of them had a very imperfect idea of how the Chapter 70 formula works. Each year the state department mimeographs the information required to compute the matching rate for each district, along with an explanation of the operation of the formula. However, this information does not include the matching rate itself, so the fact that most districts face an effective price different from one is not obvious. In addition, it is unclear how widespread the circulation of this information is. No attempt was made to interview local school administrators to determine directly whether they were aware of the price effects of the Chapter 70 formula.

41. As evidence of this, several large school districts hire administrators to maximize receipts of federal funds.

42. For an analysis of these changes and their distributive effects, see Daniere (61).

43. In this expression, property valuation per school-age child is used instead of valuation per pupil in public schools.

44. The floor and the ceiling are specified to be 75 percent and 115 percent of the state average reimburseable expenditure.

45. For more detail see Grubb (90), Appendix 3A, or Stern (243).

46. The reason is that two-stage least squares uses a linear additive form for the first-stage estimation, whereas the crucial variation in the matching rate is a nonlinear function of both property valuation and local revenue. Some results with $m$ endogenous are reported in Grubb (90), Ch. 3. The price and income effects are generally of absurd magnitudes.

47. For other such regressions, see Grubb (90), Ch. 3.

48. For example, see Musgrave and Musgrave (191), pp. 614-20.

49. Formally, total differentiation of the first-order conditions from equation (7.12) yields the following different expressions:

$$\frac{\frac{\partial R}{\partial m}}{P} = \frac{(1+m)}{P}\ \frac{\partial L}{\partial m} + \frac{L}{P} = \left(\frac{W_{22}\,L}{(1+m)P^3} - \frac{W_1}{P}\right) \Bigg/ \left(W_{11}(1+m) + \frac{W_{22}}{(1+m)P^2}\right)$$

$$\frac{\frac{\partial R}{\partial P}}{(1+m)} = \frac{\partial L}{\partial P} + \frac{L}{(1+m)}\ \frac{\partial m}{\partial P} + \left(\frac{W_{22}\,L}{(1+m)^2P^3}\right) \Bigg/ \left(W_{11}(1+m) + \frac{W_{22}}{(1+m)P^2}\right)$$

$$+ \frac{L}{(1+m)}\ \frac{\partial m}{\partial P}$$

50. The results in Table 7B-1 are not the best specifications for estimating price and income effects, but they are better suited to testing the hypotheses of this appendix than are the specifications of Table 7-3.

51. The value of $\partial m/\partial P$ is given by the formula for general school aid in Massachusetts; it is not stochastic and is not therefore estimated. Its value is – 0.0233 for districts other than those affected by one of the many ceiling or floors in the formula; most of these effectively receive nonmatching and, so $\partial m/\partial P = 0$. ($P$ is measured in thousands of dollars.)

52. For additional detail on the following derivation, see Grubb (90), Ch. 5, or Feldstein (75).

## Appendix 7 C: Means, Standard Deviations and Correlation Coefficients for the Massachusetts Sample

**Table 7C-1**
**Means and Standard Deviations**

|  | Unweighted | | Weighted by NAM | |
|  | Mean | Standard Deviation | Mean | Standard Deviation |
| --- | --- | --- | --- | --- |
| LEDR | 619.72 | 143.29 | 636.22 | 157.14 |
| CH70 | 106.51 | 37.00 | 113.77 | 39.65 |
| CSA | 50.61 | 26.19 | 46.85 | 31.44 |
| LNER | 530.14 | 264.80 | 693.92 | 422.66 |
| NESA | 148.07 | 65.51 | 182.51 | 98.55 |
| SCHRATE | 18.82 | 5.05 | 19.33 | 4.55 |
| NERATE | 19.92 | 9.44 | 27.67 | 19.62 |
| PROP | 27.83 | 11.93 | 27.066 | 9.51 |
| A | 39.02 | 51.81 | 33.01 | 48.32 |
| M | 0.168 | 0.168 | 0.195 | 0.171 |
| PRICE | 0.874 | 0.121 | 0.854 | 0.123 |
| TIT1 | 8.95 | 8.04 | 14.26 | 13.96 |
| OTHFED | 28.71 | 39.42 | 31.80 | 32.19 |
| Y | 5981 | 707.31 | 6037 | 896.91 |
| POOR | 0.108 | 0.046 | 0.111 | 0.046 |
| AFDC | 0.056 | 0.058 | 0.101 | 0.124 |
| PROF | 0.133 | 0.059 | 0.136 | 0.057 |
| ED | 11.33 | 1.36 | 11.42 | 1.34 |
| CHILD | 0.212 | 0.051 | 0.199 | 0.049 |
| OWNED | 0.702 | 0.169 | 0.626 | 0.204 |
| POPGROWTH | 0.513 | 3.099 | 0.235 | 1.701 |
| MAN | 0.404 | 0.231 | 0.383 | 0.199 |
| POP | 31559 | 56129 | 101465 | 174812 |
| POPDEN | 2962 | 5763 | 4801 | 5456 |
| SOUND | 0.887 | 0.065 | 0.884 | 0.062 |
| RES | 0.737 | 0.132 | 0.700 | 0.128 |
| NAM | 6216 | 9489 | 20610 | 26548 |

**Table 7C-2**
**Correlation Coefficients**

| | LEDR | CH70 | CSA | LNER | NESA | SCHRATE | NERATE | PROP | A | M | PRICE | TIT1 | OTHFED | Y | POOR |
|---|---|---|---|---|---|---|---|---|---|---|---|---|---|---|---|
| LEDR | 1 | -.543 | .525 | .065 | -.042 | .071 | -.204 | .644 | .071 | -.419 | .411 | -.262 | -.173 | .802 | .455 |
| CH70 | -.499 | 1 | -.311 | .316 | .443 | .522 | .630 | -.751 | -.218 | .691 | -.679 | .601 | .024 | -.593 | .523 |
| CSA | .280 | -.030 | 1 | -.284 | -.397 | .258 | -.307 | .165 | .155 | -.288 | .286 | -.368 | -.122 | .622 | -.353 |
| LNER | .326 | -.173 | -.284 | 1 | .915 | .060 | .893 | .126 | -.175 | .244 | -.227 | .846 | .097 | -.258 | .482 |
| NESA | .186 | -.022 | -.478 | .777 | 1 | .080 | .860 | .046 | -.197 | .336 | -.317 | .877 | .140 | -.359 | .601 |
| SCHRATE | .010 | .538 | .298 | .379 | -.329 | 1 | .315 | -.567 | -.081 | .344 | -.324 | .177 | .080 | .066 | .031 |
| NERATE | -.148 | .443 | -.245 | .659 | .496 | .116 | 1 | -.297 | -.251 | .488 | -.467 | .903 | .146 | -.420 | .575 |
| PROP | .541 | -.703 | -.105 | .534 | .471 | -.654 | -.216 | 1 | .148 | -.556 | .547 | -.226 | -.137 | .472 | -.260 |
| A | .002 | -.022 | .091 | -.048 | -.076 | -.015 | -.093 | .148 | 1 | -.816 | .843 | -.175 | -.152 | .160 | -.142 |
| M | -.367 | .561 | -.112 | -.104 | .009 | .306 | .297 | -.441 | -.790 | 1 | -.996 | .423 | .178 | -.453 | .398 |
| PRICE | .350 | -.550 | .102 | .105 | -.006 | -.297 | -.285 | .431 | .821 | -.994 | 1 | -.140 | -.149 | .450 | -.378 |
| TIT1 | -.158 | .300 | -.308 | .622 | .605 | -.127 | .726 | -.016 | -.011 | .145 | -.140 | 1 | .148 | -.535 | .752 |
| OTHFED | -.158 | -.142 | -.025 | -.065 | -.039 | -.001 | -.010 | -.109 | -.111 | .047 | -.029 | .011 | 1 | -.163 | .263 |
| Y | .654 | -.410 | .288 | -.037 | -.205 | .117 | -.284 | .212 | .062 | -.300 | .298 | -.468 | -.095 | 1 | -.683 |
| POOR | -.312 | .143 | -.245 | .258 | .408 | -.232 | .299 | .085 | -.045 | .134 | -.125 | .579 | .155 | -.657 | 1 |
| AFDC | -.199 | .325 | -.292 | .640 | .644 | -.117 | .790 | -.018 | -.062 | .206 | -.200 | .926 | -.008 | -.482 | .547 |
| PROF | .637 | -.469 | .261 | .045 | -.174 | .061 | -.239 | .265 | .018 | -.315 | .305 | -.385 | .068 | .762 | -.565 |
| ED | .554 | -.431 | .258 | -.033 | -.251 | .131 | -.257 | .221 | -.057 | -.237 | .224 | -.473 | .099 | .680 | -.577 |
| CHILD | .049 | -.105 | .428 | -.535 | -.610 | .319 | -.377 | -.232 | .005 | -.048 | .043 | -.550 | .238 | .249 | -.357 |
| OWNED | .158 | -.167 | .383 | -.620 | -.643 | .256 | -.611 | -.084 | .027 | -.113 | .101 | -.706 | -.119 | .434 | -.451 |
| POPGROWTH | -.008 | -.012 | -.092 | -.072 | -.025 | .015 | -.033 | -.057 | -.052 | .016 | -.028 | -.065 | -.031 | .078 | -.019 |
| MAN | -.339 | .337 | -.115 | -.163 | -.001 | .072 | .070 | -.354 | -.048 | .268 | -.261 | .091 | -.086 | -.276 | .094 |
| POP | -.008 | .183 | -.193 | .556 | .492 | .044 | .704 | -.038 | -.071 | .132 | -.127 | .605 | .056 | -.093 | .155 |
| POPDEN | .088 | -.029 | -.282 | .412 | .309 | -.119 | .388 | .060 | -.096 | .030 | -.036 | .306 | -.027 | .065 | .044 |
| SOUND | .394 | -.378 | .119 | .065 | -.062 | -.219 | -.265 | .418 | .160 | -.363 | -.357 | -.319 | -.303 | .502 | -.412 |
| RES | .094 | -.000 | .168 | -.249 | -.254 | .194 | .244 | -.042 | .097 | -.087 | .086 | -.307 | -.138 | .349 | -.192 |
| NAM | .076 | .130 | -.095 | .408 | .347 | .067 | .542 | -.077 | -.077 | .107 | -.105 | .436 | .052 | .052 | .036 |

NOTE: Correlation matrix: coefficients below the diagonal are unweighted; coefficients above the diagonal are weighted by NAM (net average membership).

**Table 7C-2 (Continued)**

| | AFDC | PROF | ED | CHILD | OWNED | POPGROWTH | MAN | POP | POPDEN | SOUND | RES | NAM |
|---|---|---|---|---|---|---|---|---|---|---|---|---|
| LEDR | -.253 | .743 | .692 | .184 | .262 | .004 | -.370 | -.108 | -.045 | .482 | .202 | .034 |
| CH70 | .615 | -.579 | -.553 | -.368 | -.503 | .044 | .181 | .529 | .281 | .582 | -.218 | .432 |
| CSA | -.317 | .464 | .482 | .507 | .461 | .002 | -.262 | -.245 | -.353 | .322 | .379 | -.223 |
| LNER | .874 | -.139 | -.174 | -.679 | -.776 | -.103 | -.287 | .854 | .755 | -.391 | -.232 | .634 |
| NESA | .895 | -.288 | -.327 | -.740 | -.828 | -.089 | -.149 | .846 | .676 | -.472 | -.278 | .677 |
| SCHRATE | .238 | .053 | .086 | .126 | -.021 | -.002 | -.107 | .328 | .013 | -.230 | .125 | .262 |
| NERATE | .958 | -.328 | -.317 | -.589 | -.765 | -.086 | .201 | .942 | .700 | -.554 | -.229 | .724 |
| PROP | -.253 | .464 | .394 | -.073 | .112 | -.029 | -.283 | -.222 | .001 | .462 | .078 | -.187 |
| A | -.206 | .145 | .042 | .110 | .180 | -.001 | .035 | -.235 | -.192 | .252 | .239 | -.304 |
| M | .451 | -.465 | -.372 | -.259 | -.390 | -.031 | .126 | .415 | .255 | -.493 | -.285 | .395 |
| PRICE | -.430 | .455 | .359 | .245 | .369 | .022 | -.125 | -.396 | -.245 | -.484 | .287 | -.395 |
| TIT1 | .969 | -.434 | -.483 | -.701 | -.852 | -.106 | -.104 | .842 | .664 | -.619 | -.300 | .620 |
| OTHFED | .156 | -.041 | -.037 | .075 | -.190 | -.051 | -.053 | .176 | .028 | -.311 | -.134 | .093 |
| Y | -.497 | .790 | .785 | .449 | .564 | .063 | -.330 | -.304 | -.241 | .647 | .461 | -.118 |
| POOR | .690 | -.642 | -.715 | -.586 | -.715 | -.064 | .108 | .461 | .343 | -.690 | -.280 | .250 |
| AFDC | 1 | -.415 | -.425 | -.650 | -.817 | -.095 | -.145 | .924 | .665 | -.605 | -.251 | .681 |
| PROF | -.430 | 1 | .842 | .469 | .513 | .063 | -.372 | -.213 | -.145 | .578 | .419 | -.085 |
| ED | -.475 | .792 | 1 | .572 | .570 | .063 | -.452 | -.175 | -.137 | .545 | .405 | .005 |
| CHILD | -.537 | .364 | .527 | 1 | .804 | -.061 | -.143 | -.500 | -.634 | .384 | .365 | -.328 |
| OWNED | -.727 | .412 | .491 | .592 | 1 | .147 | -.104 | -.649 | -.629 | .570 | .493 | -.481 |
| POPGROWTH | -.064 | .070 | .065 | -.241 | .137 | 1 | .087 | -.061 | .356 | .048 | .098 | -.077 |
| MAN | .132 | -.347 | -.418 | -.244 | -.271 | .130 | 1 | -.269 | -.200 | -.046 | -.313 | -.217 |
| POP | .714 | -.051 | -.078 | -.332 | -.414 | .067 | -.017 | 1 | .638 | -.471 | -.160 | .824 |
| POPDEN | .298 | .097 | .055 | -.459 | -.247 | .752 | .005 | .373 | 1 | -.302 | -.273 | .482 |
| SOUND | -.316 | .424 | .417 | .094 | .295 | .014 | -.165 | -.114 | .001 | 1 | .277 | -.274 |
| RES | -.313 | .292 | .331 | .233 | .454 | .088 | -.310 | -.197 | -.118 | .174 | 1 | -.221 |
| NAM | .507 | .039 | .046 | -.168 | -.296 | -.059 | -.059 | .821 | .210 | -.031 | -.185 | 1 |

# 8

## School Revenue Distributions Under
## Alternative State Aid Formulas

This chapter concludes the statistical work of this book. Based on three equations describing school district behavior, we will investigate what each district's local and total school revenue per pupil would be under different state aid formulas. This allows us to compare the current Massachusetts state school aid plan with obvious alternatives and to speculate on the effects of major reforms. We will concentrate on three alternative state aid formulations: a flat grant (no matching aid), district power equalizing (matching aid only), and restricted DPE (a flat grant with marginal matching aid).

The text presents the simplest possible simulations based on the equations of Chapter 7. In Appendix 8A we have simulated more complex interactions, including the effects of an endogenous school tax rate and of permitting changes in property value in response to educational expenditures and taxes. No qualititive conclusions are affected by the choice of text or appendix procedures.

### The Limits of Simulation

We should not present these simulations without some warning about the extent to which they are believable as predictions. Like all others, these simulations are designed to estimate what would happen in a different world from the one of our observations. There are two major weaknesses in interpreting the results too literally.

First of all, the model of Chapter 7 was estimated using variables within a given range, approximately described by the means and standard deviations in Appendix 7C. As a description of actual behavior, the model is strictly valid only for variables within that range, since behavior outside the range is not observed and cannot affect the parameters of the model.[1] In these simulations, on the other hand, we will often want to investigate state aid programs with parameters outside the range of parameters in the CH70 formula—or, for that matter, outside the range of any state's formula. In particular, we will want to simulate situations in which flat grants from the state far exceed current grant levels, and in which matching rates are allowed to be negative—as they would be under the pure form of district power equalizing.

There are three dangers to the simulations of values outside the range of observation. The first is that, since the error of any regression increases as one moves away from the means of the independent variables,[2] the expected error of the predicted variable (revenue) will be relatively larger for variables outside the range of observation. Nonetheless, our regression estimates show one possible state of the world, our best guess at the behavior of school districts. The second problem is more serious: it may well be that district behavior itself changes when exogenous variables are very different. This would make statistical estimates of current behavior irrelevant. We outlined one such possibility at the end of the previous chapter: Differences in informations flows under alternative DPE formulas might change behavior patterns. Alternatively, citizens of wealthy districts might abandon public schools if a thoroughly equalizing plan of any sort were instituted. Third, behavior may change because of the very process of changing fiscal structures. Current behavior, as we have stressed in earlier chapters, is a function not only of the current institutional setting but of its historical development. Reactions to school finance formulations might differ among states because of expectations and behavior generated by present formulations. This would be another example of the famous "Hawthorne effect," in which experimentation per se was found to produce behavioral response, independently from the specifics of the experiment.

A second major weakness in simulation is reliance on a model which is surely imperfect. The model of the previous chapter is static rather than dynamic, and therefore the simulations must abstract from the time patterns of district reactions. Certain kinds of behavior are likely to be imperfectly reflected in the model. In particular, if people choose municipal service levels by their mobility, as well as through their votes, a school finance program strong enough to affect the distribution of revenues would induce a redistribution of the population with the possibility that all socioeconomic variables would change. Finally, our equations explain only from two-thirds to three-fourths of the variance in local revenue per pupil. While this is more than respectable explanatory power, it raises the possibility that currently unobtainable variables would explain some of the remaining variance, and that our simulations without these variables are systematically biased. In addition, the presence of random elements in district behavior will make the comparison of simulations somewhat awkward, as will be described below.

If we thought these caveats destroyed the usefulness of simulations, there would be no point in proceeding. But this is not the case. The complexities of estimated district behavior are great enough that simulations prove to be necessary simply to follow the logical implications of the model. The simulations enable us to understand behavioral interactions and implications which might otherwise not be noticed.

### Evaluative Statistics

The limitations of simulation imply that predictions for individual districts would suffer from greater error than would predictions about revenue distributions in the aggregate. The simulations will therefore be described by a set of summary statistics rather than by isolating individual districts for exposition. Because of our interest in the extent of inequality per se, the initial statistic is the Gini coefficient, previously used in Chapters 3 and 4. Three statistics describe patterns in the simulated inequalities, as distinct from the amount of inequality. The first of these compares the expected revenues for the children of wealthy parents and for the children of poor parents,[3] as a measure of the social-class bias in revenue distributions. The second is the correlation between district property value and total revenue, and the third is the correlation between district income and total revenue. A final statistic descriptive of the patterns in revenue distributions is average total revenue for Massachusetts cities,[4] to be compared with the average total revenue for the sample. The purpose of including this variable is to assess the fears that cities will be made relatively worse off under various alternative financing plans. In particular, we will simulate one DPE formula especially designed to help cities.

The final two statistics are the average total revenue per pupil for the sample and the average state revenue.[5] The average revenue per pupil is of interest as a measure of whether school resources will relatively increase or decrease under different policies. Finally, one of the variables of interest to legislatures is the cost to the state of any new program. The figure for average state revenues is a net figure, the calculation of state monies distributed to districts minus revenues collected in the finance plan, if any. It therefore represents revenues required from general state revenues and can be compared with the 1968-69 level of state support ($114 per pupil) as an indication of whether more or less state revenue would be required.

### Simulations: Flat Grants and District Power Equalizing

It would be incorrect to compare the results of simulated formulas with the original data, since the original data contains some random (unexplained) variation which the simulations do not. Therefore we first simulate the revenue distribution under the current formula.[6] Table 8-1 presents the evaluative statistics derived from the original data and those derived from simulations of equations iii, iv, and v of Table 7-3.[7]

The first obvious difference between the original data and the simulations is that the Gini is lower for the simulations. The reason is that the simulations eliminate one source of variation—the variation unexplained by the estimated regressions.[8] The second obvious difference is that the correlations between total revenue and both property value and income are higher for the simulations than for the original data. Again, this result is spurious, due to the elimination of unexplained variation from the simulations.[9]  Finally, the differences among the three regressions simulated are trivial, except that the log-linear specification (equation v) tends to underpredict total revenues.

The important point to be drawn from Table 8-1 is that since simulations systematically distort the summary statistics from the revenue distributions because of the elimination of random variance, it is invalid to compare simulations with the original data in Table 8-1.[10]  We will henceforth make all comparisons with the simulations of the original equations, presented in rows 2, 3, and 4.

### Flat Grant Programs

In Table 8-2 we present simulations for flat-grant programs at state aid levels of $0, $114, $142, and $800.[11]  The first simulation estimates the prior distribution, before any state aid, as explained in Chapter 3. The second simulation allows us to determine how different the distribution of state revenues is under the actual formula than it would be under a flat grant of the same average amount. The other two simulations indicate what results might be expected from a slightly higher flat grant and from an extremely high flat grant. With a flat grant only the income effect operates because there is no matching aid. From Chapter 7, the income effect varies among the three equations simulated from -0.19 to -0.74. Therefore we will be able to see what difference various estimates of this effect have on predicted results.

For all three equations, a flat grant at the current level of state support leads to a somewhat less equal distribution than the current percentage equalizing formula, and a somewhat higher correlation between total revenue and district income. That is, under a flat-grant program, districts add local revenue to state aid on the basis of income, wealth, socioeconomic status, and property composition. Even a moderately higher level of state aid ($142 per pupil), although it lowers the Gini coefficient, does not result in as equal a distribution as the current formula. However, the flat grant near the current level of *total* revenue substantially reduces inequality. That a flat grant is equalizing relative to a prior distribution with no state aid is obvious from Table 8-2.

It is unclear from these results whether the percentage equalizing formula in Massachusetts has been effective—since the distribution is more equal than the same amount of state aid distributed as a flat grant would produce—or ineffective.[12]  But we find the reduction in the Gini coefficient below that which would have been produced by a flat grant surprisingly small, given claims made for the equalizing effect of percentage equalizing formulas. This is an indication of how seriously the effect of a pure formula can be undermined by legislative modifications.

As we would expect from the argument of Chapter 4, increases in state aid

**Table 8-1**
**Simulations of the Current Formula**

| | Gini | $\dfrac{TER_{rich}}{TER_{poor}}$ | $\rho_{TER, PROP}$ | $\rho_{TER, Y}$ | $TER_{urban}$ | TER | State |
|---|---|---|---|---|---|---|---|
| *Original Data* | 0.0854 | 1.117 | 0.328 | 0.579 | 871 | 828 | 114 |
| *Equation iii* | 0.0648 | 1.089 | 0.459 | 0.716 | 882 | 834 | 114 |
| *Equation iv* | 0.0643 | 1.101 | 0.446 | 0.700 | 868 | 829 | 114 |
| *Equation v* | 0.0718 | 1.114 | 0.466 | 0.684 | 841 | 816 | 114 |

Note: "Rich" is defined as family income greater than $25,000.
"Poor" is defined as U.S. census poverty level (adjusted for family composition) or less.

**Table 8-2**
**Simulations of Flat Grants**

| | Gini | $\dfrac{TER_{rich}}{TER_{poor}}$ | $\rho_{TER,PROP}$ | $\rho_{TER,Y}$ | $TER_{urban}$ | TER | State |
|---|---|---|---|---|---|---|---|
| **I. Equation iii** | | | | | | | |
| 1. Data Estimates | 0.0645 | 1.089 | 0.455 | 0.713 | 882 | 834 | 114 |
| 2. $K = \$0$ | 0.0705 | 1.114 | 0.518 | 0.723 | 822 | 793 | 0 |
| 3. $K = \$114$ | 0.0679 | 1.109 | 0.518 | 0.723 | 852 | 823 | 114 |
| 4. $K = \$142$ | 0.0673 | 1.108 | 0.518 | 0.723 | 859 | 830 | 142 |
| 5. $K = \$800$ | 0.0544 | 1.086 | 0.472 | 0.691 | 1030 | 1005 | 800 |
| **II. Equation iv** | | | | | | | |
| 6. Data Estimates | 0.0643 | 1.101 | 0.446 | 0.700 | 868 | 829 | 114 |
| 7. $K = \$0$ | 0.0798 | 1.165 | 0.628 | 0.705 | 701 | 733 | 0 |
| 8. $K = \$114$ | 0.0722 | 1.149 | 0.628 | 0.705 | 778 | 810 | 114 |
| 9. $K = \$142$ | 0.0705 | 1.146 | 0.628 | 0.705 | 797 | 829 | 142 |
| 10. $K = \$800$ | 0.0458 | 1.094 | 0.628 | 0.705 | 1244 | 1276 | 800 |
| **III. Equation v** | | | | | | | |
| 11. Data Estimates | 0.0718 | 1.114 | 0.466 | 0.684 | 848 | 816 | 114 |
| 12. $K = \$0$ | 0.0996 | 1.204 | 0.659 | 0.685 | 664 | 714 | 0 |
| 13. $K = \$114$ | 0.0850 | 1.173 | 0.653 | 0.681 | 747 | 794 | 114 |
| 14. $K = \$142$ | 0.0821 | 1.167 | 0.652 | 0.681 | 774 | 821 | 142 |
| 15. $K = \$800$ | 0.0451 | 1.090 | 0.650 | 0.679 | 1421 | 1467 | 800 |

do reduce inequality among districts. However, the correlation coefficients remain unchanged because of the linear form of the income effect in these specifications.[13] In the extreme case where the state provides all revenue, these correlations would be zero;[14] but the simulations indicate that, at least up to $800 of state aid, many districts would still prefer to increase revenues.[15]

Finally, the differences among the three equations are small, despite different values of in the income effect. The income effect explains a relatively small percentage of the variation in local revenues, and therefore differences in the income change the predicted outcomes relatively little. Whether this pattern of behavior would remain constant if state grants as large as $800 were instituted remains a matter for speculation, but for the purposes of simulation we can ignore the differences among the three regressions.

### District Power Equalizing Programs

While flat-grant programs involve only an income effect, the pure district power equalizing formulas whose simulations are presented in Table 8-3 illustrate response to only a price effect.[16] The alternative formulas simulated represent two alternative parameters which the state could use. One ($27,066) is equivalent to the state average property valuation per pupil in the sample,[17] but requires only a small amount of net revenue from the state. The alternative, with $k = \$35,000$, illustrates a larger amount of state support.

The most striking figures in Table 8-3 are the negative correlations between total revenue and property. The relationship between wealth and school revenue has been reversed by the change in state aid formula. Yet the Gini coefficients show that the overall inequality *increases* with the introduction of a DPE formula. Furthermore, except for equation iii, the negative correlation between property and total revenue becomes stronger as state support increases, and the Gini increases as well.

The first conclusion to be drawn is that the price response of districts is so strong that, in conjunction with the price variation under typical district power equalizing formulas, DPE plans more than correct the present positive correlation between property valuation and revenues per pupil.[18] Secondly, district power equalizing shows no signs of reducing the Gini coefficient, despite changes in the correlation coefficients. Hence DPE formulas have the power to change the pattern of school finance inequities, but apparently not their absolute magnitude.

Both district power equalizing simulations also reduce the correlation between district income and total revenue, but not to as great an extent as the correlation with property valuation. In terms of the implications of DPE for poor children rather than for property-poor districts, this result is more important than the change in the correlation with property value. As the figures in column 2 of Table 8-3 indicate, district power equalizing does improve the position of poor children in terms of expected total resources.

Finally, increases in state aid raise average total revenues, as we would expect. As in the case of flat grants, the increase in total revenue per pupil is less than the increase in average state aid per pupil. Interestingly, row 6 of Table 8-3 indicates that a pure DPE formula with the same amount of state aid as the current program would result in higher average total revenue, $866 versus $829. A pure DPE formula with a price effect applicable to all districts succeeds in stimulating greater local revenue through the price effect than does the current formula, under which a zero matching rate applies to about half the districts in the sample.

### Modifications of District Power Equalizing

The DPE formulas simulated so far have been of the simplest form possible. There are limitless modifications which can be made to such formulas, some of which are designed to give greater equalizing power, and others designed to spare wealthy districts the full impact of DPE and therefore unequalizing—such as the modifications made in the CH70 formula. In this section, we will present simulations based on four of the possible modifications, the first two designed to benefit specific groups of districts, and the second two illustrative of "political" modifications.

Progressive district power equalizing represents an attempt to incorporate district income variations as well as property value differences into a DPE formula.[19] In this version, the matching rate varies inversely with district income as well as with property valuation,[20] so that districts which are poor in terms of income rather than property are better off than under the usual DPE formula. The results in Table 8-4 indicate that, as intended, such formulas decrease the correlation between district income and revenue more than do the usual ones. Again, the strength of the price response is illustrated by the fact that this correlation becomes negative. In addition, progressive DPE programs benefit poor children and urban districts relatively more.

The results of Chapter 7 indicated that local nonschool revenues reflect factors usually associated with urban communities—population, population density, and a concentration of poor families. Similarly, the ratio of the school tax rate to the total tax rate, denoted by $q$, is clearly related to the characteristics of cities in Massachusetts.[21] Hence a DPE formula intended to benefit cities could use the variable $q$ to modify the measure of "relative fiscal capacity" in a district power equalizing formula. The result of such an experiment,[22] presented in rows 3, 9, and 14 of Table 8-4, indicates that such a program would clearly benefit urban districts, which would spend 50 percent more than the state average. In addition, it also benefits children of poor families relative to

**Table 8-3**
**Simulations of District Power Equalizing**

| | Gini | $\dfrac{TER_{rich}}{TER_{poor}}$ | $\rho_{TER,PROP}$ | $\rho_{TER,Y}$ | $TER_{urban}$ | TER | State |
|---|---|---|---|---|---|---|---|
| **I. *Equation iii*** | | | | | | | |
| 1. Data Estimates | 0.0645 | 1.089 | 0.455 | 0.713 | 882 | 834 | 114 |
| 2. $K = \$27,066$ | 0.0731 | 1.007 | -0.612 | 0.357 | 907 | 809 | 29 |
| 3. $K = \$35,000$ | 0.0674 | 1.019 | -0.540 | 0.439 | 1004 | 904 | 205 |
| **II. *Equation iv*** | | | | | | | |
| 4. Data Estimates | 0.0643 | 1.101 | 0.446 | 0.700 | 868 | 829 | 114 |
| 5. $K = \$27,066$ | 0.0944 | 0.994 | -0.479 | 0.057 | 879 | 802 | 36 |
| 6. $K = \$30,000$ | 0.1004 | 0.996 | -0.531 | 0.099 | 968 | 865 | 114 |
| 7. $K = \$35,000$ | 0.1200 | 0.996 | -0.509 | 0.086 | 1122 | 980 | 242 |
| **III. *Equation v*** | | | | | | | |
| 8. Data Estimates | 0.0718 | 1.114 | 0.466 | 0.684 | 848 | 816 | 114 |
| 9. $K = \$27,066$ | 0.0867 | 1.017 | -0.365 | 0.136 | 851 | 787 | 24 |
| 10. $K = \$35,000$ | 0.1181 | 1.014 | -0.474 | 0.123 | 1103 | 976 | 236 |

**Table 8-4**
**Modifications to District Power Equalizing**

| | Equation iii | Gini | $\dfrac{TER_{rich}}{TER_{poor}}$ | $\rho_{TER,PROP}$ | $\rho_{TER,Y}$ | $TER_{urban}$ | $TER$ | $State$ |
|---|---|---|---|---|---|---|---|---|
| I. | | | | | | | | |
| 1. | Data Estimates | 0.0645 | 1.089 | 0.455 | 0.713 | 882 | 834 | 114 |
| 2. | Progressive DPE, $k = 27{,}066 \cdot \bar{y}$ | 0.0768 | 0.937 | -0.743 | -0.040 | 950 | 815 | 41 |
| 3. | DPE with Urban Factor | 0.0986 | 0.913 | -0.429 | 0.089 | 1107 | 867 | 137 |
| 4. | $k = 35{,}000$ with Non-Negative $m$ | 0.0636 | 1.042 | 0.067 | 0.574 | 1013 | 919 | 234 |
| 5. | $k = 35{,}000$ with Save-Harmless | 0.0634 | 1.045 | -0.031 | 0.586 | 1014 | 921 | 244 |
| II. | Equation iv | | | | | | | |
| 6. | Data Estimates | 0.0643 | 1.101 | 0.446 | 0.700 | 868 | 829 | 114 |
| 7. | Progressive DPE, $k = 27{,}066 \cdot \bar{y}$ | 0.1064 | 0.896 | -0.568 | -0.253 | 974 | 817 | 55 |
| 8. | Progressive DPE, $k = 29{,}200 \cdot \bar{y}$ | 0.1139 | 0.895 | -0.553 | -0.224 | 1047 | 868 | 114 |
| 9. | DPE with Urban Factor | 0.1747 | 0.800 | -0.347 | -0.179 | 1485 | 932 | 190 |
| 10. | $k = 35{,}000$ with Non-Negative $m$ | 0.1154 | 1.023 | -0.378 | 0.153 | 1132 | 994 | 272 |
| 11. | $k = 35{,}000$ with Save-Harmless | 0.1115 | 1.028 | -0.327 | 0.164 | 1134 | 1002 | 282 |
| III. | Equation v | | | | | | | |
| 12. | Data Estimates | 0.0718 | 1.114 | 0.466 | 0.684 | 848 | 816 | 114 |
| 13. | Progressive DPE, $k = 27{,}066 \cdot \bar{y}$ | 0.1005 | 0.912 | -0.462 | -0.243 | 951 | 808 | 43 |
| 14. | DPE with Urban Factor | 0.1827 | 0.800 | -0.197 | -0.156 | 1516 | 931 | 188 |
| 15. | $k = 35{,}000$ with Non-Negative $m$ | 0.1169 | 1.042 | -0.348 | 0.207 | 1111 | 990 | 268 |
| 16. | $k = 35{,}000$ with Save-Harmless | 0.1138 | 1.040 | -0.338 | 0.202 | 1112 | 994 | 279 |

those of rich families, and reduces the correlation between income and revenues more than the standard DPE formula does.[23]

A commonly accepted modification of district power equalizing is to truncate the matching rate at zero.[24] This means that wealthy districts need not remit revenues to the state, as they must under the pure form of DPE. Of the nine states which incorporated DPE provisions in their legislation during 1972-73, only one—Maine—presently provides for negative matching rates (commonly known as recapture), and Michigan will permit negative matching rates three years in the future. The simulations without recapture are presented in rows 4, 10, and 15 of Table 8-4. The modification decreases the impact of DPE on the correlations between revenue, income, and property valuation, as might be expected, but it has little effect on the Gini coefficient. Not surprisingly, one of its strongest effects is to increase greatly the required amount of state aid from general revenue. The modification is precisely what it intends to be—tax relief for wealthy districts.

A further modification, again reflecting a political reality, is to guarantee to each district nearly as much state aid in the new law as it received in the old. This is called a "save-harmless" provision.[25] Rows 5, 11, and 16 of Table 8-4 present the simulations of a DPE formula with the provision that each district receive at least 90 percent of 1968-69 state aid. The results are similar to those for the DPE formula with lack of recapture, since the most important effect of such a save-harmless clause would be to eliminate negative matching rates. However, even more state revenue is required under the save-harmless provision.

The only real generalization which can be made about the four modifications to district power equalizing described in Table 8-4 is that once we understand how the basic DPE formula affects district behavior and revenue distributions, the various modifications which can be devised for specific purposes have precisely the predicted effects. However, in the next section a major modification to DPE will be described for which this is not true, whose effects are not self-evident without the use of simulation.

In the simulations presented so far, the differences among the three equations have been small. We will therefore present the results only for equation iv in the more complex simulations in the rest of this chapter and in Appendix 8A. Not only did this equation have the best explanatory power, but in terms of simulations it gives results intermediate between the other two.

### Combining District Power Equalizing and Nonmatching Aid

The most serious problem with district power equalizing is that it fails to reduce revenue inequality. Because of the specific pattern of incentives and disincentives, DPE allows a number of districts to raise relatively small amounts of local revenue and to levy relatively low tax rates. Flat grants, on the other hand, have greater power to reduce inequalities among districts, but fail to change the patterns of these inequalities significantly—the same districts remain at the top and bottom as is currently true. An obvious solution is to combine nonmatching and matching aid, by setting a floor $t^*$ to the tax rate. Applying the district power equalizing formula

$$S_i + L_i = k \cdot t \qquad\qquad (8.1)$$

to the case where the tax rate is $t^*$, total local plus state revenue per pupil associated with the minimum tax rate is simply $k \cdot t^*$. Each district thus receives per pupil state aid of

$$S_i = (k - P_i)t^* \qquad\qquad (8.2)$$

under the minimum provision, where $P_i$ is the property value per pupil in district $i$. This amount is negative for districts with property valuation per pupil greater than $k$. But while districts can spend more than $k \cdot t^*$ per pupil by increasing their tax rate above $t^*$, they cannot lower either the tax rate below $t^*$ or the amount of local revenue generated below $t^* \cdot P_i$. Hence there is no price effect associated with the state aid of equation (8.2), since nothing the district can do will change this amount of state aid. Furthermore, the tax rate $t^*$ amounts to a statewide property tax, since all taxable property within the state is subject to at least that tax rate. Each district receives nonmatching aid equivalent to the amount in equation (8.2), plus an amount (positive or negative) which depends on the tax rate in excess of $t^*$.[26]

There are two different ways to visualize this process, and they imply different methods of simulation. The alternatives depend on how district residents perceive the flow of funds from the state under the minimum tax provision, which might in turn depend on how the school aid plan was administered. They might, on one hand, see the funds which they raise through the minimum tax, $t^* \cdot P_i$, as local funds, with nonmatching aid from the state being the difference between this amount and the entitlement $t^* \cdot k$, or $t^* \cdot (k - P_i)$. This is a "net flow" concept of the nonmatching aid.[27] On the other hand, they could conceive of $t^* \cdot P_i$ as a state tax which they pay regardless of what other resources are generated locally or received from the state for schooling, akin to any other state tax like the sales tax or income tax.[28] In this case, they would react to the entire amount $t^* \cdot k$ as a flat grant to the district. This is a somewhat myopic view, recognizing gross flows from the state but not the tax attached to these flows. Although conceptually weaker than the net flow version, it is simulated in the second part of Table 8-5.[29]

The tax constraints for the simulations of Table 8-5 are the mean tax rate, one-half, and one standard deviation above the mean. As expected, the initial

**Table 8-5**
**District Power Equalizing With Minimum Tax Rates**

| | | Gini | $\frac{TER_{rich}}{TER_{poor}}$ | $\rho_{TER,PROP}$ | $\rho_{TER,Y}$ | $TER_{urban}$ | $TER$ | State |
|---|---|---|---|---|---|---|---|---|
| I. | Equation iv | | | | | | | |
| 1. | DPE, $k=30,000$ | 0.1004 | 0.996 | -0.539 | 0.099 | 968 | 865 | 114 |
| II. | Net Flow | | | | | | | |
| 2. | $t* = 18.82$ | 0.0769 | 1.024 | -0.573 | 0.239 | 868 | 816 | 98 |
| 3. | $t* = 21.33$ | 0.0649 | 1.029 | -0.462 | 0.278 | 855 | 817 | 92 |
| 4. | $t* = 23.86$ | 0.0440 | 1.021 | -0.304 | 0.278 | 870 | 841 | 88 |
| III. | Gross Flow | | | | | | | |
| 5. | $t* = 18.82$ | 0.0519 | 1.013 | -0.330 | 0.202 | 717 | 687 | 71 |
| 6. | $t* = 21.33$ | 0.0283 | 1.004 | -0.192 | 0.132 | 754 | 737 | 72 |
| 7. | $t* = 23.86$ | 0.0220 | 0.996 | -0.157 | 0.003 | 828 | 809 | 79 |

effect of the tax constraint is to reduce the Gini coefficient. Increasing the minimum tax decreases the Gini. State aid (from general revenue) is lower, since the minimum constraint taxes wealthy districts which would have liked to respond to the high price for school funds with a tax lower than $t^*$. Raising their tax rate raises more net revenue for the state, reducing the need to draw general revenues into the system.

While imposing a required tax rate decreases state revenues, this constraint also increases the spending of wealthy districts, and thus—at least for $t^*$ greater than 18.82—increases the correlation between total revenues and property valuation. Similarly, the correlation between district income and revenue increases under a minimum tax, with undesirable consequences for poor children.

Average total revenues decrease under the minimum tax rate (although increasing $t^*$ increases average revenue because of the increase in required local revenue). The decrease is due to the truncation of the price effect, which would otherwise stimulate higher spending.[30] Furthermore, urban districts do relatively worse under the minimum tax rate. Once again, the price the system pays to get funds from wealthy districts is that these districts spend more on themselves, increasing the correlation between property and school revenues, and decreasing the relative flow of funds to urban areas.

Table 8-5 brings out the tradeoffs in the district power equalizing concept, tradeoffs which have been obscured in discussions focused on less specific measures of revenue distributions. When state support comes from *general* funds, residents of wealthy districts may pay large tax bills but they do not respond to these taxes as school districts. The dissociation of revenue raising from school district decisions means that general fund taxes (sales and income taxes, by and large) do not affect school decisions, which respond instead to the matching rate with which they can reclaim funds from the state. Under DPE, a good deal of revenue must be raised by inducing or forcing wealthy districts to tax themselves as districts. By making the price of funds high for these districts, enough revenue can be raised to increase total educational funds and reverse the relationship between property value and school revenues (Table 8-3). But overall inequality increases, because the wealthy districts reduce their tax rates and school expenditures. To counter this inequality, one immediately thinks of putting a floor on the tax rate. The results which follow reverse the previous gains, producing a positive correlation between income and school revenue, lower total school revenue, and a worsening of the relative flows to urban districts. We can begin to draw the conclusion that this is an arbitrary and unreliable way to manipulate results. If the state evaluates the results of its school finance program along more than one dimension—particularly, in terms of both overall inequality and the pattern of inequality—it will find manipulating district behavior via price and income adjustments a difficult way to achieve any desired goal. In general, the major difficulty with district power equalizing proposals is that they combine taxes with revenue distributions in a single formula. Manipulations of the formula have both tax and revenue effects, the results of which are obvious but not necessarily desirable when they are designed to favor special groups, but complex and unobvious when they combine several modifications.

*Effects of Alternate Formulas with State*
*Revenue Constant*

For comparative purposes, Table 8-6 summarizes the simulations of alternative state programs—a flat grant, a pure district power equalizing plan, and progressive DPE—which require the same amount of net state revenue as in 1968-69. That flat grants are more equalizing than the DPE formulas is clear, as are the changes in patterns of inequality induced by any of the DPE formulas. DPE clearly has a stimulative effect on average total revenues. However, none of the alternatives presented in Table 8-6 reduce inequalities among districts below that resulting from the present formula. For this to happen, either the state must constrain local behavior by imposing a higher minimum tax rate, as in Table 8-5, or it must directly limit local options.

### Judging the Outcomes

There remain two problems in applying these results to policy making. The first is empirical: while the information existed in Massachusetts for the estimation of price and income effects and the simulation of alternative programs, the estimation of price effects in almost all other states is either extremely difficult or simply impossible because of the lack of matching grants and therefore of price differences.[31] For Massachusetts it would be possible to develop a "menu" of alternative policies from which to choose,[32] but uncertainty about price responses means that in most states the effects of a school finance formulation which depends on manipulating district behavior will be unestimable in advance.

The conceptual difficulty in evaluating school finance reform proposals comes not so much from simulating their effects, but in judging these effects. The theory behind much of the current reform movement is that districts choose to spend on schools because of several factors. A district choice function can be presented as:

Total revenue = $F$ (wealth, income, preferences for education,
percentage of adults who have school-age                    (8.3)
children, . . .)

The dominant legal arguments have contended that the appearance of wealth (property value) in this function is illegitimate, that wealth should not appear

**Table 8-6**
**District Formulas with Equal State Aid**

| Equation iv | Gini | $\dfrac{TER_{rich}}{TER_{poor}}$ | $\rho_{TER, PROP}$ | $\rho_{TER, Y}$ | $TER_{urban}$ | $TER$ | State |
|---|---|---|---|---|---|---|---|
| 1. Current allocation | 0.0643 | 1.101 | 0.446 | 0.700 | 868 | 829 | 114 |
| 2. Flat Grant | 0.0722 | 1.149 | 0.628 | 0.705 | 778 | 810 | 114 |
| 3. DPE, $k = 30{,}000$ | 0.1004 | 0.996 | -0.531 | 0.099 | 968 | 865 | 114 |
| 4. Progressive DPE, $k = 29{,}200 - \bar{y}$ | 0.1139 | 0.895 | -0.553 | -0.224 | 1047 | 868 | 114 |

as an argument of the function $F$.[33]  The proponents of district power equalizing
have claimed that it would remove wealth from the function $F$: with a matching
rate $m = k/P - 1$, the yield per mill of tax is equivalent to that of a district with
property value per pupil of $(1 + m) \cdot P$ or $k$, and therefore $k$ rather than local
property value appears in the function $F$. We have argued in Appendix 7B that
this is an empirically inappropriate conception of how school districts behave.
But even if it were appropriate, a simulated revenue distribution indicates a
serious problem with the "equal property base" concept. Table 8-7 compares
the results under a DPE formula with $k = 30,000$ to the hypothetical distribution which would result if every district had a property base per pupil of
$35,000.

The two simulations predict very different results. Relative to DPE, the
constant property simulation reduces inequality, does not require as much
revenue from the state, and lowers average revenue per pupil. Most importantly,
it does not reduce the correlation between actual property value and revenue
to zero, even though variation in property did not enter the simulation. This
occurs because other variables in the function $F$ are correlated with property.[34]
The correlation with income increased and the relative position of poor children
worsened in this simulation. Even if income were held equal, there would
remain a correlation with income and property, because the socioeconomic
variables which induce school expenditures are correlated with income as well
as with property value.

The question remains: If we could devise a formula which removed wealth
effects in its *structure*, would that formula be acceptable if its effect were to
permit a correlation between wealth and school revenue? There are, in other
words, two concepts of the role of wealth: *de jure* and *de facto*. In the *de jure*
scheme, variation in property is not directly an argument in the choice function,
but a *de facto* correlation between property value and revenue may remain.
However, district power equalizing formulas do not necessarily result even in a
*de jure* elimination of the effects of wealth, as the argument of Appendix 7B
indicates.


## Conclusion

Although they seem designed to provide solutions to the mandate of no
wealth relation, DPE formulas do not necessarily eliminate either *de facto*
or *de jure* correlations between wealth and property valuation. Instead of
manipulating the "effective property base" of districts, DPE programs vary
the price of total revenues among districts. Responses to such manipulation
are not always obvious and are different from what one would predict on the
basis of equalizing "effective" property value. Of course, by modifying the
parameters of a DPE formula, elimination of either the *de facto* or the *de jure*

**Table 8-7**
**Comparison of DPE and "Constant Property" Simulations**

| Equation iv | Gini | $\dfrac{TER_{rich}}{TER_{poor}}$ | $\rho_{TER,PROP}$ | $\rho_{TER,Y}$ | $TER_{urban}$ | $TER$ | State |
|---|---|---|---|---|---|---|---|
| 1. Current Formula | 0.0643 | 1.101 | 0.446 | 0.700 | 868 | 829 | 114 |
| 2. DPE, $k = 30,000$ | 0.1004 | 0.996 | -0.531 | 0.099 | 968 | 865 | 114 |
| 3. Constant Property, PROP = $30,000 for All Districts | 0.0622 | 1.141 | 0.256 | 0.878 | 632 | 657 | n.c.[a] |

[a]Not computed.

relationship could be achieved, but there are two drawbacks to such a manipulation. First of all, it would have to be quite precise; that is, it would be necessary to choose a parameter $k$ with full knowledge of the effects of a DPE formula on district behavior.[35] This is impossible in most states because of the lack of information, and difficult in all others because of the errors and uncertainty associated with statistical models. But such manipulation would affect many other statistics which concern most individuals, especially the extent of overall inequality, the relative position of poor children, and the relative position of urban districts. Furthermore, the modifcations of district power equalizing which we have simulated in this chapter all involve unpleasant tradeoffs—between increased revenue equality at the expense of a biased pattern of inequality, between political acceptability and effectiveness in eliminating patterned inequality, between greater effectiveness and increased state revenues.

## Appendix 8 A: Simulations with Several Endogenous Variables

Given the presentation of a multiple equation system in several variables, the most complete simulations would be based on reduced form equations, in which all endogenous variables are expressed as functions of exogenous variables only. There are several reasons why this is impossible. Most importantly, some of the equations, especially those for LEDR and PROP are nonlinear in the endogenous variables, and therefore an analytic solution for the reduced form is unobtainable. Secondly, a reduced form would require using the equation for PROP, in which we have little confidence. Finally, some of the parameters estimated in the model are difficult to interpret, and the meaning of simulation is therefore unclear. For example, we are not sure how much of the estimated effect of the school matching rate on local nonschool revenue is a shift of resources from nonschool to school services and how much represents the shifting of identical services from one budget category to another.

Because of these difficulties, the simulations in the body of Chapter 8 utilized only the structural equations for LEDR, ignoring the effects on local (and total) revenues per pupil of changes in other endogenous variables. In this appendix we analyze the effects of state aid on local revenue, considering the school tax rate and property valuation as endogenous.

Two other patterns of interaction should be mentioned. Equation vi of Table 7-5 indicated that local nonschool revenues (and thus nonschool services) are responsive to the price of school revenues. Thus the prices produced by DPE will affect local nonschool revenues, although whether these changes will reflect the kinds of services provided or merely shifts from one local account to another is unclear. A distribution of total school revenues which considers changes in nonschool revenues as budgetary manipulations only can be simulated, to see whether this effect is potentially unequalizing.[36] However, the magnitude of change in LNER is small enough that this effect can safely be ignored.[37]

Finally, changes in school matching rates will affect local nonschool revenues, according to equation vi of Table 7-5; and changes in local nonschool revenues will in turn affect local school revenues, according to equation iv. However, as one might expect, the magnitude of this effect is trivial. Even in Boston, where the impact of LNER on LEDR is the largest, an increase in the price of school funds of 0.50 will decrease local school revenue in this particular manner by only $0.77 per pupil.

### Simulations of Endogenous SCHRTE

In equations iv and v of Table 7-3, the price effect is a function of the
school tax rate, with the strength of the response to price decreasing as the
tax rate increases. Strictly speaking, this particular finding describes the price
response at the margin—the elasticity $\eta_{\text{LEDR, PRICE}}$—and not necessarily the
price response given a large change in price. When the price change is no longer
infinitesimal, the school tax rate changes as local revenue changes, and therefore the price response itself will vary. This particular interaction was not
considered previously, but Table 8A-1 presents simulations of equation iv
with the school tax rate and hence the price effect changing as local revenue
changes.[38] Comparing the evaluative statistics with those in Tables 8-3 and
8-4, the only substantial difference from allowing the price response to vary
is that the magnitude of interdistrict inequality increases. All other qualitative conclusions remain the same. The reason appears to be that variations
in the school tax rate affect the strength of the price response relatively little,
at least as compared with the variation in prices among districts under the
various DPE formulas. Given the stability of the results, we feel justified in
not further considering variations in the school tax rate as an argument of
the price response.

### Simulations of Endogenous PROP

A considerably more difficult problem is that of analyzing potential
changes in property value as a result of changing programs of state aid. We
have repeated our qualms about the equation for PROP several times, and
because of these caveats the results of any simulations are highly specula-
tive. Nonetheless, we present them here for completeness.

Table 8A-2 presents the evaluative statistics for a number of alternative
formulas with property valuation endogenous.[39]   The qualitative conclusions from Tables 8-3, 8-4, and 8-5 are by and large preserved in these
simulations with property valuation endogenous: District power equalizing
formulas reverse the present correlation between revenue and property
while flat grants do not; DPE does not reduce the Gini coefficient unless
a minimum tax rate is imposed. Progressive DPE helps income-poor districts, urban districts, and children of poor families. However, the simulations summarized in rows 2, 4, and 10 of Table 8A-2 greatly over-
predict total revenue and the amount of required state general revenue.
The reason can be seen from Table 8A-3: for these simulations, average
district property value falls drastically, so that more districts appear poor
and increase their spending in response to positive matching rates. In part,
this result is artificial. The iterative algorithm does not allow property value

**Table 8A-1**
**Simulations with School Tax Rate Endogenous**

| | Gini | $\frac{TER_{rich}}{TER_{poor}}$ | $\rho_{TER,PROP}$ | $\rho_{TER,Y}$ | $TER_{urban}$ | TER | State |
|---|---|---|---|---|---|---|---|
| *Equation iv* | | | | | | | |
| 1. Data Estimates | 0.0643 | 1.101 | 0.446 | 0.700 | 868 | 829 | 114 |
| 2. DPE, $k = 27,066$ | 0.1179 | 0.977 | -0.498 | 0.014 | 884 | 819 | 49 |
| 3. DPE, $k = \$35,000$ | 0.1934 | 0.952 | -0.471 | 0.030 | 1309 | 1075 | 293 |
| 4. Progressive DPE | 0.1297 | 0.883 | -0.525 | -0.184 | 987 | 834 | 67 |
| 5. DPE with Urban Factor | 0.1847 | 0.794 | -0.392 | -0.172 | 1487 | 944 | 196 |
| 6. DPE, $k = \$35,000$ with Non-Negative $m$ | 0.1873 | 0.978 | -0.378 | 0.063 | 1320 | 1092 | 322 |
| 7. DPE, $k = \$35,000$ with Save-Harmless | 0.1834 | 0.983 | -0.359 | 0.068 | 1322 | 1099 | 332 |

**Table 8A-2**
**Simulations with Property Value Endogenous**

| Equation iv | Gini | $\dfrac{TER_{rich}}{TER_{poor}}$ | $\rho_{TER,PROP}$ | $\rho_{TER,Y}$ | $TER_{urban}$ | $TER$ | State |
|---|---|---|---|---|---|---|---|
| **I. DPE, $k = 27{,}066$** | | | | | | | |
| 1. Structural Model | 0.0944 | 0.994 | -0.479 | 0.057 | 879 | 802 | 36 |
| 2. PROP Endogenous | 0.1971 | 0.951 | -0.509 | 0.029 | 1219 | 1015 | 270 |
| **II. DPE, $k = 30{,}000$** | | | | | | | |
| 3. Structural Model | 0.1004 | 0.996 | -0.531 | 0.099 | 968 | 865 | 114 |
| 4. PROP Endogenous | 0.2097 | 0.974 | -0.468 | 0.092 | 1367 | 1077 | 345 |
| **III. DPE, $k = 30{,}000$, $t^* = 18.82$** | | | | | | | |
| 5. Structural Model | 0.0769 | 1.024 | -0.573 | 0.239 | 868 | 816 | 98 |
| 6. PROP Endogenous | 0.1248 | 1.065 | -0.377 | 0.161 | 847 | 789 | 81 |
| **IV. DPE, $k = 30{,}000$, $t^* = 21.33$** | | | | | | | |
| 7. Structural Model | 0.0649 | 1.029 | -0.462 | 0.278 | 855 | 817 | 92 |
| 8. PROP Endogenous | 0.1301 | 1.056 | -0.356 | 0.115 | 853 | 807 | 86 |
| **V. Progressive DPE, $k = 27{,}066 \cdot \bar{y}$** | | | | | | | |
| 9. Structural Model | 0.1064 | 0.896 | -0.568 | -0.253 | 974 | 817 | 55 |
| 10. PROP Endogenous | 0.2080 | 0.838 | -0.544 | -0.082 | 1376 | 1019 | 283 |
| **VI. Flat Grant, $k = \$114$** | | | | | | | |
| 11. Structural Model | 0.0722 | 1.149 | 0.466 | 0.684 | 848 | 816 | 114 |
| 12. PROP Endogenous | 0.0723 | 1.147 | 0.629 | 0.706 | 779 | 811 | 114 |

Table 8A–3
Evaluative Statistics for Endogenous Simulations

| Equation iv | Average Hypothetical PROP | Number of Property Limits | Correlation between Actual and Hypothetical PROP |
|---|---|---|---|
| I.   DPE, $k$ = 27,066 | 21,603 | 54 | 0.967 |
| II.  DPE, $k$ = 30,000 | 22,076 | 52 | 0.967 |
| III. DPE, $k$ = 30,000, $t^*$ = 18.80 | 26,951 | 47 | 0.896 |
| IV.  DPE, $k$ = 30,000 $t^*$ = 21.33 | 26,824 | 38 | 0.898 |
| V.   Progressive DPE, $k$ = 27,066·$\bar{y}$ | 21,815 | 55 | 0.966 |
| VI.  Flat Grant, $k$ = \$114 | 27,092 | 27 | 0.964 |

to change more than 33 percent from its 1968-69 level. A larger number of districts were constrained by this limit in the three simulations which predict a lowering of property values than in the other simulations, as Table 8A-3 indicates. Thus statistically, lowered property values are associated with nonconvergent systems.

Of those districts which failed to converge, almost all were initially below the average property valuation for the sample. Districts above the sample average, on the other hand, tended to converge almost all of the time. Furthermore, they tended if anything to increase in average property valuation per pupil. If there are any implications from these simulations for property values, it is that wealthy districts will not necessarily suffer property losses under DPE formulas. In fact, property values under DPE follow a remarkably stable pattern, as the third column of Table 8A-3 indicates.

The experiments with letting property value be endogenous are not particularly informative about changes in property value because of the lack of detail in the description of property markets and because of problems with convergence. However, it is comforting to find the same qualitative conclusions about the effects of alternative state aid formulas, since it indicates stability of the conclusions under alternate techniques of simulation.

Notes

1.   An example may clarify the problem. Suppose we observe points along

the equation $y = x^2$, in the range $1 \leqslant$ to $\leqslant 2$, not knowing the actual relationship. We could describe our observations by the equation $y = 3x - 2$, and, within the observed range, error from this approximation would be negligible. If we want to predict $y$ from an observation of $x = 4$, we predict $y = 12$, but from the actual relationship $y = 16$, and our estimate errs by 25 percent! Even more serious errors occur if we want to simulate $y$ when $x$ becomes negative. If $x = -1$, we will predict $y = -1$ when $y$ is actually $+1$. For many purposes, the difference in sign will be more important than the absolute error of the prediction. All errors are due to having a restricted range of points from which to estimate a relation between $x$ and $y$.

2. See, e.g., Johnston (130).

3. The expected revenue figures are averages weighted by the percentage of *families* who are rich and poor, since data on the income backgrounds of public school-attending children is unavailable on a district level. This unavoidable omission biases the results slightly, but in an unknown direction. Rich families are defined as those with incomes over $25,000 in 1969, and poor families are those below the poverty line as defined by the 1970 census.

4. Cities are defined as those places with a 1970 population over 100,000.

5. These are not district averages but pupil averages, obtained by weighting district figures by net average membership.

6. This procedure amounts to eliminating the unexplained variation from the original data, for each of the three equations for LEDR (iii, iv, and v of Table 7-3).

7. Equations iii and iv contain denominators with the expression $(1 + bM_i)$ where $M_i$ is the district's matching rate. (In equation iv, $b$ is a function of the school tax rate, but is kept constant in text simulations and varied in Appendix 8A.) When $M_i$ is negative and $b$ is less than 1, this denominator is a small fraction and the implied LEDR is very large. This occurs in no more than 7 percent of the sample, all small districts. In these cases, we set the denominator at 0.33. Since the descriptive statistics are weighted by district size, the effect of this restriction is negligible.

8. The relationship between a Gini coefficient and the variance of the associated distribution is not necessarily monotonic. However, in our case where the eliminated variation is random, the two statistics will move together except under the most bizarre circumstances.

9. The correlation coefficient between two variables $y$ and $x$ can be expressed:

$$\rho_{xy} = \frac{\text{cov}(x,y)}{\sigma_x \sigma_y}$$

Since the estimating equation does not capture all the variation, the estimated data has less variation in the dependent variable, say $\sigma_y$. This increases the value of the correlation but has no necessary implication for the pattern of overall inequality.

10. The fact that estimated Gini coefficients are lower than the actual ones is at least partly responsible for Stern's (244) finding that district power equalizing will narrow the distribution of school resources. He compared data from an estimated distribution under district power equalizing with actual current data, similar to comparing simulations with row 1 of Table 7-3 rather than with the other rows. This comparison makes DPE look more equalizing—in the sense of lowering the Gini coefficient—than the correct comparison.

11. The formula for state aid is simply

$$S_i = K$$

where $K$ is the amount of aid per pupil, constant for all districts.

12. One problem is that the Gini coefficient is an ordinal measure only, and thus does not permit us to establish a standard by which effectiveness could be measured.

13. As state aid decreases, total revenue changes in every district by a constant, and therefore the correlation coefficient remains unchanged.

14. In such a case, state aid is a constant, and the correlation between a constant and any variable is zero.

15. We should note that $800 is so far outside the range of 1968-69 state aid levels that this conclusion is probably overstated.

16. The formula for a district power equalizing plan, following Chapter 4, is

$$S_i + L_i = k \cdot T_i$$

implying a matching rate $m_i$ of

$$m_i = \frac{k}{PROP_i} - 1 .$$

17. In common parlance, every district would have the same yield per mill of tax as the mean district. But see Appendix 7B for reasons why it is inappropriate to view districts as facing an "effective property base" of $k$.

18. This unintuitive result has also been obtained by Feldstein (75), who came to the same conclusion for Massachusetts with a less elaborate analysis, but not, we should note, with precisely the same data as we use here.

19. For a more complete discussion of progressive DPE formulas, see Benson et al. (18).

20. In place of the matching rate given in note 16, the matching rate under a progressive district power equalizing formula is

$$m_i = \frac{k}{PROP_i \cdot Y_i} - 1.$$

In the case where $k = \overline{PROP} \cdot \overline{Y} = 27,066 \cdot 5981 = 161.9 \times 10^6$, the district at the mean for both property value and income has a matching rate of 0. When $k = 29,900 \cdot \overline{Y}$ and state aid averages $114, then a district with a zero matching rate is slightly above average in either property valuation or income.

21. An ordinary least-squares regression for $q$ yields the following:

(1)  $q = -0.0022$ PROP $+ 0.000023$ Y $- 0.000008$ POPDEN $- 0.47$ AFDC
        (0.00043)        (0.0000089)   (0.0000018)              (0.13)

    $+0.146$ OWNED $+ 0.36$        $R^2 = 0.64$
    (0.046)              (0.059)

22. Specifically, in this form the matching rate is

$$m_i = \frac{k}{q_i \cdot PROP_i} - 1.$$

For the formula simulated in Table 8-4, the value of $k$ is the state average for the product $q \cdot$ PROP, or $13,368. An intuitive interpretation of $q \cdot$ PROP is the district property valuation per pupil which supports local school revenues rather than nonschool revenues.

23. This simulation is calculated for illustrative purposes only, and not as advocacy for such a municipal overburden correction. The use of $q$ in this way creates undesirable incentives to shift resources into the nonschool sector.

24. This form is called a "resource equalizer" in Benson (15).

25. The ubiquity of save-harmless provisions in the recent bills incorporating district power equalizing formulas into state aid programs is discussed in Grubb (91).

26. More generally, state aid is given by

$$S_i = (k_1 - P_i) \cdot t^* + \left( \frac{k_2}{P_i} - 1 \right) \cdot (L_i - t^* P_i)$$

If $k_1$ and $k_2$ are different, it simply means that the yield per mill is different for $t^*$ and for tax rates in excess of $t^*$. However, in the simulations in Table 8-5, $k_1$ and $k_2$ have been taken to be identical.

27. For example, the recent school finance bill of Montana explicitly utilizes the net flow approach, in that each district receives only $t^* \cdot (k - P_i)$ from the state (or remits this amount to the state if $P_i$ is greater than $k$).

28. If the minimum tax were paid directly to the state rather than to the local district, this would be a more plausible view.

29. The two views differ only in the district's conception of the amount of nonmatching aid, and thus in the magnitude of the substitution effect. The actual amount of state nonmatching revenues available for school spending is in both cases $t^* \cdot (k - P_i)$.

30. The lower average revenues under the gross flow concept are due to a larger substitution (or income) effect.

31. To repeat the findings mentioned in Chapter 6, the only other state with a sufficient number of districts for simultaneous estimation, with a reasonably simple district structure, and with a matching grant in 1970-71 was Iowa. While a number of additional states passed school aid formulas incorporating matching rates during 1972-73, the presence of save-harmless and transitional provisions will obscure the operation of price effects for some years to come.

32. For example, the policy simulated in row 3 of Table 8-5 appears to be a good one in terms of reducing the correlations between property and income without increasing the Gini coefficient.

33. That is, the partial derivative $\partial F/\partial \text{PROP}$ should be zero, where $F$ represents a cross-district relationship.

34. Referring back to the previous footnote, the correlation coefficient can be expressed by the *total* derivative $dF/dP$, given by the expression

$$dF/dP = \frac{\partial F}{\partial P} + \Sigma_i \frac{\partial F}{\partial x_i} \cdot \frac{\partial x_i}{\partial P}$$

where $x_i$ represents the other arguments of $F$. Clearly $\partial F/\partial P$ can be zero without $dF/dP$, the correlation coefficient, being zero. For an analysis of an "optimal" formula based on this distinction, see Feldstein (75) or Grubb (90), Ch. 5.

35. To summarize the analytic framework of Feldstein (75), we start with the relationship

$$R = F(P, \tau, x_1 \ldots x_n)$$

where $\tau$ is the price of total revenue, $1/1 + m$. The correlation coefficient $dR/dP$ is given by the expression

$$\frac{dR}{dP} = \frac{\partial F}{\partial P} + \frac{\partial F}{\partial \tau} \cdot \frac{\partial \tau}{\partial P} + \sum_i \frac{\partial F}{\partial x} \cdot \frac{\partial x_i}{\partial P}$$

and for this to be zero (elimination of the *de facto* relation),

$$\frac{\partial \tau}{\partial P} = - \frac{\dfrac{\partial F}{\partial P} + \sum_i \dfrac{\partial F}{\partial x_i} \cdot \dfrac{\partial x_i}{\partial P}}{\partial F/\partial \tau}$$

implying a matching rate of

$$m = \frac{1}{c - \left( \dfrac{\partial F}{\partial P} + \sum_i \dfrac{\partial F}{\partial x_i} \cdot \dfrac{\partial x_i}{\partial P} \; P \right) \Big/ \dfrac{\partial F}{\partial \tau}} - 1$$

In the usual DPE formula, the constant $c$ (which is a constant of integration) is taken to be zero, and the parameter $k$ is precisely

$$k = - \frac{\dfrac{\partial F}{\partial \tau}}{\dfrac{\partial F}{\partial P} + \sum_i \dfrac{\partial F}{\partial x_i} \cdot \dfrac{\partial x_i}{\partial P}}$$

On the other hand, to eliminate the *de jure* relation,

$$\frac{\partial R}{\partial P}$$

must equal zero, and this can be achieved if

$$\frac{\partial F}{\partial \tau} \cdot \frac{\partial \tau}{\partial P} = - \frac{\partial F}{\partial P} \rightarrow \frac{\partial \tau}{\partial P} = - \frac{\dfrac{\partial F}{\partial P}}{\dfrac{\partial F}{\partial \tau}}$$

implying a parameter $k$ of

$$k = -\frac{\frac{\partial F}{\partial \tau}}{\frac{\partial F}{\partial P}}.$$

36. Such budget manipulation is potentially antiequalizing because the effect of price on LNER increases with socioeconomic status (PROF). Thus for a district in which PROF is one standard deviation above the mean, a doubling of the price of school resources (from 1 to 2) would increase local nonschool resources by $51.28. A district one standard deviation below the mean with a price 0.5 instead of 1 would increase LNER by only $3.51.

37. For the relevant simulation, see Grubb (90), Ch. IV, Table IV-9.

38. The simulations are obtained by iteration. Each district is assumed to respond to the price effect of a particular DPE formula, move one-third of the way to the simulated level of local revenue, recalculate its price response on the basis of a new tax rate, and proceed in this way until changes in the simulated local revenue fall below a critical level. This procedure always yields convergence, while an analytic solution sometimes yields unreal numbers.

39. Again, the simulation uses an iterative rather than an analytic technique, since the analytic solution requires the simultaneous solution of two nonlinear and one linear equations. Each district is assumed to respond initially to a new state aid program by calculating a new level of local revenue, but it moves only one-third of the way to the new level. Then a new school tax rate is calculated, and property value changes on the basis of the new level of total revenue and the new school tax rate. Next, a different level of local nonschool revenue based on the revised property valuation is calculated. The local school revenue is then based on the revised property valuation and the previously revised school tax rate, and the iteration repeats itself—except that changes in property valuation respond to changes in school revenues, nonschool revenues, and in both the school and the nonschool tax rate. Convergence is defined by a change in local school revenue of less than one dollar per pupil. However, a limitation is imposed to keep some districts from blowing up or oscillating: if the change in property value per pupil is greater than 33 percent of the original property value, then the "equilibrium" position of the district is calculated at this limit.

# 9

## The Implications for State Aid Programs

In the preceding eight chapters we have analyzed school finance from historical, theoretical, and empirical perspectives, looking within school districts occasionally but emphasizing the behavior of districts and differences among districts. Our task here is to integrate these various views to draw some conclusions about desirable and feasible policies for financing public schools.

The first task is straightforward: in the initial section of this chapter, we will outline the implications of the analysis for state finance programs. In particular we will distinguish between several issues which are sometimes confused, and indicate which reforms address which issues. In the second section we discuss the results of state manipulation of prices and propose modifications of district power equalizing. Because of its relevance to our conclusions, we will look briefly at recent school finance legislation. In the third section we discuss features of a complete school finance allocation formula, paying attention to recent literature on the costs and idiosyncracies of providing "equivalent" services in different places to different children. A final brief section places our recommendations in historical perspective, and suggests what the limitations of school finance reform are.

### State Aid and District Behavior

Two descriptions of inequality are conceptually and empirically separable. One is the measure of the extent of inequality without regard for which districts occupy high and low positions—for example, the Gini coefficient. The other we have called *patterned inequality*. It describes the situation when districts at the top or bottom of unequal distributions can be identified by some characteristics. Thus not only do some districts currently spend more on schools than others, but these tend to be the districts whose residents are identifiable by their high socioeconomic status, high family incomes, or high property values.

A major difference in approaches to school finance reform is that between opposition to patterns of inequality and opposition to inequality per se. The dominant litigative approach to schooling inequality has attacked only the pattern, the basis upon which the state allows differential resources to flow to children. According to such an approach, inequalities in school finance are allowable if they are based on a set of adult characteristics which does not

189

include wealth.[1] Other interpretations of the Constitution suggest that inequalities in school finance per se are unjustified, but arguments to this effect have not been presented in court.[2]   We have seen in Chapter 8 that these do seem to be separable issues: district power equalizing formulas are able to reverse the correlation between wealth and school revenue, and bring the correlation between family income and school revenue to zero, *without* reducing the amount of inequality among districts.

The two conceptions of inequality are not always distinguished because patterns of inequality are usually quite constant—the same kinds of people are always at the top (or the bottom) of different distributions. With respect to the quality of jobs, for example, it is usually true that the worst jobs (according to generally accepted norms) are also the most poorly paid—that is, the same individuals are at the bottom of both pay scales and the range of job conditions.[3] The usual reform proposals specify either that the worst jobs be eliminated or that the worst jobs be better paid. Both deal with the amount of inequality but not its pattern.[4] Other proposals involve job rotation and sharing to eliminate the patterns of inequality and the hierarchy implied by inequality.[5]

Compensation for inequality occurs to a slight degree in the market place. Thus there are better and worse places to live, and the better ones cost more. Inequality in living conditions is patterned because the better places go to the wealthy, but the greater expense for better location neither balances the scales nor goes to the poor to compensate them for worse conditions. For many of the social goods we care about, one could conceive of an ethical equivalent to strict equality if alternatives exist which balance inequality in one distribution with an inversely patterned inequality in another. Such a possibility seems inconceivable, however, for education, health care, nutrition, and in general for those goods for which there are no substitutes and whose consequences are irreversible. If the two conceptions of inequality are empirically separable—in that policies which change patterns of inequality do not necessarily reduce the magnitude of inequality, as described in Chapter 8—and if there can be no compensation for inferior schooling in terms of other social goods, then it becomes necessary to specify which of the two is more important.

Recent reformers have by and large viewed unequal school finance as they might see job quality or housing quality: the pattern, not inequality per se, is the problem. We disagree with this judgment. We can find no rationale for any group of children being advantaged by state policy. Resources should flow to children because of their own characteristics, not those of their parents. Children are very much the "victims" of circumstance, greatly affected by the families into which they are born. But the state has assumed responsibility for formally educating children as a class defined by their age only. Within that class it allows nepotism—some children favored over others because of characteristics of their families. We know of no theory of the state which presents an ethical justification of such unequal treatment.

The difference between patterned inequality and simple measures of magnitude in school finance reform comes down to the issue of parental choice. Reform measures which allow parents to choose, but change the terms of this choice, are likely to reproduce inequality while changing the placement of individual children along the distribution of funds. Our stand for school finance independent of the characteristics of the parents is a stand against parental or district choice over funding levels.

Given our position on school resource inequalities, the logical policy for us to support is commonly referred to as *full state funding,* the distribution of all school resources by the state on a nonmatching basis. Such a program need not allocate the same resources to each child. There may be justifiable reasons for variation based on the characteristics of children or districts, as discussed below. But even a grant based on the characteristics of children comes to districts as nonmatching aid, and such a grant can induce no local district response. Full funding by the state eliminates both the income and the price effects and thus eliminates the source of expenditure inequalities which would exist under other state aid plans, including district power equalizing.

There is in addition to this equity-based argument an efficiency argument for full state funding in preference to schemes which manipulate local decisions via price effects. The equations of Chapter 7 indicated that nonschool revenues are responsive to the price of school revenues—or more precisely, to the relative price of school and nonschool expenditures. Hence price manipulation in one sector affects the other as well. While the magnitude of this effect was small in Massachusetts, the larger price effects which would be necessary under most DPE formulas might be expected to change this result, to induce large substitutions of expenditures and functions among local sectors. Full state funding avoids this possibility by eschewing price manipulation.

Our conclusions based on the econometric results of the previous two chapters are consistent with the much less sophisticated data presented in Chapter 4. There we demonstrated the increasing levels of state aid over time have decreased inequalities among districts, and that the amount of state aid appears more important in achieving greater equality than the manner of its distribution. Thus both sets of evidence support the use of greater proportions of state revenue in place of local funding, in preference to using more complex formulas to allocate limited state funds.

Unfortunately, political reality usually constrains the set of available choices among distribution formulas and levels of state funding, and it may be necessary to choose from a set of second-best solutions. In particular, although the levels of state aid have increased greatly in the past decade or so,[6] few legislatures appear ready to increase state support to the levels required for full state funding. Hence the practical choice is usually among a set of alternative distribution formulas at a level of state support which is considerably less than 100 percent. In the next section, therefore, we will

discuss mechanisms to modify district power equalizing formulas and to narrow
the extent of inequality.

### Modifying District Power Equalizing

A district power equalizing program can be described, as in Chapter 4, by
the formula

$$S + L = k \cdot t$$

where $k$ is a number (or function) specified by the state. If the restriction
$t^* \leqslant t_i$ is added, where $t^*$ is a minimum tax rate set by the state, there is a guaranteed revenue of

$$S + L = k \cdot t^*$$

which can be larger or smaller than the revenue raised locally with a tax rate $t^*$.
The locally raised revenue $t^* \cdot \text{PROP}_i$ amounts to a statewide property tax
because all taxable property is taxed at a minimum of $t^*$, and this tax rate is
invariant to local spending decisions. There is no price effect attached to the
minimum funding level $kt^*$ because of the absence of local choice.

In Chapter 8 we simulated a state formula with minimum tax rates. Such
plans reduced the extent of inequality (as measured by the Gini coefficient),
compared to those without a minimum tax. This result was due to restrictions
in the range of permissible expenditures, cutting off those levels below $k \cdot t^*$.
In Massachusetts, where districts respond noticeably to prices, district power
equalizing with a minimum tax rate also increased the correlation between total
revenues on the one hand and property valuation and district income on the
other. That is, as compared with an unmodified DPE plan, the modified formula worsened the patterns of inequality. Again, it did this by restricting the
operation of the price effect, which normally makes increased spending expensive for wealthy districts. In a state where price responses are somewhat weaker,
the effect of a minimum tax rate in increasing these correlations should not be
as marked.

However, in our view the worsening of wealth-based patterns of inequality
in these simulations was relatively small, at least for a range of minimum tax
rates. The important point is that such a restriction does enable a district
power equalizing program to reduce the extent of interdistrict inequalities.[7]
Given this conclusion based on econometric evidence, it is gratifying to find that
a number of states have recently adopted such a limited DPE system. Of the
nine states which incorporated matching rates into the modifications of their
school aid programs in 1972-73, four of them—Florida, Maine, Montana, and

Utah—restricted the range over which the matching provision can operate by requiring a minimum tax rate—as we have simulated—and also by setting a maximum expenditure level above which the matching provision fails to operate.[8]

A final restriction—adopted by Colorado, California, and Wisconsin in 1973—takes the form of limiting the growth rates of expenditures over time. In the most sophisticated versions such as those of Colorado and California, the allowable growth rates are designed to narrow the distribution of expenditures over time by permitting low-spending districts to increase expenditures at a faster rate than high-spending districts. As in the case of ceilings on tax rates or on the range of expenditures subject to matching aid, these limitations can be overriden in some cases. But what is important is the perception by a number of states that formulas permitting extensive local choice, like unrestricted district power equalizing formulas, are likely to have relatively little effect in reducing inequalities per se.

### Distributing School Funds

In addition to the current push for equality in funding, or for equality in the power of districts to choose funding levels, others involved with finance reform have argued that equality in terms of dollars per pupil is not equitable because school districts vary in their abilities to provide schooling services for a given expenditure level.[9] Sometimes this normative argument is confused by the presentation of evidence that a district *does* spend a lot of money for some children,[10] but the argument is generally one of straightforward necessity, bypassing the rebuttal of administrative inefficiency.

We do not want to judge the acceptability of these various arguments here. Most people appear convinced that *some* characteristics of children and districts justify expenditure variations. The arguments are over which specific characteristics merit additional resources, and how much. Our task is to categorize arguments for divergences from strict dollar equality and to show how legitimate differences can be incorporated into funding formulas. We will specify three categories, and distinguish the kinds of arguments which might justify placing specific characteristics in these categories.

*Pupil Characteristics*

We start with a flat-grant formula

$$TER_i = C \cdot P_i \qquad\qquad (9.1)$$

where *TER* is total educational revenue, *C* is the flat grant, and *P* is the number of pupils. The subscript *i* represents individual districts. The first claim is that not all pupils are "alike"; that is, some pupils are more expensive to educate than others. Many state formulas have categorized kindergarten and high school pupils this way and most states allow extra aid for handicaps such as blindness, deafness, and mental retardation.[11]

Distinguishing categories of children is simple. We use the subscript *j* to denote different classifications of children. Rather than $P_i$ children in a district, there are $\sum_j P_{ij}$ children, where $P_{ij}$ denotes the number of *j*-type children in district *i*. The most common adjustment of the state's flow of funds is a weighting factor, some number which indicates how much more expensive one type of child is to educate than another. If $d_j$ is the additional weighting for the child of subscript *j* (i.e., $d = 0$ for the "ordinary" child), the *j*-type child receives $C \cdot (1 + d_j)$ from the state, and the district receives:

$$TER = C \cdot \sum_j (1 + d_j) \cdot P_{ij} \ . \tag{9.2}$$

If there are no *j*-type children, or no category is deemed legitimate, then either all $P_{ij} = 0$ except where *j* indicates the "normal" category, or all $d_j = 0$. In either case equation (9.2) collapses to equation (9.1).

How would one argue that some $d_j \neq 0$ is legitimate? At this point, the arguments must be purely political. This does not make them invalid, but it does take them out of the realm of "scientific" evidence and into the realm of values. Some advocates have hoped to find evidence from the literature on the effects of school resources, but this literature has so far provided only a source of references for political arguments of every variety and little consensus.[12] In any event, the production function literature has not even addressed the issues of relative resources for children distinguished by age, by physical, mental, or emotional handicaps or by curriculum. These pupil characteristics have been widely accepted—without any objective evidence—as justifications for different allocations under state and programs. Our advocacy of "equality" should not be interpreted as opposition to such adjustments.[13] Incorporating them into an equalizing scheme like full state funding and or district power equalizing presents no substantial problem.[14]

### District Characteristics

Some districts also argue that, even if they had children with equivalent characteristics, it would be more difficult for them to provide services to children than for other districts. Assuming that their argument is not based on teacher bargaining power, this is an argument about real resources: it says that some districts absorb more inputs for the same output, not because of misadministration, but because of some inherent characteristic of the district. Vandalism is one example; high costs of property and construction are others. If the district suffers from air pollution, teachers may become ill and be absent more than usual, requiring additional substitute funds. This problem should be amenable to technical analysis, since—unlike the case of pupil characteristics— the criterion of equality (cost per unit of input) is uncontroversial. A district claiming cost difference should be able to demonstrate the source and magnitude of the extra cost. The state's adjustment would be on a district basis and would be affected by the numbers of pupils but not by the characteristics of children. The adjustment can take the form of a factor $F_i$ which increases an exceptional district's allocation:

$$TER_i = (1 + F_i) \cdot C \cdot \sum_j (1 + d_i) P_{ij}$$

For the ordinary district $F_i = 0$, and equation (9.3) reduces to equation (9.2). By and large the only such factors which have been widely accepted by state legislatures are those which compensate small districts for presumed diseconomies of scale. A few states also distribute additional aid to large districts, although whether this is intended to compensate for pupil characteristics, district characteristics, or municipal overburden is unclear.[15]

A more difficult problem is the claim that the high price of teachers constitutes a factor justifying compensation. The inherent characteristics of the district, according to this claim, reduce the supply of qualified teachers, and thus drive up the equilibrium wage level.[16] Combat pay for inner cities and reservation pay for Indian reservations have typically been justified by such arguments. *In principle* there are better jobs and worse jobs and, as we have already indicated, in a fair world worse jobs would receive higher compensation. This argument, then, becomes political, since it depends on the evaluation about job quality and the ethical stand on equity the state is willing to make.

One state, Florida, has incorporated into its state aid formula a factor for costs-of-living differentials among the different counties.[17] The state has calculated an index for each county according to the methodology of the consumer price index and compensates districts accordingly. In most states, where the residence of the teacher cannot be so easily ascertained, such a correction would be difficult. But we surely have no objection to school fund distribution based on concepts of teacher salary equity.

### Noneducational Services

One major argument about expenses of districts involves the provisions by the school department of services which are not themselves educational, but which may be prerequisites for education. These include security patrols, heat, light, building maintenance, transportation, and school lunches. These expenses may vary by district. If not considered by the state, they must differentially reduce districts' abilities to finance educational services. Historically, for example, state legislatures have been willing to bear the cost of pupil transportation, although this has been partly to induce small districts to consolidate.

The argument for special consideration of expenditures required for schooling but unproductive of schooling services is more powerful if state action has intensified the need for additional services. If zoning laws and the operation of markets in residential property localizes vandalism in certain districts, for example, the state may prefer to pay the higher costs than to attempt a redistribution of the causes of those costs. A correction for noneducational costs, $N$, seems reasonable.[18] Districts advocating exceptions to equal dollar funding would do well to consider which kinds of expenditure belong in this category.

The logic behind this categorization implies that local choice over noneducational services is inappropriate. Even if one argues that the state should increase the amount of real choice which local districts can exercise in funding schooling services, it follows that fiscal burdens on school districts which do not increase resources directly related to learning should be equalized before districts choose funding levels. Otherwise their choices—and hence the distribution of expenditures—will be influenced by local cost conditions which should be irrelevant. The policy implication, clearly, is that the state should assume the burden of all such noneducational costs.

### Municipal Overburden

The final plea for relief comes from cities who claim their nonschool expenditures are so high they cannot adequately finance schools. We have presented some evidence in Chapter 7 that municipal overburden may exist. The question remains whether a state finance plan based on district choice should consider constraints imposed by nonschool expenditures.

We have argued above that price manipulation as a solution to school inequities is unsatisfactory, potentially inequitable, and imprecise. The same criticisms extend to the use of corrections in school aid formulas to compensate for the burden imposed by other municipal services.[19] Instead, cities that have inordinate nonschool expenditures should argue for state financing of these expenditures. The noneducational expenditures which are allowable in the school finance formula are those which operate through the school department, and directly provide services to schools. Other municipal services should be evaluated on their own merits, with the state deciding—in a political process—whether such costs are in fact imposed on urban districts or are the results of local choice. We see no reason to inflict this additional burden on the already overloaded debate about school finance.

### The Prospects for School Finance Reform

We end where we began—with a historical perspective on the role of financing in the schools. The first conclusion from a historical view is that finance reforms have repeated themselves over and over—in the "discovery" of inequities, in the arguments for greater equality versus local control (or some variant), and in the structure of state programs designed to correct perceived inequities. We can only expect that this cycle will recur, that the reforms stimulated by the current court cases, the citizens' committees, and the legislative battles will prove to be inadequate—perhaps because of the lack of "recapture" from wealthy districts or of insufficient attention to the pupil and district characteristics reviewed earlier in this chapter, or perhaps because wealthy districts manage to evade the intent of equalizing programs.[20] We can expect that successive reformers will find the changes of our period as insubstantial as we have found earlier reforms.

Yet, unlike some other aspects of political behavior, each wave of finance reform has tended to reinforce rather than reverse the previous one, particularly in efforts to reduce resource inequalities among districts. The current reform movement is somewhat different from previous ones, not only in using courts to rectify inequities but in concentrating more on the pattern of inequality than on its magnitude. The shift in emphasis is regrettable, since eliminating patterns of inequality need not reduce the extent of inequality (although the reverse is necessarily true). Nonetheless, the legislation which has been stimulated, however indirectly, by the court cases of the past four years has combined measures to correct wealth-based patterns in resource availability with provisions intended to narrow expenditure disparities directly. If this legislation is indicative of the impact that courts will eventually prove to have on school financing, then the trend of the past seventy years will be reinforced and extended. From our present perspective, the logical conclusion—however far in the future it may be—is a situation where the only school resource inequalities will be those which can be justified on the basis of pupil or district characteristics rather than on the characteristics of parents.

If the most important conclusion from Chapter 2 is correct—that patterns of school finance have essentially worked to reinforce the class stratification function of schooling—then such a situation could occur in only two ways: either in a classless society where stratification is nonexistent, or in one where the financing of public schools has become increasingly irrelevant to stratification in the economic system as a whole. Ignoring the first of these as implausible in the near future, we face the hypothesis that school resources are becoming increasingly irrelevant, or are finally being seen as irrelevant to the equity of the schooling process. This might be happening not because resources are unproductive—in the sense that more resources fail to produce more of some criterion, all other factors equal—but because as the variation in funding among districts decreases, resource inequalities become overwhelmed in importance by other sources of inequitable treatment. These include bias in classroom activity, in the administration of funds on a district and school level, in the tracking and placement system, in access to different kinds of colleges, and—particularly as college attendance begins to dominate the variation in years of schooling—bias within the college system.[21]

This hypothesis must be tentative, based as it is on the extrapolation of historical evidence. But more plausibly, it raises the familiar problem that winning a legislative or judicial victory asks more questions than it answers. For example, we have not looked at school administration to see whether funds are in general "well" or "poorly" spent or at the range of discriminatory mechanisms which might undo the effects of more equal funding. We have not dealt here with the larger context of the schooling institution, in which "well spent" and "poorly spent" funds must be defined, and in which the discriminatory effects of schooling might be clearer than they are in finance mechanisms.

Nor, having spent this much time analyzing an institution which so dominates the lives of children between the ages of six and sixteen, have we asked whether the kind of service provided is optimal (or by what criteria we could make such a judgment), whether the current provision of minor amounts of non-educational services—in school lunches and health care, for example—should be greatly extended. Implicitly, we have accepted what it is most important to question: what services are provided in schools, how, and for whose benefit? Equitable funding for schools is therefore a necessary step, worth the efforts which have been expended over the past few years, but only preliminary to the more fundamental questions which remain to be investigated.

### Notes

1. See Coons, Clune, and Sugarman (52), or state court decisions such as *Serrano* v. *Priest* or *Robinson* v. *Cahill*. See also the discussion in Chapter 8 indicating the confusion between *de jure* and *de facto* wealth correlation.
2. See Wise (279).
3. Lucas (158). For most job characteristics, his results do *not* confirm the "compensating differential" hypothesis of neoclassical wage theory, which would predict that jobs with poor working conditions would be paid more, *ceteris paribus*.
4. On Cuba's investment policy to eliminate the worst jobs, see Bowles (32). On labor credit systems designed to compensate people for taking jobs which displease them, see Skinner (241). A labor credit system following Skinner has been instituted at the Twin Oaks commune in Virginia; see (144).
5. For readings on changing job structure and content, see Hunnius, Garson, and Case (115).

6. This was particularly evident in the 1972-73 legislation; Grubb (91).

7. The use of a DPE system with a minimum tax rate was proposed in California as a mechanism for moving from district power equalizing to full state funding over a number of years. See Benson et al. (18).

8. The imposition of a maximum on the range over which DPE operates is clearly an effort to narrow the range of permissible expenditures from the top as well as from the bottom. Often, however, such a maximum can be overriden by local vote. In such cases—of which Montana is an illustration—a ceiling designed to reduce the amount of inequality within a state may have precisely the opposite effect. If the only districts affected are those property-poor districts who can receive no matching aid above the ceiling, while property-rich districts are able to use their tax base without penalty to raise additional revenue, then the ceiling on matching funds may promote greater inequality.

   We should note, however, that in the *absence* of district power equalizing, tax rate limitations simply serve to limit the expenditures of low-wealth districts relative to high-wealth districts, and thus can only exacerbate the wealth-based inequalities. This issue was aired in *Hargrave* v. *Kirk.*

9. See, for example, Callahan, Wilkin, and Sillerman (43), or Drachler (68).

10. Drachler (68), for example, presents figures for the average per pupil expenditure in Detroit for exceptional (handicapped and retarded) children. This shows what expenditures *are*, not what they *should* be. The National Educational Finance Project has been particularly guilty of this confusion; see Johns, Alexander, and Rossmiller (127).

11. We should point out that extra funds for diagnosed handicapped children leads to potential abuses in diagnosis. Any state funding which compensates districts for characteristics of children must assure that the extra funds are spent on those children, and should in some way monitor the diagnosis of handicaps and retardation.

12. Furthermore, we would argue that this approach is not likely to yield reliable evidence, at least in the foreseeable future. See Michelson (173).

13. For evidence that such adjustments can significantly vary the average expenditure per (unweighted) child, see the Utah Foundation's report on the probable effects of the 1973 bill.

14. The attack of Callahan, Wilken, and Sillerman (43) on full state funding and district power equalizing options sets up straw versions of these plans in which there is no variation among children based on their characteristics, and shows that such plans would discriminate against districts with high proportions of children who deserve and require extra resources. Their conclusion is more a political point than a technical argument against certain kinds of distribution mechanisms. If children with special needs are not explicitly considered, they will not receive additional resources no matter what distribution formula is used.

15. One exception is Michigan where additional aid is specifically directed to districts where the nonschool tax rate is extraordinarily high, a clear attempt to compensate for municipal overburden.

16. For evidence claiming this to be true, see Toder (258). However, there is some question whether his results reflect "compensating differentials" or union power.

17. Curiously, the cost-of-living correction is the only part of the recently enacted legislation to be challenged in court. Observers feel that this is due to the fact that the cost corrections involve parameters similar to the $F_i$ of equation (9.3) which are *negative*—that is, the cost-of-living index is centered on one instead of taking zero as the minimum point—so that low-cost districts have interpreted the provision as taking funds away from them.

18. Note that the noneducational costs $N$ might be a function of the number of pupils. They might even be a function of the pupil characteristics, but these refinements add nothing to our categorization of costs and the relevant arguments. The complete formulation is:

$$TER_i = (1 + F_i) \cdot C \cdot \sum_j (1 + d_i) P_{ij} \quad + N$$

19. This assumes that municipal overburden does exist. There is very little other evidence comparable to the regressions of Chapter 7, where the concept is not strongly supported.

20. This is particularly possible because, as state programs become more equalizing, the incentives for wealthy districts to evade their controls become stronger.

21. For documentation of the growth of a relatively new mechanism reinforcing the stratification function of schooling as a whole, see Karabel's (135) analysis of junior college expansion.

## Cases Cited

Bradley v. Milliken, 433 F2d 897 (6th Cir 1970), *appeal after remand,* 438
    F2d 945 (6th Cir 1971)
    Plan to decentralize Detroit schools held unconstitutional because it
    would thwart desegregation. Detroit required to submit metropolitan
    area-wide desegregation plan, upheld 468 F2d 902 (6th Cir 1973).
    Appealed to U.S. Supreme Court, Cert. granted.
Brown, Cortez et al. v. Board of Education of the City of Chicago, Federal
    District Court, N.D. Ill., No. 71-C-694
    In active litigation (6/74).
Brown v. Board of Education, 347 US 483 (1954)
    Mr. Chief Justice Warren delivered unanimous opinion overturning
    segregated schooling in Topeka, Kansas. For relief, see 349 US 294
    (1955).
Burruss v. Wilkerson, 310 F Supp 572 (WD Va 1969), *aff'd mem,* 397 US 44
    (1970)
Douglas Independent School District No. 3 v. Jorgenson, 293 F Supp 849 (1968)
Hargrave v. Kirk, 313 F Supp 944 (MD Fla 1970), *vacated,* 401 US 476 (1971)
Hobson v. Hansen I, 269 F Supp 401 (DDC 1967), *aff'd en banc sub nom,*
    Smuck v. Hobson, 408 F2d 175 (DC Cir 1969)
    Opinion by Judge J. Skelly Wright finding racial segregation, unequal
    allocation of resources, and misclassification of students in the public
    schools of Washington, D.C.
Hobson v. Hansen II, 327 F Supp 844 (DDC 1971)
    J. Skelly Wright, now Circuit Judge sitting as District Judge, ordering
    equalization of expenditures per pupil among District of Columbia
    public schools to enforce ruling in Hobson v. Hansen I. No appeal.
Hawkins v. Town of Shaw, 437 F2d 1286 (5th Cir 1971)
    Orders equal provision of town services.
Hollins v. Shoftstall, No. C-253652, Super Ct Ariz, January 13, 1972
Lau v. Nichols, 94 S. Ct. 786 (1974)
    Overturns lower courts' "adverse disposition of a civil rights class action
    filed by appellants to compel the San Francisco Unified School District
    to provide all non-English-speaking Chinese students attending district
    schools with bilingual compensatory education in the English language";
    from opinion by Trask, Circuit Judge, 483 F2d 791 (9th Cir 1973)
McInnis v. Shapiro, 293 F Supp 327 (ND Ill 1968), *aff'd sub nom,*

McInnis v. Olgilvie, 394 US 322 (1969)

Mission Coalition et al., v. San Francisco Unified School District, No. C-70-2627
(ND Cal)

Filed December 9, 1970 in Federal District Court. Dropped when School
District submitted desegregation and equalization plan.

Robinson v. Cahill, 62 NJ 473, 303 A2d 273 (1973)

New Jersey school finance law declared unconstitutional.

San Antonio Independent School District et al. v. Rodriguez, 411 US 1 (1973)
Also cited as 93 S. Ct. 1278 (1973). Complaint filed in 1968, that Texas
school finance law was unconstitutional. District Court finds for plaintiffs, 337 F Supp 280. Overturned by U.S. Supreme Court 5-4. Opinion
of the Court by Mr. Justice Powell. Dissent by Mr. Justice Marshall at
93 S. Ct. 1315.

Thompson v. Engel King, No. 47055, Dist. Ct. Ada County, Idaho. Decision
November 16, 1973.

# Bibliography

1. Advisory Commission on Intergovernmental Relations (ACIR), *Fiscal Balance in the American Federal System,* Volumes I and II, U.S. Government Printing Office, 1967.
2. _____, *Implications for Intergovernmental Relations in Central Cities and Suburbs,* U.S. Government Printing Office, 1965.
3. _____, *State Aid to Local Government,* U.S. Government Printing Office, 1969.
4. _____, *State and Local Finances: Significant Features, 1967 to 1970,* U.S. Government Printing Office, 1969.
5. Aigner, D.J., and A.J. Heins, "A Social Welfare View of the Measurement of Income Inequality," *Review of Income and Wealth* 13 (1967).
6. Arrow, Kenneth J., "The Organization of Economic Activity: Issues Pertinent to the Choice of Market Versus Non-Market Allocation," in Robert Haveman and Julius Margolis, editors, *Public Expenditures and Policy Analysis,* Markham, 1970.
7. Averch, Harvey, Stephen Carroll, Theodore S. Donaldson, Herbert J. Kiesling, and John Pincus, *How Effective Is Schooling?* Rand Corporation, 1972.
8. Bahl, Roy W., "Studies on Determinants of Public Expenditures: A Review," appendix to Selma J. Mushkin and John F. Cotton, *Sharing Federal Funds for State and Local Needs: Grants-in-Aid and PPB Systems,* Praeger, 1969.
9. Bailey, Stephen K., Richard T. Frost, Paul E. Marsh, and Robert C. Wood, *Schoolmen and Politics: A Study of State Aid to Education in the Northeast,* Syracuse University Press, 1962.
10. Bailyn, Bernard, *Education in the Forming of American Society*, Vintage Books, 1960.
11. Barlow, Robin, "Efficiency Aspects of Local School Finance," *Journal of Political Economy* 78 (1970).
12. Barro, Stephen M., *Theoretical Models of School District Expenditure Determination and the Impact of Grants in Aid,* Rand Corporation Monograph R-867-FF, 1972.
13. Becker, Gary, *Human Capital,* Columbia University Press, 1964.
14. Beman, Lamar, *The Towner-Sterling Bill,* H.W. Wilson, 1922.
15. Benson, Charles, *The Cheerful Prospect,* Houghton Mifflin, 1965.
16. _____, *The Economics of Public Education,* Houghton Mifflin, 1961.
17. _____, *The Economics of Public Education,* 2nd edition, Houghton Mifflin, 1968.

18. Benson, Charles, Paul Goldfinger, E. Gareth Hoachlander, and Jessica Pers, *Planning for Educational Reform: Financial and Social Alternatives,* Dodd, Mead & Co., 1974.

19. Benson, Charles, and Peter B. Lund, *Neighborhood Distribution of Local Public Services,* Institute of Governmental Studies, University of California, 1969.

20. Berg, Ivar, *Education and Jobs: The Great Training Robbery,* Praeger, 1970.

21. Berke, Joel S., with Stephen K. Bailey, Alan K. Campbell, and Seymour Sacks, *Federal Aid to Public Education: Who Benefits?* Syracuse University Press, 1971.

22. Berke, Joel S., James A. Kelly and John Callahan, "The Financial Aspects of Equality of Educational Opportunity," Select Committee on Equal Educational Opportunity, U.S. Government Printing Office, 1972.

23. Berke, Joel S., and Michael W. Kirst, "The Federal Role in American School Finance: A Fiscal and Administrative Analysis," *Georgetown Law Journal* 61 (1973).

24. ———, *Federal Aid to Education: Who Benefits? Who Governs?* Lexington Books, 1972.

25. Bishop, George, "Stimulative versus Substitutive Effects of State School Aid in New England," *National Tax Journal* 17 (1964).

26. Bloom, Benjamin S., "Innocence in Education," *School Review,* May 1972.

27. Boardman, Anthony, *Simultaneous Equations Estimates of the Educational Process,* Ph.D. dissertation (School of Urban and Public Affairs), Carnegie-Mellon Institute, 1975.

28. Bond, Horace Mann, *Negro Education in Alabama: A Study in Cotton and Steel,* Atheneum Press, 1969; originally The Associated Publishers, 1939.

29. Bowles, Samuel, "Towards an Educational Production Function," in W. Lee Hansen, editor, *Education, Income and Human Capital,* National Bureau of Educational Research, 1970.

30. ———, "Unequal Education and the Reproduction of the Social Division of Labor," in R. Edwards, M. Reich, and T. Weisskopf, editors, *The Capitalist System*, Prentice-Hall, 1972.

31. ———, "Contradictions in U.S. Higher Education," in James Weaver, editor, *Readings in Political Economy,* Allyn and Bacon, 1973.

32. ———, "Cuban Revolution and The Revolutionary Ideology," *Harvard Educational Review* 41 (1971).

33. Bowles, Samuel, and Herbert Gintis, "IQ In The U.S. Class Structure," *Social Policy,* January/February 1974.

34. Bradford, David, and Wallace Oates, "Towards A Predictive Theory of Intergovernmental Grants," *American Economic Review* 61 (May 1971).

35. Brazer, Harvey, *City Expenditures in The United States,* National Bureau of Economic Research, 1959.

36. ———, "The Variable Cost Burdens of State and Local Governments," in *Financing State and Local Government,* Federal Reserve Bank of Boston, 1970.

37. Brittain, John A., "The Incidence of Social Security Payroll Taxes," *American Economic Review* 61 (1971).

38. Brown, Byron, "A Model of Educational Expenditure and Its Relationship To Past Empirical Studies," Harvard University (unpublished), 1971.

39. Burke, Arvid, *Financing Public Schools In The United States,* Harper and Brothers, 1957.

40. Burkhead, Jesse, *Input and Output in Large-City High Schools,* Syracuse University Press, 1967.

41. ———, *State and Local Taxes for Public Education,* Syracuse University Press, 1967.

42. Bussard, Mary Rachael, *Economy, Efficiency and Equality: The Myths of Rural School Consolidation,* Harvard Graduate School of Education (unpublished), 1972.

43. Callahan, John, William H. Wilkin, and M. Tracy Sillerman, *Urban Schools & School Finance Reform: Promise & Reality,* The National Urban Coalition, 1973.

44. Callahan, Raymond, *Education and the Cult of Efficiency,* University of Chicago Press, 1962.

45. Campbell, Roald F., and Robert A. Bunnell (editors), *Nationalizing Influences on Secondary Education,* Midwest Administration Center, University of Chicago, 1963.

46. Charters, W.W., "Social Class Analysis of the Control of Public Education," *Harvard Educational Review* 23 (1953).

47. Churgin, Michael, Peter Ehrenberg, and Peter Grossi, "A Statistical Analysis of the School Finance Decision: On Winning Battles and Losing Wars," *Yale Law Journal* 81 (1972).

48. Clark, Burton R., "The 'Cooling Out' Function in Higher Education," *American Journal of Sociology* (1960).

49. Cohen, David K., and Marvin Lazerson, "Education and the Industrial Order," *Socialist Revolution,* March 1970.

50. Cohen, David K., Walter McCann, Jerome Murphy, and Tyll R. Van Geel, "The Effects of Revenue Sharing and Block Grants on Education," Harvard Graduate School of Education, 1970.

51. Coleman, James S., et al., *Equality of Educational Opportunity,* U.S. Office of Education, 1966.

52. Coons, John E., William H. Clune III, and Stephen D. Sugarman, *Private Wealth and Public Education,* Belknap Press, 1970.

53. Counts, George S., *Secondary Education and Industrialism,* Harvard University Press, 1929.

54. ———, *The Social Composition of Boards of Education,* University of Chicago Press, 1922.

55. Cremin, Lawrence, *American Education: The Colonial Experience 1607-1783,* Harper & Row, 1970.

56. ———, *The Transformation of the American School,* Alfred A. Knopf, 1961.

57. Cubberley, Elwood P., *Changing Conceptions of Education,* Houghton Mifflin, 1909.

58. ———, *Public School Administration,* revised edition, Houghton Mifflin, 1929.

59. ———, *School Funds and Their Apportionment,* Teachers College, 1905.

60. Daly, Charles (editor), *The Quality of Inequality: Urban and Suburban Public Schools,* University of Chicago Press, 1968.

61. Daniere, Andre, "Cost-Benefit Analysis of General Purpose State School-Aid Formulas in Massachusetts," Report to the Massachusetts Advisory Council on Education, 1969.

62. Davis, Otto A., "Empirical Evidence of Political Influence Upon the Expenditure Policies of Public Schools," in Julius Margolis, editor, *The Public Economy of Urban Communities,* Johns Hopkins University Press, 1965.

63. ———, "Quality and Inequality: Some Economic Issues Related to the Choice of Educational Policy," in Charles Daly, editor, *The Quality of Inequality: Urban and Suburban Public Schools,* University of Chicago Press, 1968.

64. Deitch, Kenneth M., "An Econometric Analysis of the Demand for American Education in the 1960's with a Statement of the General Economic Case for Public Education," Ph.D. dissertation (Economics), Harvard University, 1966.

65. Denison, Edward F., *The Sources of Economic Growth in the United States and The Alternatives Before Us,* Supplementary Paper No. 13, Committee for Economic Development, 1962.

66. de Leeuw, Frank, "The Demand for Housing: A Review of Cross-Section Evidence," *Review of Economics and Statistics* 53 (1971).

67. Domhoff, William, *Who Rules America?,* Prentice-Hall, 1967.

68. Drachler, Norman, "The Large-City School System: It Costs More To Do The Same," in *Equity for Cities in School Finance Reform,* Potomac Institute, 1973.

69. Dreeben, Robert, *On What Is Learned In School,* Addison-Wesley, 1968.

70. Dunn, Richard S., *Puritans and Yankees: The Winthrop Dynasty of New England, 1630-1717,* Princeton University Press, 1962.

71. Dye, Thomas, "Governmental Structure, Urban Environment, and Educational Policy," *Midwest Journal of Political Science* 11 (1967).

72. Educational Finance Inquiry Commission, *Bibliography on Educational Finance,* Macmillan, 1924.

73. Edwards, Richard C., *Alienation and Inequality: Capitalist Relations of Production in Bureaucratic Enterprises,* Ph.D. dissertation (Economics), Harvard University, July 1972.

74. Fairlie, John A., *The Centralization of Administration in New York State,* Teachers College, New York, 1898.

75. Feldstein, Martin, "Wealth, Neutrality, and Local Choice in Public Education," Discussion Paper No. 293, Harvard University Institute of Economic Research, May 1973.

76. Finn, Chester, and Leslie Lenkowsky, " 'Serrano' vs. The People," *Commentary* 54 (1972).

77. Fisher, Franklin, *The Identification Problem in Econometrics,* McGraw-Hill, 1966.

78. Fisher, Glenn, "Determinants of State and Local Government Expenditures: A Preliminary Analysis," *National Tax Journal* 14 (1961).

79. _____, "Interstate Variation in State and Local Government Expenditure," *National Tax Journal* 17 (1964).

80. Freeman, Roger, *Taxes For The Schools,* Volume 2 of *Financing The Public Schools,* Institute for Social Science Research, 1960.

81. Friedenberg, Edgar Z., *Coming of Age In America,* Random House, 1965.

82. Gintis, Herbert, "Education, Technology, and Worker Productivity," *American Economic Review* 61 (May 1971).

83. Goetz, Charles J., and Charles R. McKnew, Jr., "Paradoxical Results in a Public Choice Model of Alternative Government Grant Formulas," in James Buchanan and Robert Tollison, editors, *Theory of Public Choice,* University of Michigan Press, 1972.

84. Goldstein, John, "The Effectiveness of Manpower Training Programs: A Review of Research On The Impact On The Poor," Joint Economic Committee, November 1972.

85. Gordon, David, "From Steam Whistles to Coffee Breaks," *Dissent* 19 (1972).

86. _____, *Theories of Poverty and Underemployment,* Lexington Books, 1972.

87. Greer, Scott, *Governing the Metropolis,* John Wiley, 1962.

88. Greven, Philip, *Four Generations: Population, Land and Family in Colonial Andover, Massachusetts,* Cornell University Press, 1970.

89. Grubb, W. Norton, "A Review of the National Education Finance Project," *Harvard Educational Review* 42 (1972).

90. _____, *Intergovernmental Aid and Resource Disparity: School Finance in Massachusetts,* unpublished draft, Childhood and Government Project, University of California, August 1973.

91. _____, "New Programs of State School Aid," *Law and Contemporary Problems* 39 (1974).

92. _____, "The Distribution of Costs and Benefits in an Urban Public School System," *National Tax Journal* 24 (1971).

93. ———, "The Impact of the Vocational Education Movement After 1910," typescript, Harvard University, 1971.

94. Grubb, W. Norton, and Marvin Lazerson, "Vocational Education in American Schooling: Historical Perspectives," *Inequality In Education* No. 16 (March 1974).

95. ———, *Vocationalism and Education: A Documentary History, 1870-1970,* Teachers College Press, 1974.

96. Grubb, W. Norton, and Stephan Michelson, "Public School Finance in a Post-Serrano World," *Harvard Civil Rights-Civil Liberties Law Review* 8 (1973)

97. Gurley, John, "Federal Tax Policy," *National Tax Journal* 20 (1967).

98. Guthrie, James, Henry M. Levin, George B. Kleindorfer, and Robert T. Stout, *Schools and Inequality,* MIT Press, 1972.

99. Hansen, W. Lee, and Burton A. Weisbrod, "The Distribution of Costs and Direct Benefits of Public Higher Education: The Case of California," *Journal of Human Resources* 4 (1969).

100. Hanson, Nels, "Economy of Scale As A Cost Factor In Financing Public Schools," *National Tax Journal* 17 (1964).

101. Hanushek, Eric, *Education and Race,* Lexington Books, 1973.

102. Harlan, Louis R., *Separate and Unequal: Public School Campaigns and Racism in the Southern Seaboard States, 1901-1915,* Atheneum Press, 1969; originally University of North Carolina Press, 1958.

103. Harris, William, "The Political Economy of School Finance," *Educational Review* 29 (1905).

104. Harrison, Forrest W., and Eugene P. McLoone, *Profiles in School Support: A Decennial Overview,* U.S. Office of Education, 1965.

105. Hartman, Robert, "Evaluation of Multi-Purpose Grant-in-Aid Programs," Department of Health, Education, and Welfare, 1968.

106. Haskins, George Lee, *Law and Authority in Early Massachusetts,* Macmillan, 1960.

107. Heins, A. James, "State and Local Response to Fiscal Decentralization," *American Economic Review* 61 (May 1971).

108. Henderson, James, "Local Government Expenditures: A Social Welfare Analysis," *Review of Economics and Statistics* 50 (1968).

109. Herndon, James, *The Way It 'Spozed To Be,* Simon and Schuster, 1968.

110. Hettich, Walter, "Equalization Grants, Minimum Standards, and Unit Cost Differences in Equation," *Yale Economic Essays* 8 (1968).

111. Hirsch, Werner Z., "Determinants of Public Education Expenditures," *National Tax Journal* 13 (1960).

112. ———, "The Supply of Urban Public Services," in Harvey S. Perloff and Lowdon Wingo, editors, *Issues in Urban Economics,* Resources For The Future, 1968.

113. Hollingshead, August de Belmont, *Elmtown's Youth,* John Wiley, 1949.

114. Horowitz, Ann, "A Simultaneous Equation Approach to the Problem of Explaining Interstate Differences in State and Local Expenditure," *Southern Economic Journal* 34 (1968).

115. Hunnius, Gerry, G. David Garson, and John Case, *Workers' Control: A Reader On Labor and Social Change,* Random House, 1973.

116. Hutchins, Clayton, and Albert R. Munse, *Expenditures for Education at the Midcentury,* U.S. Office of Education, 1953.

117. Hyman, Herbert, "The Value Systems of Different Classes," in Reinhard Bendix and Seymour M. Lipset, editors, *Class, Status and Power,* Free Press of Glencoe, 1961.

118. Iannaccone, Laurence, *Politics In Education,* Center for Applied Research in Education (New York), 1967.

119. Inman, Robert P., "Efficiency, Equity and School Financing: The Implementation and Implications of *John Serrano* v. *Ivy Baker Priest,*" Fels Discussion Paper No. 16, The Fells Center of Government, University of Pennsylvania, March 1972.

120. Jackson, George Leroy, *The Development of School Support in Colonial Massachusetts,* Teachers College, 1909.

121. _____, *The Development of State Control of Public Instruction in Michigan,* Michigan Historical Commission, 1926.

122. James, H. Thomas, James A. Kelly, and Walter I. Garms, *Determinants of Educational Expenditures in Large Cities of the United States,* Stanford University Press, 1966.

123. James, H. Thomas, J. Alan Thomas, and Harold Dyck, *Wealth, Expenditure, and Decision-Making for Education,* Stanford University School of Education, 1963.

124. Jencks, Christopher S., "The Coleman Report and The Conventional Wisdom," in Frederick Mosteller and Daniel P. Moynihan, editors, *On Equality of Educational Opportunity,* Random House, 1972.

125. Jencks, Christopher S., Marshall Smith, Henry Acland, David Cohen, Herbert Gintis, Barbara Heyns, and Stephan Michelson, *Inequality,* Basic Books, 1972.

126. Johns, Roe L., "State Financing of Elementary and Secondary Education," in Edgar Fuller and Jim B. Pearson, editors, *Education in the States: Nationwide Development Since 1900,* National Education Association, 1969.

127. Johns, Roe L., Kern Alexander, and Richard Rossmiller, *Dimensions of Educational Need,* National Educational Finance Project, 1969.

128. Johns, Roe L., Kern Alexander, and Dewey H. Stollar, *Status and Impact of Educational Finance Programs,* National Educational Finance Project (Volume 4), 1971.

129. Johns, Thomas L., *Public School Finance Programs, 1968-69,* U.S. Office of Education, 1969.

130. Johnston, J., *Econometric Methods*, McGraw-Hill, 1963.

131. Jones, Thomas H., *Review of Existing State School Finance Programs*, U.S. President's Commission on School Finance (Volume 1), 1971.

132. Kaestle, Carl F., *The Origins of an Urban School System: New York City, 1750-1850*, Ph.D. dissertation (History), Harvard University, 1970.

133. _____, "Social Reform and the Urban School," *History of Education Quarterly* 12 (1972).

134. Kain, John, and John Quigley, "Measuring The Value of Housing Quality," *Journal of the American Statistical Association* 65 (1970).

135. Karabel, Jerome, "Community Colleges and Social Stratification," *Harvard Educational Review* 42 (1972).

136. Katz, Michael, "The 'New Departure' in Quincy, 1873-1888: The Nature of Nineteenth Century Educational Reform," *New England Quarterly* (1967).

137. _____, *The Irony of Early School Reform*, Harvard University Press, 1968.

138. _____, "The Emergence of Bureaucracy in Urban Education: The Boston Case, 1850-1884," *History of Education Quarterly* 8 (1968).

139. _____, *Class, Bureaucracy, and Schools*, Praeger, 1971.

140. _____, *School Reform: Past and Present*, Little, Brown, 1971.

141. Katzman, Martin T., *The Political Economy of Urban Schools*, Harvard University Press, 1971.

142. Kiesling, Herbert, *High School Size and Cost Factors*, Final Report to the U.S. Office of Education, 1968.

143. _____, "Measuring A Local Government Service: A Study of School Districts in New York State," *Review of Economics and Statistics* 49 (1967).

144. Kinkade, Kathleen, *A Walden Two Experiment*, William Morrow and Co., 1973.

145. Kirst, Michael W., *State, School and Politics*, Lexington Books, 1972.

146. Kohl, Herbert, *36 Children*, New American Library, 1967.

147. Kolko, Gabriel, *Wealth and Power in America*, Praeger, 1962.

148. Kozol, Jonathan, *Death At An Early Age*, Houghton Mifflin, 1967.

149. Krug, Edward A., *The Shaping of The American High School, 1880-1920*, Harper & Row, 1964.

150. Lazerson, Marvin, "Revisionism and American Educational History," *Harvard Educational Review* 43 (1973).

151. Levin, Betsy, Thomas Muller, William J. Scanlon, and Michael A. Cohen, *Public School Finance: Present Disparities and Fiscal Alternatives*, The Urban Institute, 1972.

152. Levin, Henry M., "Concepts of Economic Efficiency and Educational Production," in *Education As An Industry*, National Bureau of Economic Research, 1972.

153. _____, "The Effect of Different Levels of Expenditure on Educational Output," in *Economic Factors Affecting The Financing of Education,* National Educational Finance Project (Volume 2), 1970.

154. _____, (editor), *Community Control of Schools,* Brookings Institution, 1970.

155. Levine, Ralph S., "Massachusetts' New Equalization Formula for Education," Harvard University Graduate School of Education, 1967.

156. Lindahl, Erik, "Just Taxation: A Positive Solution," in Richard Musgrave and Alan Peacock, editors, *Classics in the Theory of Public Finance,* International Economic Association, 1958.

157. Listokin, David, *Funding Education: Problems, Patterns, Solutions,* Rutgers University, 1972.

158. Lucas, Robert E.B., *Working Conditions, Wage-Rates and Human Capital: A Hedonic Study,* Ph.D. dissertation (Economics), Massachusetts Institute of Technology, 1972.

159. Lynd, Robert S., and Helen M. Lynd, *Middletown,* Harcourt, Brace, 1929.

160. McClure, Charles, "The Interstate Exporting of State and Local Taxes: Estimates for 1962," *National Tax Journal* 20 (1967).

161. McGuire, Martin C., and Henry Aaron, "Efficiency and Equity in the Optimal Supply of a Public Good," *Review of Economics and Statistics* 51 (1969).

162. McMahon, Walter, "An Economic Analysis of Major Determinants of Expenditures on Public Education," *Review of Economics and Statistics* 52 (1970).

163. Maisel, Sherman, James Burnham, and John Austin, "The Demand for Housing: A Comment," *Review of Economics and Statistics* 53 (1971).

164. Malinvaud, E., *Statistical Methods of Econometrics,* North-Holland, 1970.

165. Margolis, Julius "A Comment on the Pure Theory of Public Expenditure," *Review of Economics and Statistics* 37 (1955).

166. Martin, George H., *The Evolution of the Massachusetts Public School System,* D. Appleton, 1915.

167. Martin, Ruby, and Phyllis McClure, *Title I of ESEA: Is It Helping Poor Children?* Washington Research Project, and Legal Defense and Education Fund, 1969.

168. Masters, Nicholas A., Robert H. Salisbury, and Thomas H. Eliot, *State Politics and the Public Schools,* Alfred A. Knopf, 1964.

169. Michelman, Frank, "Forward: On Protecting the Poor Through the Fourteenth Amendment," *Harvard Law Review* 83 (1969).

170. Michelson, Stephan, "The Association of Teacher Resourceness With Children's Characteristics," in Alexander Mood, editor, *Do Teachers Make A Difference?* U.S. Office of Education, 1970.

171. _____, "Economics in the Courts: Equal School Resource Allocation," *Journal of Human Resources* 7 (1972).

172. ———, "Equal Protection and School Resources," *Inequality In Education* No. 2 (December 1969).

173. ———, "The Further Responsibility of Intellectuals," *Harvard Educational Review* 43 (1973).

174. ———, *Incomes of Racial Minorities,* unpublished manuscript, The Brookings Institution, 1968.

175. ———, "On Public School Finance Reforms," *Law and Contemporary Problems* 39 (1974).

176. ———, "The Political Economy of Public School Inequalities," in Martin Carnoy, editor, *Schooling In A Corporate Society,* David McKay, 1972.

177. ———, "Principal Power," *Inequality In Education* No. 5 (June 1970).

178. Mieszkowski, Peter, "Tax Incidence Theory: The Effect of Taxes On The Distribution of Income," Journal of Economic Literature 7 (1969).

179. ———, "The Property Tax: An Excise Tax or A Profits Tax?" *Journal of Public Economics* (1972).

180. Miller, Herman P., *Income Distribution In The United States,* U.S. Department of Commerce, 1966.

181. Miner, Jerry, *Social and Economic Factors in Spending for Public Education,* Syracuse University Press, 1963.

182. Morrison, Henry C., *School Revenue,* University of Chicago Press, 1930.

183. Morss, Eliot, "Some Thoughts on the Determinants of State and Local Expenditures," *National Tax Journal* 19 (1966).

184. Mort, Paul, *State Support for Public Education,* American Council on Education, 1933.

185. Mosteller, Frederick, and Daniel P. Moynihan (editors), *On Equality of Educational Opportunity,* Random House, 1971.

186. Moynihan, Daniel P., "Equalizing Education—In Whose Benefit?" *The Public Interest* 29 (1972).

187. Munger, Frank J., and Richard Fenno, Jr., *National Politics and Federal Aid to Education,* Syracuse University Press, 1962.

188. Munse, Albert R., *Revenue Programs for the Public Schools in the United States, 1959-60,* U.S. Office of Education, 1961.

189. ———, *State Programs for Public School Support,* U.S. Office of Education, 1965.

190. Murphy, Jerome T., "Title I of ESEA: The Politics of Implementing Federal Education Reform," *Harvard Educational Review* 41 (1971).

191. Musgrave, Richard, and Peggy Musgrave, *Public Finance in Theory and Practice,* McGraw-Hill, 1973.

192. National Educational Finance Project, *Alternative Programs for Financing Education,* National Educational Finance Project (Volume 5), 1971.

193. Netzer, Dick, *Economics of The Property Tax,* The Brookings Institution, 1966.

194. Norton, James K., and Eugene S. Lawler, *An Inventory of Public School Expenditures in the United States,* American Council on Education, 1944.

195. Norton, John, *The Ability of the States to Support Education,* National Education Association, 1926.

196. Oates, Wallace, "The Effects of Property Taxes and Local Public Spending On Property Values: An Empirical Study of Tax Capitalization and the Tiebout Hypothesis," *Journal of Political Economy* 77 (1969).

197. O'Brien, Thomas, "Grants-in-Aid: Some Further Answers," *National Tax Journal* 24 (1971).

198. Oldman, Oliver, and Henry Aaron, "Assessment-Sales Ratios Under the Boston Property Tax," *National Tax Journal* 18 (1965).

199. Osman, Jack, "On The Use of Intergovernmental Aid As an Expenditure Determinant," *National Tax Journal* 21 (1968).

200. Owen, John, "The Distribution of Educational Resources in Large American Cities," *Journal of Human Resources* 7 (1972).

201. ———, "Inequality and Discrimination in the Public School System: Some Empirical Evidence," in David Mermelstein, editor, *Economics: Mainstream Readings & Radical Critiques,* 1st edition, Random House, 1970.

202. Parsons, Talcott, "The School Class as Social System: Some of Its Functions In American Society," *Harvard Educational Review* 39 (1969).

203. Pechman, Joseph, "The Distributional Effects of Public Higher Education in California," *Journal of Human Resources* 5 (1970).

204. Perkinson, Henry J., *The Imperfect Panacea: American Faith In Education 1865-1965,* Random House, 1968.

205. Peterson, George, "The Regressivity of the Residential Property Tax," Urban Institute Working Paper 1207-10, 1972.

206. Pidot, George, "A Principle-Components Analysis of the Determinants of Local Government Fiscal Patterns," *Review of Economics and Statistics* 51 (1969).

207. Piore, Michael, "Notes for a Theory of Labor Market Stratification," Working Paper No. 95, Department of Economics, Massachusetts Institute of Technology, 1972.

208. ———, "On-the-job Training In The Dual Labor Market," in Arnold Weber, Frank Cassell, and Woodrow Ginsberg, editors, *Public-Private Manpower Policies,* University of Wisconsin Press, 1969.

209. Pirenne, Henri, *Economic and Social History of Medieval Europe,* Harvest Books, 1937.

210. Pogue, Thomas, and L.G. Sgontz, "The Effects of Grants-in-Aid on State-Local Spending," *National Tax Journal* 21 (1968).

211. Polanyi, Karl, "Aristotle Discovers the Economy," in George Dalton, editor, *Primitive, Archaic and Modern Economics,* Doubleday, 1968.

212. ———, "Our Obsolete Market Mentality," in George Dalton, editor, *Primitive, Archaic and Modern Economics,* Doubleday, 1968.

213. ———, *The Great Transformation,* Beacon Press, 1944.

214. Powell, Sumner C., *Puritan Village: The Formation of A New England Town,* Wesleyan University Press, 1963.

215. Quincy, Josiah, *The History of Harvard University,* edited by J. Owen, Cambridge, Mass., 1840.

216. Reischauer, Robert D., and Robert W. Hartman, *Reforming School Finance,* The Brookings Institution, 1973.

217. Renshaw, Edward, "A Note on the Expenditure Effect of State Aid To Education," *Journal of Political Economy* 68 (1960).

218. Ribich, Thomas I., "The Problem of Equal Opportunity: A Review Article," *Journal of Human Resources* 7 (1972).

219. Ritterband, Paul, "Race, Resources and Achievement," *Sociology of Education* 46 (1973).

220. Rivlin, Alice, Review of Guthrie et al., *Schools and Inequality,* in *Journal of Politics* 35 (1973).

221. Rosett, Richard N., "Inequity in the Real Property Tax of New York State and the Aggravating Effects of Litigations," *National Tax Journal* 23 (1970).

222. Ross, Myron H., "The Property Tax Assessment Review Process: A Cause For Regressive Property Taxation," *National Tax Journal* 24 (1971).

223. Rothenberg, Jerome, unpublished data from the Urban Modeling Project at Massachusetts Institute of Technology, described in Robert Engel, "De Facto Discrimination in Residential Assessments," Working Paper No. 119, MIT Department of Economics, November 1973.

224. Sacks, Seymour, with David Ramsey and Ralph Andrew, *City Schools/ Suburban Schools: A History of Fiscal Conflict,* Syracuse University Press, 1972.

225. Sacks, Seymour, and Robert Harris, "The Determinants of State and Local Government Expenditure and Intergovernmental Flows of Funds," *National Tax Journal* 17 (1964).

226. Sacks, Seymour, and William F. Hellmuth, *Financing Government in a Metropolitan Area,* Free Press, 1960.

227. Samuelson, Paul, "The Pure Theory of Public Expenditure," *Review of Economics and Statistics* 36 (1954).

228. Schiller, Bradley R., *The Economics of Poverty and Discrimination,* Prentice-Hall, 1973.

229. Schmandt, Henry, and G. Ross Stephens, "Measuring Municipal Output," *National Tax Journal* 13 (1960).

230. Schultz, T. Paul, "Secular Trends and Cyclical Behavior of the Income Distribution in the United States: 1944-1965," in Lee Soltow, editor, *Six Papers on the Size Distribution of Income,* National Bureau of Economic Research, 1969.

231. Scott, Stanley, and Edward Feder, "Factors Associated With Variations in Municipal Expanditure Levels," Bureau of Public Administration, University of California (Berkeley), 1957.

232. Sennett, Richard, and Jonathan Cobb, *The Hidden Injuries of Class,* Alfred A. Knopf, 1972.

233. Sexton, Patricia, *Education and Income,* Viking Press, 1964.
234. Sharkansky, Ira, *Spending In The American State,* Rand McNally, 1968.
235. Shapiro, Sherman, "Some Socio-Economic Determinants of Expenditures for Education: Southern and Other States Compared," *Comparative Education Review* 6 (1962).
236. Shibata, Hirofumi, "A Bargaining Model of the Pure Theory of Public Expenditure," *Journal of Political Economy* 79 (1971).
237. Shurtleff, Nathaniel B. (editor), *Records of the Governor and Company of the Massachusetts Bay,* Commonwealth of Massachusetts, 1854.
238. Siegel, Barry N., "On the Positive Theory of State and Local Expenditures," in Paul Kleinsorge, editor, *Public Finance and Welfare: Essays in Honor of C. Ward Macy,* University of Oregon, 1966.
239. Silard, John, and Sharon White, "Intrastate Inequalities in Public Education: The Case for Judicial Relief Under the Equal Protection Clause," *Wisconsin Law Review,* 1970.
240. Silberman, Charles, *Crisis In The Classroom,* Random House, 1970.
241. Skinner, B.F., *Walden Two,* Macmillan, 1948.
242. Stauffer, Alan C., *Major School Finance Changes in 1973,* preliminary version, Education Commission of the States, Report No. 40, June 1973.
243. Stern, David, *The Limits of Equalization: State Aid to Local Schools in Massachusetts,* Ph.D. dissertation (economics), Massachusetts Institute of Technology, 1971.
244. _____ , "The Effects of Alternative Formulas for Distributing State Aid to Schools in Massachusetts," *Review of Economics and Statistics* 55 (1973).
245. Stone, Kathy, "The Origins of Job Structures in the Steel Industry," *Review of Radical Political Economics* (forthcoming).
246. Strayer, George D., Jr., *Centralizing Tendencies in the Administration of Public Education,* Teachers College, 1934.
247. _____ , *City School Expenditures,* Teachers College, 1905.
248. Strayer, George D., and Robert M. Haig, *The Financing of Education in the State of New York,* American Council on Education, 1924.
249. Struyk, Raymond J., "Effects of State Grants-in-Aid on Local Provisions of Education and Welfare Service in New Jersey," *Journal of Regional Science* 10 (1970).
250. Summers, Anita A., and Barbara L. Wolfe, "Philadelphia's School Resources and The Disadvantaged," *Business Review,* Federal Reserve Bank of Philadelphia, March 1974.
251. Swift, Fletcher, *A History of Permanent Common School Funds in the United States, 1795-1905,* H. Holt, 1911.
252. _____ , "A Survey of Public School Finance in the United States," in U.S. Commissioner of Education, *Biennial Survey of Education, 1920-22.*
253. _____ , *State Policies in Public School Finance,* Bureau of Education Bulletin No. 6, 1922.

254. Thomas, J. Alan, *School Finance and Educational Opportunity in Michigan,* Michigan Department of Education, 1968.

255. Tiebout, Charles, M., "A Pure Theory of Local Expenditures," *Journal of Political Economy* 64 (1956).

256. Tiedt, Sidney W., *The Role of the Federal Government in Education,* Oxford University Press, 1966.

257. Toby, Jackson, "Orientation to Education as a Factor In the School Maladjustment of Lower-Class Children," in Robert Winch, Robert McGinnis, and Herbert Barringer, editors, *Selected Studies in Marriage and The Family,* Holt, Rinehart and Winston, 1962.

258. Toder, Eric, "The Supply of Public School Teachers To An Urban Metropolitan Area: Possible Source of Discrimination In Education," *Review of Economics and Statistics* 54 (1972).

259. Tyack, David, "Bureaucracy and the Common School: The Example of Portland, Oregon, 1851-1913," *American Quarterly* 19 (1967).

260. _____, *Turning Points in American Educational History,* Blaisdell, 1967.

261. Updegraff, Harlan, *Rural School Survey of New York State: Financial Support,* Cornell University Press, 1922.

262. U.S. Commission On Civil Rights, *Racial Isolation in the Public Schools,* U.S. Government Printing Office, 1965.

263. U.S. Department of Commerce, *Statistical Abstract of the United States,* 1970.

264. U.S. Department of Labor, *Formal Occupational Training of Adult Workers: Its Extent, Nature and Use,* Manpower/Automation Research Monograph No. 2, 1962.

265. U.S. Office of Education, *Digest of Educational Statistics,* 1969.

266. Usdan, Michael D., *The Political Power of Education in New York State,* Teachers College, 1963.

267. Vassar, Rena L. (editor), *Social History of American Education,* Rand McNally, 1965.

268. Vieg, John A., Hubert Armstrong, Frank Farner, Gerhard Rostvold, John P. Shelton, and Proctor Thomson, *California Local Finance,* Stanford University Press, 1960.

269. Wasserman, William, *Educational Price and Quantity Indexes,* Syracuse University Press, 1963.

270. Weber, William, "Public Schooling and Changing Ruling Class Hegemony: Education in Boston," Harvard University Graduate School of Education, 1972.

271. Webster, William C., *Recent Centralizing Tendencies in State Educational Administration,* Columbia University, 1897.

272. Weinberg, Joel, *State Aid To Education in Massachusetts,* New England School Development Council, 1962.

273. Weisbrod, Burton, *External Benefits of Public Education*, Industrial Relations Section, Princeton University, 1964.

274. Weiss, Steven, *Existing Disparities in Public School Finance and Proposals for Reform*, Research Report for the Federal Reserve Bank of Boston, 1970.

275. Wilde, James, "The Expenditure Effect of Grant-in-Aid Programs," *National Tax Journal* 21 (1968).

276. Wicksell, Knut, "A New Principle of Just Taxation," in Richard Musgrave and Alan Peacock, editors, *Classics in the Theory of Public Finance*, International Economic Association, 1958.

277. Winkler, Donald R., "School Inputs, Educational Production, and the Achievement Gap Between Blacks and Whites," paper delivered at the Econometric Society, December 28, 1972.

278. Wirt, Frederick M., and Michael Kirst, *The Political Web of American Schools*, Little, Brown, 1972.

279. Wise, Arthur, *Rich Schools, Poor Schools*, University of Chicago Press, 1968.

# Index

# Index

Alabama, 53, 68n*1*, 77, 84
Alaska, 53, 68n*1*
Arizona, 5

Bureaucracy, 22

California, 4, 79, 84n*15*, 148n*11*, 149n*27*;
district power equalizing, 199n*7*; recent
legislation, 193
Class structure, 18; function of schools, 19,
21-24, 29-30, 67, 197, 200n*21*
Cognitive skill, 8-9
Coleman Report, 8, 13n*8*, 51n*11*
Colorado, 80; recent legislation, 193
Combat pay, 195
Connecticut, 51n*10*
Control of schools, 30-32, 37n*64*, 38n*72*,
51n*10*

Delaware, 53, 84n*12*
District power equalizing: defined, 75; modifications, 164-67, 192-93, 199n*8*; district
behavior under, 141-42, 158; simulations
of 163-71, 178; argument against, 79,
145-46, 171-75; mentioned, 135, 191,
199n*14*

Economies of scale, 84n*13*, 96, 109n*12*, 195

Federal aid to schools, 4, 53-55
Flat grant: defined, 72; modifications, 193-95;
in state laws, 73-74; and income effect, 92,
111n*33*; and equalization, 51n*9*, 76, 79,
85n*25*; simulated, 160-63, 168, 171-72,
178
Florida: recent legislation, 79, 80, 192, 200n*17*;
teacher pay, 195
Formulas, school finance: pure, 71-75; modifications, 71, 75-78, 160, 193-96; effect of,
29, 60-61, 67. *See also* District power
equalizing; Flat grant; Foundation plan;
Full state funding; Percentage equalizing
Foundation plan, 28-29, 72, 76-77; in state
laws, 73-74, 84n*15*; and income effect,
92, 111n*33*
Full state funding, 191

Gini coefficient: defined, 41-42, 49n*1*; characteristics of, 68n*5*, 183n*12*; comparisons,
44-46, 54-60 *passim,* 69n*10*, 183n*10*;
from simulations, 159-74 *passim,* 179-80;
mentioned, 189

Hawaii, 68n*1*, 68n*2*

Idaho, 5
Illinois, 80

Income effect: defined, 92, 98; theory, 99,
106; estimated 122-26; mentioned, 111n*33*,
141, 142, 191
Inter-district finance, 4-5, 11, 27, 29, 55-61
Interstate school finance. *See* Federal aid to
schools
Intra-district finance, 5, 61-66
Iowa, 79, 106

Lorenz curve, 41-43

Maine, 79; recent legislation, 167, 192
Massachusetts, 12, 20, 22, 152n*51*; characteristics of districts, 119, 128, 150n*37*;
inequality of school revenues, 41-43,
78-79, 84n*16*, 160; matching rate, 105,
106; flat grant, 160-63; district power
equalizing, 163-71, 192; mentioned,
115, 146, 149n*27*, 157. *See also* Percentage equalizing
Matching rate, 93, 98-105, 116; in percentage equalizing, 118, 138; in district
power equalizing, 167; state adoption,
192; response to, 122-26, 141-46,
151n*40*; calculated, 149n*28*; mentioned, 92
Michigan, 80, 200n*15*; recent legislation,
167
Minnesota, 4
Mississippi, 69n*6*, 69n*10*
Montana, 79; recent legislation, 185n*27*,
192, 199n*8*
Municipal overburden, 94, 104; in state
school aid, 76, 196; 200n*19*; school
expenditures, 97; mentioned, 48, 195,
110n*12*

Nebraska, 77
Nevada, 68n*1*
New Hampshire, 53
New Jersey, 4-5, 15n*30*, 77, 84n*14*
New York, 53, 77, 79, 84n*14*, 106
North Dakota, 79

Oklahoma, 77
Oregon, 68n*1*

Pennsylvania, 77, 106
Percentage equalizing: formula, 35n*47*, 74,
118, 137; modifications, 36n*49*, 76-78,
85n*21*, 111-33, 118, 137-38; in state
laws, 28, 35n*48*, 73-74; in Massachusetts,
36n*49*, 78, 83n*1*, 87n*32*, 137-38; effect
of, 29, 35n*4*, 160-61; mentioned, 115
Power equalizing. *See* District power equalizing

221

Price effect: theory, 99, 106; estimated, 125-46, 178; mentioned, 141, 142, 111n*33*, 191

Price of local school funds. *See* Matching rate

Property value: and school revenue, 95, 120, 127-30, 178-81; and nonschool revenue, 149n*29*; assessment, 86n*31*, 147n*8*, 147n*9*; incidence, 86n*31*, 110n*15*, 132-33; in district power equalizing, 168; estimated, 131-33; mentioned, 189

Rhode Island, 77, 79, 106

Scale. *See* Economies of scale

Simulations: caution about, 135, 157-59; flat grant, 159-63; district power equalizing, 163-71; endogenous, 177-81; conclusions from, 115, 146, 173-75

South Carolina, 149n*27*

South Dakota, 77, 84n*12*

Social class: measure of, 95-96, 134-135; of

districts, 127-28, 133; and school cost, 97

Substitution of state for local funds: theory, 43-46, 53-54, 99; estimates, 122-28

Tax rate, 143; floor, 170; relationship to property value, 120, 126, 178-81; relationship to price effect, 125-26

Taxes, 46, 49, 77; distribution of, 80-82

Texas, 4, 7

Title I, 116; disbursement, 119, 133, 134; and local revenue, 127

Utah, 79, 80, 84n*10*, 106; recent legislation, 193

Utility theory, 122, 142; approach to estimation, 98-101, 112n*39*

Virginia, 77

Wealth, in school finance, 172-73

Wisconsin, 77, 79, 80, 106; recent legislation, 193

## About the Authors

**W. Norton Grubb** is a Research Associate with the Childhood and Government Project at the University of California at Berkeley; he received the B.A. from Harvard College and is a candidate for the Ph.D. in economics at Harvard University. He is coauthor of *American Education and Vocationalism* (Teachers College Press, 1974) and has contributed to various professional journals.

**Stephan Michelson** is Senior Economist at the Center for Community Economic Development in Cambridge, Mass; he received the B.A. from Oberlin College and the M.A. and Ph.D. from Stanford University. He is coauthor of *Educational Vouchers, A Preliminary Report* (Center for the Study of Public Policy, 1970), *An Impact Study of Day Care* (Center for the Study of Public Policy, 1971), and *Inequality: A Reassessment of the Effect of Family and Schooling in America* (Basic Books, 1972; Harper Torchbooks, 1973). Dr. Michelson has also contributed numerous articles to books and professional journals.